YOUR recipe could appear in our next cookbook!

Share your tried & true family favorites with us instantly at
www.gooseberrypatch.com
If you'd rather jot 'em down by hand, just mail this form to...
Gooseberry Patch • Cookbooks – Call for Recipes
PO Box 812 • Columbus, OH 43216-0812

If your recipe is selected for a book, you'll receive a FREE copy!

Please share only your original recipes or those that you have made your own over the years.

Recipe Name:

Number of Servings:

Any fond memories about this recipe? Special touches you like to add
or handy shortcuts?

Ingredients (include specific measurements):

Instructions (continue on back if needed):

Special Code: **cookbookspage**

Over ➤

Extra space for recipe if needed:

Tell us about yourself...

Your complete contact information is needed so that we can send you your FREE cookbook, if your recipe is published. Phone numbers and email addresses are kept private and will only be used if we have questions about your recipe.

Name:

Address:

City: State: Zip:

Email:

Daytime Phone:

Thank you! Vickie & Jo Ann

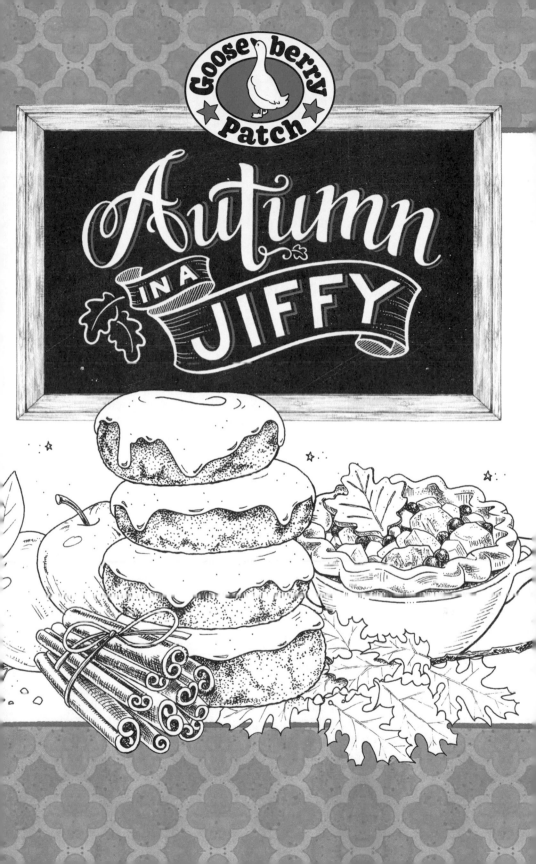

Gooseberry Patch

An imprint of Globe Pequot
246 Goose Lane
Guilford, CT 06437

www.gooseberrypatch.com

1•800•854•6673

Copyright 2022, Gooseberry Patch 978-1-62093-469-2

Do you have a tried & true recipe...

tip, craft or memory that you'd like to see featured in
a **Gooseberry Patch** cookbook? Visit our website at
www.gooseberrypatch.com and follow the easy steps
to submit your favorite family recipe.
Or send them to us at:

Gooseberry Patch
PO Box 812
Columbus, OH 43216-0812

Don't forget to include the number of servings your recipe makes,
plus your name, address, phone number and email address. If we
select your recipe, your name will appear right along with it...
and you'll receive a **FREE** copy of the book!

Contents

Dedication

To busy moms who want to spend more time with family this fall and less time in the kitchen.

Appreciation

A big thanks to everyone who shared their can't-miss recipes for the season with us.

Oven Omelet Brunch

Gladys Kielar
Whitehouse, OH

Breakfast for a bunch is so fast and easy with this recipe! Add a basket of muffins and brunch is served. If you aren't feeding a crowd, it's simple to cut the recipe in half.

1/4 c. butter, sliced
1-1/2 doz. eggs
1 c. milk
1 c. sour cream

1 t. salt
1 c. shredded Cheddar cheese
1/4 c. green onions, chopped

Place butter in a 13"x9" baking pan. Melt in a 325-degree oven, tilting pan to cover bottom completely; set aside. In a large bowl, beat eggs, milk, sour cream and salt until blended. Stir in cheese and onions; pour into baking pan. Bake, uncovered, at 325 degrees until eggs are set, about 30 to 35 minutes. Cut into squares. Makes 10 to 12 servings.

The first day back to school usually means a busy morning, so why not make a simple overnight breakfast dish? Putting it together the night before means less fuss in the morning and the kids get off to a great start.

Hanna's Favorite French Toast

Hanna Donner
Grandview, MO

My mother taught me this recipe when I was young...I still love it!

2 eggs, beaten
2 T. milk
1/2 c. sugar
1 t. cinnamon
1 t. vanilla extract

1 T. butter, divided
4 slices honey wheat bread
Garnish: creamy peanut butter,
    maple syrup, powdered sugar

In a shallow dish, beat eggs with milk, sugar, cinnamon and vanilla; set aside. Melt half of butter in a skillet over medium heat. Dip 2 bread slices in egg mixture, coating well on both sides; add to skillet. Cook for about 2 minutes, until golden; turn and cook other side. Repeat with remaining butter and bread. Serve slices topped with peanut butter and maple syrup; sprinkle with powdered sugar. Makes 4 servings.

French toast can be frozen, how handy! Make French toast
the usual way and cool completely. Layer slices with wax paper
and place in a plastic freezer bag. To serve, simply pop
a slice in the toaster until crisp.

Bubble Breakfast Pizza

Linda Kilgore
Kittanning, PA

A quick, delicious breakfast that's a family favorite! Try it with crisp bacon instead of sausage too.

16-oz. pkg. ground pork
  breakfast sausage
1 doz. eggs
1/2 c. milk
1 T. butter

16-oz. tube refrigerated jumbo
  biscuits
8-oz. pkg. pasteurized process
  cheese spread, sliced

Brown sausage in a large skillet over medium heat; drain and set aside. Whisk together eggs and milk in a large bowl. Wipe out skillet; melt butter over low heat and add egg mixture. Cook and stir until eggs are lightly scrambled. While eggs are cooking, separate biscuits and press into a greased 13"x9" baking pan, forming a crust. Spoon scrambled eggs over biscuits; top with sausage and cheese. Bake, uncovered, at 375 degrees for 30 minutes, or until biscuits are set and cheese melts. Serves 8.

Many farmers' markets are open well into autumn. Visit a nearby market for just-harvested fruits & vegetables, eggs, baked goods, jams & jellies...perfect for farm-fresh breakfasts.

❧ *Breakfast* ❧
ON THE GO

Mama Meg's Breakfast Biscuits

Megan Kreplin
Coxsackie, NY

My sons are big breakfast fans. The first time I made these, the boys took a taste and their eyes really lit up. It's so handy to keep the biscuits frozen for a quick breakfast on the way out.

8-oz. tube refrigerated biscuits
4 eggs, beaten
1 T. milk
salt and pepper to taste

2 t. butter
8 slices American cheese
8 thin slices cooked deli ham or
    crisply cooked bacon

Bake biscuits according to package directions; cool for 5 minutes. Meanwhile, in a bowl, whisk together eggs, milk and seasonings. Melt butter in a skillet over medium heat. Add egg mixture; scramble to desired doneness. Top eggs with cheese; let stand until melted, then slice eggs into 8 equal pieces. Split biscuits. Top each biscuit bottom with egg, ham or bacon and biscuit top. Serve immediately. To freeze, wrap each biscuit in plastic wrap. Place all biscuits in a plastic zipping bag and freeze. To serve, remove from freezer and microwave for 45 seconds. Makes 8 servings.

Fall conjures up so many memories! September reminds me of new school clothes and freshly sharpened pencils. It's time to make the house cozy, warm and inviting. I love everything about October. It is the month my daughter Keli was born and I can sense that a change is coming...it's time for pumpkins and gourds, Indian corn and sunflowers. On a crisp day when the colors of autumn are at their peak, I visit my favorite cider mill and bring home a jug of fresh cider just off the apple presses and an abundance of pumpkin doughnuts. My favorite time of year!

–Sherry Svoboda, Bel Air, MD

Apple Ring Pancakes

Becky Drees
Pittsfield, MA

You just have to try these! They're like a scrumptious cross between pancakes, apple pie and fried dough.

1 c. biscuit baking mix
1/2 c. milk
1 egg, beaten
1 t. pumpkin pie spice

zest of 1/2 lemon
2 apples, peeled
Garnish: pancake syrup

Combine biscuit mix, milk, egg, spice and zest in a bowl. Stir until blended; set aside. Cut apples horizontally into 1/8-inch slices, coring out the centers to make rings. Dip apple rings into batter; add to a greased griddle over medium heat. Cook on both sides until golden. Serve with syrup. Serves 2.

Cinnamon-Pumpkin Pancakes

Paula Johnson
Center City, MN

Everyone loves this cinnamon and pumpkin combination. Yum!

1 c. whole-wheat flour
1 T. sugar
2 t. baking powder
1/4 t. salt
1/2 t. cinnamon

1 c. skim milk
1/2 c. canned pumpkin
2 eggs, separated and divided
1-1/2 T. oil

In a large mixing bowl, combine flour, sugar, baking powder, salt and cinnamon. In a separate bowl, blend together milk, pumpkin, beaten egg yolks and oil. Add pumpkin mixture to flour mixture all at once, stirring until just blended. Beat egg whites with an electric mixer on high speed until stiff peaks form, then gently fold into pancake batter. For each pancake, spoon 2 to 3 tablespoons batter onto a griddle sprayed with non-stick vegetable spray. Cook until bubbles begin to form around edges; turn and cook until second side is golden. Makes 2 dozen, serves 6.

Take your family's breakfast outdoors! Spread a quilt on the picnic table and enjoy the cool morning air.

◉ *Breakfast* ◉
ON THE GO

Oven Pancake

Paulette Alexander
Newfoundland, Canada

I love being able to bake this pancake in the oven. It frees up the stovetop to cook breakfast bacon or ham at the same time.

3 eggs, beaten
1/2 c. milk
1/2 c. all-purpose flour

1/4 t. salt
1 T. butter, melted
Garnish: pancake syrup

In a bowl, whisk together eggs, milk, flour and salt until smooth. Spread butter in a 9" pie plate; add batter. Bake at 400 degrees for about 20 minutes, until cooked through. Serve with pancake syrup. Serves 4.

Cinnamon-Maple Apples

Andrea Heyart
Savannah, TX

Delicious as a pancake topping or as a side dish for sausages or pork chops. A family favorite for sure!

2 T. butter
3 to 4 apples, peeled, cored and
    sliced into wedges
1/4 c. maple syrup

1/4 c. brown sugar, packed
1 t. cinnamon
1/4 t. nutmeg

In a skillet over medium heat, melt butter and add sliced apples. Toss to coat; simmer until apples begin to soften. Add remaining ingredients to skillet. Simmer over medium heat, stirring often, until sauce is thickened and bubbly. Serves 4.

Fresh eggs can safely be kept in the refrigerator for four to five weeks...go ahead and stock up when they're on sale.

Snookie's Coffee Cake

Julie Wiesen
Houston, TX

I have made this coffee cake at least 75 times over the past six years for my children and their friends, sports teams and teachers. It is crazy how it has become such a hit with my kids and their school!

2/3 c. brown sugar, packed	4 eggs, beaten
4 t. cinnamon	2/3 c. oil
18-1/2 oz. pkg. butter golden cake mix	1 c. buttermilk
	1/4 c. sugar

Mix brown sugar and cinnamon in a cup; set aside. In a large bowl, combine dry cake mix and remaining ingredients. Beat for 3 to 4 minutes with an electric mixer on medium speed. Pour half of batter into a greased 13"x9" baking pan; sprinkle with half of brown sugar mixture. Repeat layers; swirl through both layers with a table knife. Bake at 325 degrees for 40 minutes, or until set. Remove pan to a wire rack, being very careful not to shake the pan, as the cake will sink in the center if you do. Drizzle Powdered Sugar Icing over cooled cake; cut into squares. Makes 10 to 12 servings.

Powdered Sugar Icing:

1 to 1-1/2 c. powdered sugar	1 t. vanilla extract
1 to 2 T. milk, divided	

Beat together powdered sugar and one tablespoon milk. Beat in more milk as needed for a drizzling consistency. Stir in vanilla.

Drizzle a frosting glaze over breakfast treats in a jiffy. Spoon glaze into a plastic zipping bag, snip off a tiny corner and drizzle away. Then just toss away the bag... couldn't be simpler!

🌾 *Breakfast* 🌾
ON THE GO

Butterscotch Bubbles

Joyce Keeling
Springfield, MO

I received this recipe from a pen pal when I was just ten years old. It was the first recipe that I made by myself, and I was thrilled that my family liked it so much. Whenever company arrived, Mom would tell me, "Go make some of your bubbles." I was so proud when I served them... after just one taste, they'd ask for my recipe!

1/4 c. butter, melted
1/4 c. brown sugar, packed
1/4 c. chopped nuts

1/2 t. cinnamon
8-oz. tube refrigerated biscuits,
   quartered

Place melted butter in a shallow dish; set aside. In a shallow dish, mix together brown sugar, nuts and cinnamon. Dip biscuit pieces into butter, then into brown sugar mixture. Arrange biscuits on ungreased baking sheets. Bake at 475 degrees for 10 minutes, or until lightly golden. Serve warm. Makes about 3-1/2 dozen pieces.

A mini photo album is just right for keeping go-to recipes handy on the kitchen counter. Tuck in a few photos of happy family mealtimes too!

Banana-Oat Breakfast Cookies

Sandra Sullivan
Aurora, CO

Need something new for breakfast? These satisfying cookies are great with a glass of cold milk or a cup of hot coffee.

1/2 c. ripe banana, mashed
1/2 c. crunchy peanut butter
1/2 c. honey
1 t. vanilla extract
1 c. quick-cooking oats,
   uncooked

1/2 c. whole-wheat flour
1/4 c. powdered milk
2 t. cinnamon
1/4 t. baking soda
1 c. sweetened dried cranberries
   or raisins

In a large bowl, stir together banana, peanut butter, honey and vanilla; set aside. In a small bowl, combine oats, flour, powdered milk, cinnamon and baking soda. Add oat mixture to banana mixture; stir until blended. Fold in cranberries or raisins. Lightly coat 2 baking sheets with non-stick vegetable spray. Drop mounds of dough onto baking sheets by 1/4 cupfuls, 3 inches apart. With a spatula dipped in water, flatten each mound into a 2-3/4 inch circle, about 1/2-inch thick. Bake at 350 degrees, one sheet at a time, for 14 to 16 minutes, until golden. Transfer cookies to wire racks to cool. Store in an airtight container up to 3 days. Cookies may also be cooled, wrapped and frozen; thaw before serving. Makes one dozen.

Egg dishes are a terrific way to use up tasty tidbits from the fridge...chopped veggies, deli meats and cheese. Warm ingredients briefly in the skillet before scrambling in the eggs.

Chocolate-Peanut Butter Granola Bars

Amy Bradsher
Roxboro, NC

We keep these sweet & satisfying bars stashed in the fridge for on-the-go breakfasts and quick snacks. My kids love to try to sneak a taste as they help me mix them up!

2 c. quick-cooking oats, uncooked
1/2 c. sunflower seed kernels
1/2 c. unsweetened flaked coconut

1/2 c. semi-sweet chocolate chips
1/2 c. peanuts, coarsely chopped
2/3 c. creamy peanut butter
1/3 c. honey

In a bowl, mix together all ingredients except peanut butter and honey; set aside. In a small saucepan over low heat, melt peanut butter and honey together; stir until blended. Pour peanut butter mixture over oat mixture; stir until combined and mixture is sticky. If mixture is too dry, drizzle in a little bit more honey and mix well. Press into a greased 8"x8" baking pan. Bake at 225 degrees for 20 to 30 minutes; cool slightly. Cut into bars and wrap individually. For firmer bars, keep refrigerated. Makes one dozen.

A little coffee brings out the flavor in any chocolate recipe. Just dissolve a tablespoon of instant coffee granules in liquid ingredients and continue as directed.

Amy's Biscuit, Egg & Gravy Casserole

Amy Snyder
Beckley, WV

I like this hearty casserole any time of the year, but it's a true comfort meal to get a chilly day started right. It warms tummies and your family time warms your heart.

16-oz. pkg. ground pork
   breakfast sausage
16-oz. tube refrigerated jumbo
   biscuits
1 c. shredded Cheddar cheese

6 eggs, beaten
1/2 c. milk
salt and pepper to taste
1-1/2 oz. pkg. country
   gravy mix

Brown sausage in a skillet over medium heat; drain. Spray a 13"x9" baking pan with non-stick vegetable spray; set aside. Separate biscuits and tear into one-inch pieces; line the bottom of pan with biscuit pieces. Scatter browned sausage over biscuits; sprinkle sausage with cheese. Whisk together eggs, milk and seasonings; pour over cheese. Prepare gravy mix according to package directions; spoon over egg mixture. Bake, uncovered, at 350 degrees for 30 to 40 minutes, checking after 30 minutes, until firm in the center. Makes 6 to 8 servings.

Start a tailgating Saturday right...invite friends to join you for breakfast. Keep it simple with a breakfast casserole, baskets of sweet rolls and a fresh fruit salad. It's all about food and friends!

ON THE GO

Ham, Egg & Cheesewich

Wendy Jo Minotte
Duluth, MN

I taught my children how to make this quick and tasty breakfast sandwich. Enjoy with a glass of orange juice.

2 slices bread, toasted
3 t. butter, softened and divided
1 egg
1 slice American cheese

salt to taste
3 to 4 thin slices cooked
    deli ham

Spread each slice of toast with one teaspoon butter; set aside. Melt remaining butter in a skillet over medium-low heat. Crack egg into skillet; break yolk with a fork or leave whole. Cook until egg is nearly set; turn over with a spatula. Season with salt; top with cheese and remove to a plate. Add stacked ham to skillet; warm on both sides. Top ham with egg and cheese; sandwich ham and egg stack between toast slices. Makes one serving.

Breakfast Burritos

Lauren Vanden Berg
Grandville, MI

I make these breakfast treats all the time...it only takes 15 to 20 minutes to make a stack of them.

1 lb. ground pork breakfast
    sausage
1 green pepper, diced

8 eggs, beaten
1 c. shredded Cheddar cheese
8 burrito-size flour tortillas

Brown sausage with green pepper in a skillet over medium heat; drain. Add eggs and cheese to skillet; cook and stir until eggs are set. Divide mixture among tortillas; fold tortillas burrito-style. Makes 8 servings.

Paper coffee filters make tidy holders for breakfast burritos... easy for little hands to hold too.

Blueberry Cheese Danish

JoAnna Nicoline-Haughey
Berwyn, PA

I make this special treat for my daughter's teachers.
The school staff loves it...it's so simple but tastes like I have been
baking all morning! Try it with cherry pie filling too.

2 8-oz. tubes refrigerated
   crescent rolls
2 8-oz. pkgs. cream cheese,
   softened
1 egg, separated

3/4 c. sugar
1 t. vanilla extract
21-oz. can blueberry pie filling
Garnish: cinnamon-sugar

Lightly grease a 13"x9" baking pan. Unroll one tube of crescent rolls
and place in bottom of pan; set aside. In a bowl, blend cream cheese,
egg yolk, sugar and vanilla; spread over crescent rolls. Spoon pie
filling over cream cheese mixture. Unroll remaining crescent rolls and
place on top. Whisk egg white in a cup until foamy; spread over
crescents. Sprinkle with cinnamon-sugar. Bake at 350 degrees for
25 to 30 minutes. Cool completely; cut into squares. Makes 10 to
12 servings.

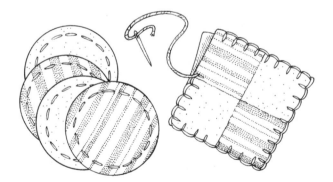

Turn old wool sweaters into a stack of cozy felt mug coasters.
Just wash sweaters in very hot water, then place them in the
dryer set to hot. When dry, cut out circles or squares. Decorate
the edges with colorful yarn in a simple whip stitch.

Berry Yummy French Toast

Sue Klapper
Muskego, WI

Start your day deliciously!

2 slices bread, cut one-inch
   thick
3 T. strawberry preserves
1 T. chopped pecans
1 egg, lightly beaten
1/3 c. milk

1-1/2 t. sugar
1/4 t. vanilla extract
2 T. butter, softened
2 T. powdered sugar, divided
1/4 c. strawberries, hulled
   and sliced

Cut a pocket in one end of each bread slice, cutting almost but not quite through to the other end. In a small bowl, mix strawberry preserves and pecans. Stuff half of the mixture into the pocket in each slice. In a pie plate, whisk together egg, milk, sugar and vanilla. Melt butter on a griddle over medium-high heat. Carefully dip bread slices into egg mixture on both sides. Cook on griddle until golden on one side; turn and sprinkle half of the powdered sugar over both slices. Cook until golden on other side. Turn again and sprinkle with remaining powdered sugar. Serve topped with strawberries. Makes 2 servings.

Stir up a super-simple fruit topping for pancakes and waffles. Combine a can of fruit pie filling and 2 tablespoons orange juice in a small bowl. Microwave for 2 to 2-1/2 minutes, stirring twice. Serve warm.

Cowboy Breakfast Casserole

Sandy Perry
Bakersfield, CA

This is an easy crowd-pleaser! It's a great way to use up leftover baked potatoes...don't be tempted to use frozen potatoes in this recipe. My whole family loves this one and they request it often.

1 doz. eggs, lightly beaten
2-1/2 c. shredded Cheddar
   cheese, divided
1 c. whipping cream
1 green pepper, chopped
1/2 c. onion, chopped

2 baked potatoes, peeled
   and chopped
salt and pepper to taste
1 lb. bacon, ground pork
   sausage or ham, cooked
Garnish: sour cream, salsa

Pour eggs into a greased 13"x9" baking pan. Sprinkle with one cup cheese; pour cream over top. Layer with remaining ingredients except garnish, ending with remaining cheese. Do not stir. Bake, uncovered, at 350 degrees for 50 to 60 minutes. Let stand for 5 minutes; cut into squares. Serve topped with sour cream and salsa. Makes 8 to 10 servings.

Whip up some special hot cocoa with a round disc of Mexican chocolate...the sugar and cinnamon are already mixed in. Bring 4 cups milk almost to a boil, add the chopped chocolate and whisk until it's melted and creamy.

Citrus-Glazed Fruit Salad

Pamela Myers
Auburn, IN

This fruit salad is the absolute best! I can't tell you how many times I've been asked for the recipe. I serve it with sweet rolls for breakfast and with cake for dessert. The glaze prevents the fruit from turning brown, so it keeps well for a few days in the refrigerator. Change up the fruit to suit your family's taste...I've also used apples and kiwi.

4 c. strawberries, hulled
   and sliced
4 c. blueberries
2 c. seedless green grapes,
   halved
2 to 3 ripe bananas, sliced
11-oz. can mandarin oranges,
   drained

20-oz. can pineapple tidbits,
   drained and juice reserved
1/3 c. orange juice
1 T. lemon juice
1/2 c. sugar
2 T. cornstarch

In a serving bowl, combine all of the fruit; set aside. In a saucepan, combine reserved pineapple juice, orange juice, lemon juice, sugar and cornstarch. Cook and stir over medium heat until thickened and bubbly. Remove from heat; set aside. Pour warm sauce over fruit and stir gently to coat. Cover and refrigerate. Makes 12 to 16 servings.

Serve pancakes with cheery pumpkin faces! Cut an apple
into thin slices, then cut triangles for the eyes and nose.
Give Jack a happy smile with an apple slice for his mouth.

Angie's Easy Pancakes

Evangeline Boston
Bradenton, FL

I have been using this recipe for more than 30 years and my kids grew up on them. It's easy, no-fail and tastes so good, even plain. There's no need to buy pancake mix...you have it all in your pantry!

2 c. all-purpose flour
1/2 c. sugar
4-1/2 t. baking powder
1 t. salt
2 eggs, beaten
2 c. milk

1/4 c. butter, melted and slightly
   cooled
Optional: 1/2 c. blueberries,
   chocolate chips or chopped
   pecans
Garnish: butter, pancake syrup

In a large bowl, combine flour, sugar, baking powder and salt; mix well and set aside. In a separate bowl, whisk together eggs, milk and melted butter. Add egg mixture to flour mixture; stir until all big lumps are gone. Stir in optional ingredients, if desired. Spoon batter onto a greased hot griddle by 1/4 cupfuls. Cook until golden on both sides. Serve topped with butter and syrup. Leftover pancakes freeze well. Makes 12 to 15, 5-inch pancakes.

Apple Cider Syrup

Samantha Starks
Madison, WI

This yummy syrup is delicious over waffles, pancakes or any kind of apple dessert.

1/2 c. sugar
4 t. cornstarch
1 t. cinnamon

1 c. apple cider or apple juice
1 T. lemon juice
2 T. butter, sliced

In a small saucepan, combine sugar, cornstarch and cinnamon. Stir in apple cider or juice and lemon juice. Cook over medium heat, stirring constantly, until thickened and bubbly. Cook and stir an additional 2 minutes. Remove from heat; stir in butter. Serve hot. Makes about 1-1/2 cups.

Autumn Amish Baked Oatmeal

Karen Sampson
Waymart, PA

My grandkids Silas and Eliza have enjoyed this tasty fall breakfast treat since they were toddlers. Especially when we top it with a splash of Grandpa's homemade maple syrup!

Optional: 1/2 c. diced apples,
   1/2 c. raisins
1-1/2 c. long-cooking oats,
   uncooked
1/2 c. brown sugar, packed
1 egg, beaten

1/4 c. oil
1 c. milk
1 t. baking powder
1 t. cinnamon
Garnish: additional milk

Layer apples and/or raisins in the bottom of a greased 9"x9" baking pan, if using; set aside. Beat together remaining ingredients except garnish with a spoon. Pour oat mixture into pan. Bake, uncovered, at 300 degrees for 30 to 35 minutes. Serve topped with milk. Serves 6.

Quick Oats for One

Wendy Jo Minotte
Duluth, MN

This makes very fluffy oatmeal for a quick, healthy breakfast, and almost no clean-up afterwards.

1 c. quick-cooking oats,
   uncooked
1-1/2 c. boiling water

Garnish: milk, sugar, cinnamon,
   dried fruit

Place oats in a heat-proof cereal bowl. Pour boiling water over oats; water should just cover oats. Cover the bowl with a plate and let stand for 5 minutes. Garnish as desired. Makes one serving.

Hang an old-fashioned peg rack inside the back door...you'll always know where to find your scarf, the kids' backpacks and the dog's leash!

23

Sweet Bacon Monkey Bread

Polly McCallum
Palatka, FL

A new take on monkey bread that everyone is sure to love!

6 slices bacon
2 T. butter
2 T. maple syrup
1/4 c. brown sugar, packed

1/4 t. cinnamon
2 8-oz. tubes refrigerated
   crescent dinner rolls

In a skillet over medium heat, cook bacon until crisp; drain on paper towels. Combine butter and syrup in a microwave-safe bowl. Microwave on high, uncovered, for 30 to 45 seconds, until hot. Add brown sugar and cinnamon; stir until dissolved. Spray an 8"x4" loaf pan with non-stick vegetable spray; gently pour butter mixture into pan. Crumble bacon over top. Unroll one tube of rolls into a large rectangle; press perforations to seal. Cut rectangle into 8 rows by 3 rows, to make 24 pieces. Repeat with remaining tube. Form each piece of dough into a ball; layer balls in pan. Bake at 350 degrees for 30 to 35 minutes, until golden. Cool in pan 5 minutes. Place a serving plate over pan; carefully turn out onto plate. Serve warm. Serves 8.

Greet guests with a harvest wreath on the front door. To a straw wreath, hot-glue sunflower heads and mini gourds. Tie on a big bow of homespun fabric and it's ready to display.

Whole-Wheat Pumpkin Bread

Julie Dossantos
Fort Pierce, FL

Toasted pumpkin bread with cream cheese is our breakfast tradition for Halloween and Thanksgiving. Also wonderful for a late-night snack!

3-1/2 c. whole-wheat flour
3 c. sugar
2 t. baking soda
1-1/2 t. salt
2 t. cinnamon
2 t. nutmeg

1 c. oil
15-oz. can pumpkin
4 eggs, beaten
2/3 c. water
1-1/2 t. vanilla extract

Spray two 9"x5" loaf pans with non-stick vegetable spray; set aside. In a large bowl, combine flour, sugar, baking soda, salt and spices; mix well. Add oil, pumpkin, eggs, water and vanilla. Beat with an electric mixer on low speed until combined. Pour half of batter into each loaf pan. Bake at 350 degrees for 55 minutes to an hour, until loaves test done with a toothpick inserted in the center. Cool loaves in pans on a wire rack for 15 minutes; turn out of pans. Makes 2 loaves.

One of my favorite fall memories is of when my Uncle Kenny would hook up his small flatbed trailer to his lawn tractor for a ride in the woods. Grandma and Aunt Becky, who both had difficulty with walking and balance, would sit in old recliner chairs on the trailer and all the kids and other adults would huddle around them. By being so creative, my uncle made it possible for all of the family to enjoy the colors and scents of autumn. Afterwards we would have a bonfire snuggled under blankets and roasting marshmallows and hot dogs, and just enjoy talking and being together.

–Emily Edwards, Alliance, OH

Cinnamon Roll Breakfast Bake

Cheryl Culver
Perkins, OK

I like to have an easy tasty breakfast on weekends because I have so much to do. This breakfast bread pudding goes together in about ten minutes. I always gets requests for repeats...it's just so yummy!

4 eggs, beaten
1 c. plus 2 T. milk
2 T. sugar
1 t. vanilla extract

1/2 t. cinnamon
12 slices cinnamon raisin swirl
    bread, quartered

Spray a 9"x9" baking pan with cooking spray; set aside. In a large bowl, combine eggs, milk, sugar, vanilla and cinnamon; beat until smooth. Add bread pieces to bowl and stir into egg mixture, breaking bread into chunks, until liquid is absorbed. Let stand 5 minutes; transfer to baking pan. Bake at 350 degrees for 30 to 40 minutes, until puffed and a knife tip inserted near center tests clean. Spread Icing over warm casserole; cut into squares. Serves 9.

Icing:

2 c. powdered sugar
2 T. butter, softened

2 to 3 T. milk
1/4 t. vanilla extract

In a large bowl, combine powdered sugar, butter, 2 tablespoons milk and vanilla. Beat with an electric mixer on low speed until sugar is moistened. Increase to medium speed. Beat until smooth and spreadable, adding a little more milk if necessary.

I'm so glad I live in a world where there are Octobers.

–Lucy M. Montgomery

Breakfast
ON THE GO

Melt-in-Your-Mouth Pecan Rolls

Joyceann Dreibelbis
Wooster, OH

Your family will love these quickie sticky buns! They're easy to put together too...you'll be enjoying them in no time at all.

1/2 c. brown sugar, packed
1/2 c. butter, softened
1/4 c. corn syrup
2 8-oz. tubes refrigerated
   crescent dinner rolls

2/3 c. chopped pecans
1/4 c. sugar
1 t. cinnamon

In a small bowl, blend brown sugar, butter and corn syrup. Divide mixture between 2 greased 8"x8" baking pans; spread to coat bottoms and set aside. Unroll each tube of dough into a rectangle; press to seal perforations. Combine pecans, sugar, and cinnamon; sprinkle over dough. Separately roll up each rectangle, jelly-roll style, starting on one long side; seal edges. Cut each roll into 16 slices. Place slices cut-side down in pans. Bake at 375 degrees for 13 to 16 minutes, until golden. Cool in pans for one minute; turn rolls out onto serving plates Makes about 2-1/2 dozen.

Mismatched glass salt & pepper shakers make sweet mini vases for the breakfast table. Simply remove the tops, fill with water and tuck in a big blossom. Place one at each table setting for a colorful accent.

Bacon & Cheese Muffins

Tina Butler
Royse City, TX

*These savory breakfast muffins are perfect for on-the-go mornings
and busy school days. They can be frozen and reheated too.*

1/2 lb. bacon, diced
2 c. all-purpose flour
2 t. baking powder
1/4 t. salt
1/4 t. pepper
1-1/4 c. milk

1 egg, beaten
1/4 c. butter, melted and
  slightly cooled
3/4 c. shredded Cheddar cheese
1/4 c. red or orange sweet
  peppers

In a skillet over medium heat, cook bacon until crisp; drain on paper
towels. Meanwhile, in a large bowl, stir together flour, baking powder,
salt and pepper. In a separate bowl, mix together milk, egg and melted
butter. Add milk mixture to flour mixture; stir just until moistened.
Fold in bacon, cheese and peppers just until combined. Fill greased
or paper-lined muffin cups 2/3 full. Bake at 400 degrees for 20 to
25 minutes, until lightly golden. Serves 6.

Serve fuss-free favorites like Bacon & Cheese Muffins...
ideal for tailgating Saturday morning. Everyone can
easily help themselves while the day's fun is beginning.

Breakfast
ON THE GO

Nell's Sausage Muffins

Lynda Zickefoose
Lubbock, TX

*A dear friend in my Sunday School class shared this recipe with me.
I have made it my own by using a variety of meats like crumbled
bacon, diced ham and pepperoni...they're all tasty!*

16-oz. pkg. ground pork
   breakfast sausage
10-3/4 oz. can Cheddar
   cheese soup

2/3 c. water
3 c. biscuit baking mix
1 c. shredded Cheddar cheese

Brown and crumble sausage in a skillet over medium heat; drain and
set aside. In a large bowl, whisk together soup and water until smooth.
Gradually add biscuit mix; stir until well blended. Add sausage and
cheese; stir well until a stiff batter forms. Grease 24 muffin cups. Fill
greased muffin cups 2/3 full. Bake at 350 degrees for 20 to
25 minutes, until golden. Makes 2 dozen.

Breakfast Taters & Bacon

Kathy Milligan
Mira Loma, CA

*I was looking for a good way to use leftover baked potatoes when
I found this marvelous little recipe. Quick & easy.*

4 slices bacon, chopped
1/2 c. onion, chopped
4 baked potatoes, peeled
   and diced

salt and pepper to taste

In a large skillet, cook bacon over medium heat until crisp; partially
drain. Add onion; cook until lightly golden. Add potatoes; season with
salt and pepper. Mix with a spatula to blend. Cook until golden, about
5 minutes. Cut into sections and flip. Keep cooking until heated
through with lots of brown spots, about 8 minutes. Add more salt
and pepper as needed. Makes 4 servings.

Ella's Easy Granola

Lynnette Jones
East Flat Rock, NC

Our son Kyle deserves the credit for this because it is his recipe that he shared with me. It's named for his little girl, who is our granddaughter. This granola is so simple to make ahead and keep on hand. It's very versatile...cut it into granola bars or crumble to use as a yogurt topping. Add any dried fruit you might like too.

4 c. old-fashioned oats, uncooked
2/3 c. oil
3 T. water
2/3 c. brown sugar, packed
2 T. molasses
2 T. maple syrup
2 T. chopped pecans
2 T. sliced almonds
1/2 t. cinnamon
1/4 t. salt

Place oats in a large bowl and add oil; mix thoroughly. In a small bowl, mix water with brown sugar. Add to oat mixture along with remaining ingredients; stir thoroughly. Line a 15"x10" jelly-roll pan with aluminum foil for easy clean-up; spray with non-stick vegetable spray. Spread mixture evenly in pan. Bake at 350 degrees for 30 to 35 minutes. Let cool completely; cut into bars or break up into serving-size pieces. Makes 8 to 10 servings.

Are breakfast smoothies a favorite at your house?
Mix them up the night before, then pour into canning jars
and tuck in the fridge. Perfect portions, ready to go!

Apple Pie Smoothie

Julie Dossantos
Fort Pierce, FL

This is the perfect breakfast smoothie for autumn.
Fruit and protein...a fine way to begin each day!

1 ripe banana, peeled
1/2 Granny Smith apple, peeled,
   cored and coarsely chopped
4-oz. container vanilla yogurt

1/4 c. applesauce
1 t. creamy peanut butter
cinnamon to taste
3 ice cubes

Place all ingredients in a blender and process well. Immediately pour into a chilled tall glass and serve. Makes one serving.

Growing up in the Houston area, there wasn't much of the traditional autumn weather, but we lived on an acre of land full of pine trees and the trees would shed their pointy needles. When the yard started to get covered in brown needles, it was the children's job to rake them up. Since we were not really amused by this, my sister and brother decided to make it more fun by making huge piles of needles and jumping in them! It made the huge chore so much fun! We did this for many years. I can't wait for my children to be old enough to enjoy the feeling of jumping into big piles of pine needles.

–Kathy Carmona, Webster, TX

Cheesy Potato & Ham Scramble

Sue Klapper
Muskego, WI

*Ever since a co-worker gave me this recipe, I've been
making it for weekend breakfasts for my family.*

8 eggs, beaten
1/4 c. milk
1/4 t. garlic salt
1/4 t. pepper
1/4 c. green onions, thinly sliced

1 T. butter, sliced
1 c. frozen shredded
hashbrowns
1/2 c. cooked ham, diced
1/3 c. shredded Cheddar cheese

In a bowl, combine eggs, milk and seasonings. Whisk until well
blended. Stir in green onions; set aside. In a large non-stick skillet,
melt butter over medium heat. Add hashbrowns and ham to skillet.
Cook for 6 to 8 minutes, stirring occasionally, until lightly golden. Add
egg mixture to skillet. Cook over medium heat without stirring until
mixture begins to set around the edges and on the bottom. Using a
large spatula, lift and fold the partially cooked egg mixture so
uncooked portion flows underneath. Continue cooking and folding
for 2 to 3 minutes, until eggs are set but still glossy and moist.
Immediately remove from heat; sprinkle with cheese. Serves 4.

Hard-boiled eggs are terrific to have on hand for speedy
breakfasts, easy sandwiches or even a quick nutritious snack.
Use eggs that have been refrigerated at least seven to
ten days...the shells will slip right off.

Breakfast
ON THE GO

Easy Egg Bake

Jennie Gist
Gooseberry Patch

I've made this dish often to share with friends. It just takes a few minutes to put together and pop in the oven! Change up the ingredients as you like...sometimes I'll omit the bacon.

20-oz. pkg. refrigerated diced
    potatoes with onions
6-oz. pkg. precooked bacon
6 to 8 eggs, beaten

1/4 c. milk
salt and pepper to taste
8-oz. pkg. shredded sharp
    Cheddar cheese

Spray a 13"x9" baking pan with non-stick vegetable spray. Spread potatoes in pan. Using kitchen scissors, snip bacon into pieces over potatoes. Bake, uncovered, at 350 degrees for about 15 minutes; remove from oven. Whisk together eggs and milk; pour over baked layer. Sprinkle with salt, pepper and cheese. Return to oven, uncovered, for 25 to 30 minutes, until eggs are set and cheese is melted. Cut into squares. Serves 8.

Brown Sugar Muffins

Jill Ball
Highland, UT

I like to make a double or triple batch of these muffins to freeze. They can be popped in the microwave for a minute to reheat. Enjoy a warm muffin on the way out the door!

2 c. all-purpose flour
1 c. brown sugar, packed
1 t. baking soda
1/4 t. salt
1/2 c. butter, softened

1 egg, beaten
1 c. milk
1 t. vanilla extract
Optional: 1/2 c. chopped nuts

Combine all ingredients in a large bowl; stir until moistened. Fill greased muffin cups about 2/3 full. Bake at 375 degrees for 10 to 12 minutes. Makes 2 dozen.

English Cream Scones

Janis Parr
Ontario, Canada

These scones are perfect to serve with afternoon tea. They are light and dainty...so good with a dab of homemade strawberry jam.

2 c. all-purpose flour
2 T. sugar
1 T. baking powder
1/2 t. salt
1/4 c. butter

2 eggs
1/3 c. light cream
Garnish: beaten egg white,
    additional sugar

Combine flour, sugar, baking powder and salt. Cut in butter with 2 knives until mixture resembles coarse cornmeal. In a separate bowl, beat eggs until light; stir in cream. Make a well in the center of flour mixture; slowly add egg mixture. Stir vigorously until dough comes away from the side of the bowl. Pat out dough 3/4-inch thick; cut into squares or triangles. Place on a greased baking sheet. Brush tops with beaten egg white; sprinkle with sugar. Bake at 450 degrees for 12 to 15 minutes. Serve warm. Makes 9 to 12.

Maple-Walnutty Spread

Sharon Demers
Dolores, CO

Perfect to spread on piping hot scones in the fall.

8-oz. pkg. cream cheese,
    softened
2 T. maple syrup

1/2 t. maple extract
1/2 c. chopped walnuts, toasted

Beat cream cheese with syrup and extract until well mixed. Fold in walnuts. Let stand 20 to 30 minutes to allow flavors to blend before serving. Keep refrigerated. Makes about 1-1/2 cups.

A basket of homemade scones with a jar of creamy spread makes a tasty teacher gift. Tuck in a tiny slate board as a clever gift tag.

Jack-o'-Lantern Jumble

Carrie Kelderman
Pella, IA

This is a sweet & savory mix that our kids request each fall. Whenever we share it with our extended family, it's gone in a flash!

8 c. bite-size crispy corn &
  rice cereal squares
1 c. dry-roasted peanuts
1/4 c. butter, sliced

1/4 c. creamy peanut butter
2-1/4 t. Worcestershire sauce
1/4 t. garlic salt
1 to 2 c. candy corn

Combine cereal and peanuts in a large bowl; set aside. In a saucepan, combine remaining ingredients except candy corn. Cook over low heat until melted, stirring frequently. Pour over cereal mixture, stirring to coat well. Spread in a lightly greased 15"x10" jelly-roll pan. Bake, uncovered, at 250 degrees for one hour. Cool to room temperature; stir in candy corn. Store in an airtight container. Makes 10 to 11 cups.

Every fall, our family heads to the local pumpkin patch with the little ones to let them pick a pumpkin. We call it "punkin' huntin'" and the kids love it! When our boys were little, it would be my husband and I taking them to a family farm about an hour from home. Now that they're in high school and college, my sister and I take my youngest granddaughter and anyone else who wants to go. It's a cherished tradition and particularly special to me as fall is my favorite time of year.

–Brenda Lenz, Georgetown, TX

Sticky Popcorn

Brittney Green
Frederick, CO

This is the first snack to go at any get-together! It always brings back special memories from when I was young and my friend's mom would make it for us. I even remember asking her for the recipe when I was ten years old, so my mom could make it for me.

5 to 6 family-size pkgs.
   microwave popcorn, popped
1 c. butter, sliced

1-1/3 c. sugar
1/2 c. light corn syrup
1 t. vanilla extract

Pop popcorn and place in a large heat-proof bowl. Discard any unpopped kernels; set aside. In a heavy saucepan over medium heat, combine butter, sugar and corn syrup. Bring to a boil; cook for about 5 minutes, until mixture reaches the soft-ball stage, or 234 to 243 degrees on a candy thermometer. Remove from heat; stir in vanilla and pour over popcorn. Toss to coat well; spread on wax paper and let cool. Makes 25 servings.

Fall Delight

Jo Ann Belovitch
Stratford, CT

A sweet treat for munching that's ready in just a minute!

1 c. candy-coated chocolates
1 c. candy corn

1 c. cashews
1 c. raisins

Toss together all ingredients in a serving bowl; serve. Makes 4 cups.

Paper cupcake liners come in all colors...great for
serving single portions of party mix.

Candy Corn Crispy Balls

Amy Jones
Graham, NC

A different take on popcorn balls...these are fun,
easy and so delicious!

4 c. crispy rice cereal
2 c. candy corn
1/2 c. creamy peanut butter

1/4 c. butter, sliced
4 c. mini marshmallows
Optional: cellophane, ribbon

Combine cereal and candy corn in a large bowl; set aside. Melt butter
and peanut butter in a large saucepan over low heat. Add
marshmallows; stir until completely melted. Pour over cereal mixture;
stir to coat. With buttered fingers, roll into balls the size of a tennis
ball. If desired, wrap each ball in an 8-inch square of cellophane;
twist ends closed and tie with ribbon. For a simpler way, press warm
mixture into a buttered 13"x9" baking pan and cut into squares.
Makes 16 balls.

Surprise a friend or neighbor with a homemade popcorn ball
in a trick-or-treat bag! It's so simple. Just place the popcorn
ball in an orange paper bag and gather together the top of
the bag; secure with a rubber band. Hide the rubber
band with green florists' tape.

Spicy Vanilla-Glazed Pretzels

Jonni Sue Wilhelm
Hebron, MD

Every Sunday at church I set out bowls of pretzels for people to snack on with their coffee. This slightly sweet pretzel is a bit spicy too! I like to make one bowlful using sugar and one bowlful using sweetener so that people who need sugar-free snacks can enjoy them too. They have been a big hit!

14-oz. pkg. pretzel sticks or
   mini pretzel twists
2 egg whites
2 T. vanilla extract
1/2 c. sugar, or 3/4 c. powdered
   calorie-free sweetener

1 T. cinnamon
1/2 t. cayenne pepper
1/2 t. salt

Pour pretzels into a large heat-proof bowl; set aside. In a small bowl, beat egg whites and vanilla until foamy; pour over pretzels and toss to coat. In a separate medium bowl, combine sugar or sweetener, spices and salt; mix well. Pour mixture over pretzels; toss again to coat evenly. Spread on a greased 15"x10" jelly-roll pan. Bake, uncovered, at 250 degrees for about one hour; let cool. Break apart. Store in airtight container. Makes 15 to 20 servings.

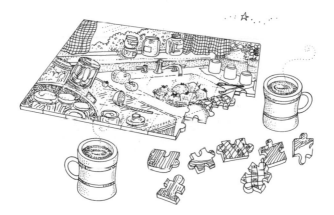

Family night! Serve a simple supper, then spend
the evening assembling jigsaw puzzles or
playing favorite board games together.

Harvest Apple Cheese Ball

Lorrie Coop
Munday, TX

My daughter Brittany started making this cheese ball as a young 4-H'er as part of her fall foods project. It adds a little whimsy to any holiday table.

8-oz. pkg. cream cheese,
   softened
1 c. shredded Cheddar cheese
1/4 t. cinnamon
3/4 c. dried apples, finely
   chopped

1/3 c. chopped nuts
Garnish: 2-inch cinnamon stick,
   bay leaf
assorted crackers

In a large bowl, beat cream cheese, Cheddar cheese and cinnamon until blended. Stir in dried apples. Form mixture into an apple shape; roll in chopped nuts. Insert cinnamon stick and bay leaf on top to resemble an apple's stem and leaf. Cover and refrigerate until firm. Serve with crackers. Makes 10 servings.

Still too warm for a fire? Give your fireplace a welcoming autumn glow...fill it with pots of flame-colored orange and yellow mums.

Toffee Apple Dip

Kim McCallie
Guyton, GA

*My friends & family always request this dip. Chill overnight to soften
the toffee bits and create luscious ribbons of toffee.*

8-oz. pkg. cream cheese,
  softened
1/4 c. butter, softened
3 T. powdered sugar

1/2 c. brown sugar, packed
1 t. vanilla extract
8-oz. pkg. toffee bits, divided
sliced apples, graham crackers

Combine cream cheese and butter in a large bowl. Beat with an
electric mixer on low speed until blended. Add sugars and vanilla; mix
well. Set aside 1/4 cup toffee bits; add remaining toffee bits to cream
cheese mixture. Stir until well blended. Cover and refrigerate
overnight, if possible. Just before serving, sprinkle remaining toffee
bits on top of dip. Serve with sliced apples and graham crackers for
dipping. Serves 8 to 10.

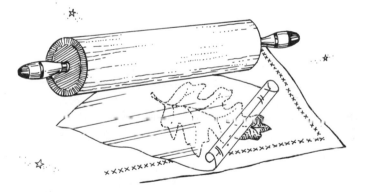

A tried & true kid craft...leaf art! Have kids hunt for colorful
leaves, then press the leaves in a heavy book between pieces of
wax paper for a few days. Glue leaves to colored paper to form
a picture. Twigs, seed pods and acorn caps can be added too.
Finish by drawing on details.

Cranberry-Jalapeño Salsa

Bonnie Waters
Bloomington, IN

This salsa has been a family favorite at Thanksgiving and other gatherings for many years. I have to make two or three batches! We grow our own jalapeños and green onions, so when in season, it's fresh from our garden. This salsa is also delicious as a sauce over roast turkey or pork for a meal or sandwich.

14-oz. can whole-berry
   cranberry sauce
1 jalapeño pepper, halved,
   seeded and diced
1/4 c. fresh cilantro, snipped

2 green onions, sliced
1 t. lime juice
1/4 t. ground cumin
tortilla chips

In a bowl, combine all ingredients except tortilla chips. Stir until well blended. Serve at room temperature or cover and chill. Serve with tortilla chips. Makes 8 servings.

Plenty of ready-to-eat goodies can be found at farmers' markets and roadside stands. Tuck a basket filled with picnic supplies into the car trunk along with a quilt to sit on. Instant picnic!

Snacks & Appetizers
❂ TO SHARE ❂

Cheesy Jack-o'-Lantern

Lori Simmons
Princeville, IL

*This cheese ball looks just like a pumpkin...great for Halloween!
If you have extra pepperoni, chop it finely and stir into
the cream cheese mixture for a tasty addition.*

3 green onions, divided
2 8-oz. pkgs. cream cheese,
  softened
8-oz. pkg. shredded Cheddar
  cheese, divided

1/4 c. red pepper, finely chopped
Garnish: several slices pepperoni
assorted crackers

Cut a 4-inch "stem" from the green part of one onion; chop remaining onions and set aside. In a bowl, beat together cream cheese and 1-1/4 cups Cheddar cheese. Stir in remaining onions and red pepper; cover and refrigerate one hour. Form into a ball; roll in remaining Cheddar cheese. Cut pepperoni slices into triangle shapes for eyes, nose and mouth; press into cheese ball to make a face. Insert reserved onion piece into top. Makes 3 cups.

Pepper Jelly Cream Cheese

Holly Child
Parker, CO

*With just a few ingredients on hand, I can always whip up this
quick appetizer for any type of gathering. Easy to put together
and always a big hit with its spicy-sweet flavor.*

8-oz. pkg. cream cheese,
  softened
1/4 c. medium salsa

1/4 c. orange marmalade
assorted crackers

Unwrap cream cheese and place the block on a serving dish. Mix together salsa and marmalade in a bowl; spoon evenly over cream cheese. Serve with assorted crackers. Makes 10 to 12 servings.

Glazed Sausage Balls

Beth Wajts
Sterling Forest, NY

This is a terrific appetizer for watching those football games that have you sitting on the edge of your seat, or a fun night at home playing games and sharing snacks with friends.

16-oz. pkg. ground hot
  pork sausage
1 egg, beaten
2 c. saltine crackers, finely
  crushed

2-1/2 c. tomato juice, divided
2 T. oil
3/4 c. brown sugar, packed
1/4 c. vinegar
2 T. dry mustard

In a large bowl, combine sausage, egg, crackers and 1/2 cup tomato juice. Mix well; form into small meatballs. In a large skillet, brown meatballs in oil; drain and set aside. Add remaining tomato juice and other ingredients to skillet; mix well. Return meatballs to tomato mixture. Reduce heat to medium-low. Cover and simmer for about 30 minutes. May be kept warm in a slow cooker on low setting. Makes about 3 dozen.

Pick up a dozen pint-size Mason jars for entertaining...
they're fun and practical for serving frosty root beer
or chilled apple cider.

Barbecue Drummies

Debi King
Reisterstown, MD

My friend Sharon gave me the idea of using drumsticks instead of wings, since they are less messy. I like to pack the baking dish of drummies in a portable carrier to take to football games.

14-oz. can whole-berry
  cranberry sauce
12-oz. bottle chili sauce
2 T. red pepper flakes

3 lbs. chicken drumsticks
2 T. olive oil
Garnish: ranch or blue cheese
  salad dressing, celery sticks

Combine cranberry sauce, chili sauce and red pepper flakes in a one-gallon plastic zipping bag. Knead bag to mix. Remove 1/2 cup of sauce mixture and refrigerate. Pat drumsticks dry with a paper towel; add to bag. Seal bag and refrigerate for at least one hour. Remove drumsticks to a greased 13"x9" glass baking pan, discarding sauce mixture in bag. Bake, uncovered, at 375 degrees for about 25 minutes. Turn drumsticks over; baste with reserved sauce mixture. Bake for another 7 to 10 minutes, until chicken juices run clear. Serve drumsticks with salad dressing and celery sticks for dipping. Makes 8 to 12 servings.

Packing for a picnic or a tailgating party? Safety first!
Keep hot foods hot, cold foods cold, and don't let any food
sit out longer than 2 hours, even if the food looks just fine.

Smoked Pimento Cheese Dip

Mary Bettuchy
Columbia, SC

We're a military family, so we've been stationed all over the country and get to try different regional foods. Here in South Carolina, one of the most delicious things I've discovered is pimento cheese! The smoky flavor is my own spin on this classic.

8-oz. pkg. smoked Cheddar
   cheese, shredded
8-oz. pkg. cream cheese,
   softened
2 4-oz. jars pimentos or
   roasted red peppers, drained
   and diced

1/4 c. mayonnaise
1/2 t. smoked salt or
   1/4 t. smoke-flavored
   cooking sauce
1/4 t. hot pepper sauce
1/4 t. red pepper flakes
pita chips

In a food processor or blender, combine all ingredients except pita chips. Pulse until combined. If mixture is too thick, add a little more mayonnaise. If more smoky flavor or heat is desired, add more smoke or hot sauce to taste. Serve with pita chips. Serves 8.

Tasty Bread Spread

Beckie Apple
Grannis, AR

Tuck this savory spread in the fridge for those hurry-up days when you want to enjoy something special.

2 c. finely shredded mozzarella
   or Parmesan cheese
4-1/4 oz. can chopped black
   olives, drained
1 c. butter, softened

1 c. mayonnaise
1 t. minced garlic or garlic
   powder
split rolls or sliced French bread

Combine all ingredients except rolls or bread and mix well. Cover and chill for one to 2 hours. To serve, spread on split or sliced dinner rolls or French bread. Place on an aluminum foil-lined baking sheet. Bake at 375 degrees for 20 to 25 minutes, until toasted. Cover and refrigerate up to 2 weeks. Makes about 4 cups.

Snacks & Appetizers
⊙ TO SHARE ⊙

Homemade Boursin Cheese

Denise Webb
Newington, GA

*Boursin cheese is a little pricey for me, so I was thrilled
to find this recipe to make my own. It's wonderful on
crackers and fabulous in sausage cheese balls.*

2 8-oz. pkgs. cream cheese,
    softened
8-oz. container whipped butter,
    room temperature
1 t. garlic salt
1/2 t. dried oregano

1/4 t. dried marjoram
1/4 t. dried thyme
1/4 t. dried basil
1/4 t. dill weed
1/4 t. pepper

Combine all ingredients in a food processor or blender. Process until
completely blended and smooth. Line a serving bowl with plastic
wrap; spoon cheese mixture into bowl. Cover and refrigerate for
several hours before serving, to allow flavors to blend. Makes 3 cups.

Need to soften cream cheese in a hurry? Simply place
an unwrapped 8-ounce block on a plate and microwave
for about a minute at 50% power.

Monterey Mushroom Squares

Jo Ann
Gooseberry Patch

*These cheesy squares are irresistible! Mix & match
different kinds of mushrooms and cheeses for variety.*

8-oz. tube refrigerated
  crescent rolls
2 c. sliced mushrooms
1/4 c. butter, melted

1/2 c. shredded Monterey
  Jack cheese
1/2 t. dried oregano
1/4 t. onion salt

Separate rolls into 2 long rectangles. Press into the bottom and
1/2-inch up the sides of a lightly greased 13"x9" baking pan. Toss
mushrooms with melted butter; spoon over dough. Sprinkle with
remaining ingredients. Bake, uncovered, at 375 degrees for 20 to
25 minutes. Cut into squares; serve warm. Makes 2 dozen.

Savory Spinach Rolls

Laurie Rupsis
Aiken, SC

*I bring these to our church's potlucks but never set them out before
the crowd comes in. The ladies working the kitchen seem to
eat a lot of them before the potluck even starts!*

2 onions, chopped
3/4 c. butter
2 10-oz. pkgs frozen spinach
3 c. stuffing mix

6 eggs, beaten
1/2 c. shredded Parmesan
  cheese

In a skillet over medium heat, sauté onions in butter until tender.
Cook spinach according to package directions; squeeze dry. In a bowl,
combine onion mixture, spinach and remaining ingredients. Shape
into 2-inch balls using a cookie scoop. Refrigerate at least one hour,
until firm. Place on a lightly greased baking sheet. Bake, uncovered,
at 350 degrees for 20 minutes. May be frozen unbaked; bake just
before serving. Serve warm or cool. Makes 3 dozen.

Country Caviar

*Kay Pyle
Stockton, MO*

One of our favorite dips! It's easy to make and keeps for days in the fridge, if it lasts that long. I have made it for ages and my grandkids love it. Great for family gatherings and football games. Spice it to suit to your taste, from mild to extra hot.

l5-oz. can black, red or
   pinto beans, drained
11-oz. can sweet corn & diced
   peppers, drained
10-oz. can mild, medium or
   hot diced tomatoes with
   green chiles, drained
6 green onions, chopped

2 c. shredded Monterey Jack,
   Pepper Jack or Cheddar
   cheese
1 c. light mayonnaise
1 c. light sour cream
hot pepper sauce to taste
pita chips, tortilla chips

Mix together all ingredients except chips in a large bowl. Cover and chill; may be kept refrigerated for several days. Serve with warm pita chips or tortilla chips. Serves 8 to 10.

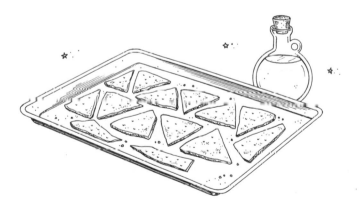

Make your own crunchy pita chips for dipping. Cut pita bread rounds into triangles, brush lightly with olive oil and sprinkle with garlic salt or herbs. Bake at 350 degrees for a few minutes, until crisp.

Corn Dog Muffins

Tina Goodpasture
Meadowview, VA

I love hot dogs any way that I can find to fix them.
This recipe is fast, easy and good!

6 hot dogs
1 c. all-purpose flour
1 c. cornmeal
1/2 c. sugar
2-1/2 t. baking powder
1 t. salt

1 c. milk
1/3 c. oil
1 egg
Garnish: catsup, mustard,
    pickle relish

In a skillet over medium heat, cook hot dogs for 5 to 8 minutes, just until starting to brown. Remove from heat. Cut each hot dog into 6 pieces; set aside. In a large bowl, combine flour, cornmeal, sugar, baking powder and salt. Add egg, milk and oil; stir until just combined. Spray mini muffin cups with non-stick vegetable spray. Spoon batter into muffin cups, filling 2/3 full. Press one piece of hot dog into the center of each muffin cup. Bake at 350 degrees for 10 minutes. Increase heat to 400 degrees. Bake another 3 to 5 minutes, watching closely, until golden. Cool in muffin tins for 5 minutes before removing. Serve muffins with your favorite condiments. Makes 3 dozen.

A muffin tin makes a terrific condiment server. Fill each cup with something different...how about catsup, mustard, relish, hot pepper sauce, horseradish and mayonnaise?

Meatball Sliders

Becky Drees
Pittsfield, MA

So easy to make...a big hit at football parties!

32 frozen Italian-style meatballs
28-oz. jar pasta sauce
2 8-oz. tubes refrigerated
    crescent rolls

11 slices mozzarella cheese,
    cut into thirds

Combine meatballs and sauce in a large saucepan. Simmer over low heat until warmed through, 5 to 10 minutes. Separate crescent rolls into triangles. Cut each triangle in half width-wise to form 2 triangles. Top each triangle with 1/3 slice cheese and one meatball; roll up. Bake, uncovered, at 375 degrees for 15 to 18 minutes, until golden. Makes 32 sliders.

When I was growing up, I couldn't wait until I was old enough to join the Grange. In the fall when the weather was crisp and trees were so beautiful, the Grange members would have a picnic. Some of the younger members would go ahead to the park and get the fire going for the delicious hot dogs and hamburgers. Then the ladies came, bringing all those luscious covered dishes for a wonderful feast. While they got the meal ready, the men would pitch horseshoes. The kids played hide & seek and put on skits. Then we all ate until we were stuffed! These are some of my best memories.
    –Barbara Feldner, Caldwell, OH

Bacon-Wrapped Pineapple Bites

Jessica Kraus
Delaware, OH

*These are so irresistible...the mixture of salty and sweet is amazing!
You should probably double the recipe, because they'll go quickly.*

1 c. brown sugar, packed
16-oz. pkg. bacon, slices cut
   in half
20-oz. can pineapple chunks,
   drained

wooden toothpicks, soaked
   in water

Place brown sugar in a shallow bowl. Dredge each half-slice of bacon
in brown sugar. Place one pineapple chunk on one end of each
bacon piece and roll up; secure with a toothpick. Sprinkle rolls with
remaining brown sugar. Arrange on a greased rack placed on a baking
sheet. Bake at 375 degrees for 25 minutes, or until bacon is crisp.
Makes 10 servings.

Smoked Kielbasa Bites

Marcia Shaffer
Conneaut Lake, PA

Perfect for football snacking!

1 lb. Kielbasa sausage, cut into
   bite-size pieces
3/4 c. ginger ale

1/2 c. brown sugar, packed
1/2 c. barbecue sauce

Place sausage in a greased 9"x9" baking pan. Mix together ginger ale,
brown sugar and barbecue sauce; spoon over sausage. Cover; bake at
300 degrees for 1-1/2 hours. Serves 6.

For a fun after-school snack
that's ready in a jiffy, stuff a
hollowed-out apple with
peanut butter and raisins.

Ranch Buffalo Wings

Phyl Broich-Wessling
Garner, IA

We love chicken wing appetizers for parties and snacks, so I'm always on the lookout for a new recipe to try, the easier the better. This one is very tasty...the secret ingredient is the vinegar.

1/2 c. butter, melted
1/4 c. hot pepper sauce,
   or to taste
3 T. white vinegar
12 chicken wings,
   cut into sections

1-oz. pkg. ranch salad
   dressing mix
1/2 t. paprika
Garnish: ranch salad dressing,
   celery sticks

In a small bowl, whisk together butter, hot sauce and vinegar. Dip wing pieces into butter mixture. Arrange in a single layer on a large cast-iron pizza pan or other baking pan. Sprinkle with salad dressing mix. Bake, uncovered, at 350 degrees for 30 to 40 minutes, until wings are golden and juices run clear, basting occasionally with pan juices. Sprinkle with paprika. Serve wings with salad dressing and celery sticks for dipping. Serves 6 to 8.

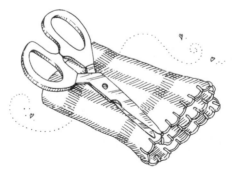

Wondering what's the best way to cut up slippery chicken wings? A pair of sturdy kitchen scissors does the job in a jiffy. Afterwards, wash the scissors well in soapy water and set on a towel to dry.

Texas Snacker Crackers

Kim Hinshaw
Cedar Park, TX

*When I served these to my bunco group, everyone wanted to play
at the table with the spicy crackers! Store-brand crackers
work great, so save yourself a little cash.*

2 c. canola oil
1-oz. pkg. ranch salad
   dressing mix
3 T. red pepper flakes

2 T. paprika
2 t. garlic, minced
16-oz. pkg. saltine crackers,
   divided

Whisk together oil, dressing mix and seasonings in a bowl, adjusting
spices to suit your taste. Add one sleeve of crackers to a one-gallon
plastic zipping bag; pour 1/4 of oil mixture over crackers. Alternately
repeat with remaining 3 sleeves and oil mixture. Seal bag. Let stand
for 24 hours, turning bag over once every hour. Makes 30 servings of
5 crackers each.

Slow-Cooked Chili Peanuts

Paula Marchesi
Lenhartsville, PA

*I love fixing quick & easy appetizers, especially during football
season. These nuts are simply awesome! You'll love the taste
and how easy they are to prepare.*

2 12-oz. cans cocktail peanuts
1/4 c. butter, melted

1-5/8 oz. pkg. chili seasoning
   mix

Place peanuts in a slow cooker. Drizzle with melted butter; sprinkle
with seasoning mix. Toss together. Cover and cook on low setting for
2 to 2-1/2 hours. Uncover and turn to high setting; cook another
10 to 15 minutes. Serve warm or cool. Makes about 5 cups.

For stand-up parties, make it easy on guests by serving foods
that can be eaten in just one or two bites.

Candied Nuts

JoAnne Hayon
Sheboygan, WI

My husband and I attended a Toys for Tots party and these nuts were going like wildfire. I knew I needed to get the recipe! Very tasty for fall and winter holidays...makes a nice hostess gift.

3 c. peanuts, mixed nuts
   or almonds
1 egg
1 t. salt
1 c. powdered calorie-free
   sweetener

Optional: 1 to 2 t. pumpkin
   pie spice or cinnamon
6 T. butter, sliced

Spread nuts on an ungreased baking sheet. Bake, uncovered, at 300 degrees for 15 minutes, or until warmed. Meanwhile, in a large bowl, beat egg and salt until foamy. Add sweetener and spice, if desired. Add warmed nuts to egg mixture; stir to coat. Melt butter in a disposable 13"x9" aluminum baking pan in the oven; spread nuts in pan. Bake, uncovered, at 300 degrees for 30 minutes, stirring every 6 to 7 minutes. Drain nuts on paper towels. Store in an airtight container. Makes about 3 cups.

For a quick & easy snack that everybody loves, nothing beats a big bowl of popcorn. Jazz it up with a sprinkle of grated Parmesan cheese or taco seasoning mix, or serve it the classic way, with butter and salt.

Kevin's Football Dip

Diana Karol
Dickerson, KS

*Sunday afternoon football games wouldn't be the same without
this hearty dip. Kevin is our son-in-law and the go-to guy for
crowd-pleasers. A slow cooker makes this dip so easy!*

1 lb. ground beef
1/2 c. onion, chopped
8-oz. jar taco sauce
10-oz. can diced tomatoes with
   hot peppers

32-oz. pkg. pasteurized process
   cheese spread, cubed
tortilla chips, cubed French
   bread

Brown beef with onion in a skillet over medium heat; drain. Transfer
beef mixture to a slow cooker; add taco sauce, tomatoes and cheese.
Cover and cook on high setting for about 45 minutes, stirring every
10 minutes, until cheese is completely melted. Reduce heat to low
setting; serve with chips and bread cubes. Makes 10 to 12 servings.

If busy kids can't get home for dinner, take it to them.
Pack a tailgating basket and enjoy picnicking with them at
the stadium. Be sure to pack extra for hungry team members!

Snacks & Appetizers
◎ TO SHARE ◎

Border Bites

Amy Hunt
Traphill, NC

My family loves Mexican dip! These zesty bites are
just the right size for snacking.

24 wonton wrappers
1 c. canned refried beans
1/4 to 1/2 c. salsa
1 T. taco seasoning mix

1 c. shredded Mexican-blend
   cheese
Garnish: sour cream, diced
   tomato, diced green onions

Spray 24 mini muffin cups with non-stick vegetable spray. Gently
press a wonton wrapper into each cup, with edges extending over
top of cups. Bake at 350 degrees for 5 minutes; let cool. Combine
beans, salsa and seasoning mix; spoon mixture into cups. Bake at
350 degrees for 10 minutes, or until heated through. Top with cheese
and bake one to 2 minutes more, until cheese melts. Garnish as
desired. Makes 2 dozen.

Cheesy Chile Artichoke Dip

Hollie Moots
Marysville, OH

This has become a staple at our get togethers. It's so easy
to prepare...and once you've tried it, you can't stop dipping!

14-oz. jar artichokes, drained
   and chopped
6-1/2 oz. jar marinated
   artichokes, drained
   and chopped

4-oz. can green chiles
1/4 c. mayonnaise
2 c. shredded Cheddar cheese
tortilla chips, snack crackers

Combine artichokes, chiles, mayonnaise and cheese in a bowl; mix
well. Transfer to a greased 8"x8" baking pan. Bake, uncovered, at
350 degrees for 20 to 25 minutes, until bubbly and cheese is melted.
Serve with tortilla chips and crackers. Serves 10 to 12.

Sarah's Special Pickles

Sarah Slaven
Strunk, KY

These fried pickles are great year 'round, but especially for tailgating, homecoming and other fall activities. Try them with homemade ranch dip on the side...yum!

1 c. cornmeal
1 c. self-rising flour
1 t. garlic powder
1 t. onion powder
1/2 t. salt

1 t. pepper
3 eggs
32-oz. jar hamburger dill pickle
   chips, well drained
oil for frying

Combine cornmeal, flour and seasonings in a shallow bowl; beat eggs in a separate shallow bowl. Coat pickle chips in cornmeal mixture, then dip in eggs. Coat again in cornmeal mixture and eggs; coat once more in cornmeal mixture. In a stockpot, heat 2 inches oil to about 375 degrees. Working in batches, add pickles to oil. Cook for about 2 minutes, until golden on both sides. Drain on paper towels. Makes 12 servings.

ooompah!

On a sunny autumn day, throw a backyard Oktoberfest party! Set a festive mood with polka music. Toss some brats on the grill to serve in hard rolls, topped with sauerkraut. Round out the menu with potato salad, homemade applesauce and German chocolate cake for dessert. Sure to be fun for all!

Snacks & Appetizers
⚬ TO SHARE ⚬

Sweet & Spicy Pickles

Shirley Morris
Clarks Summit, PA

*I first tried this recipe for a Fathers' Day gift and
25 years later, it's still my most-requested recipe.*

32-oz. jar whole dill pickles,
    drained, rinsed and sliced
3 to 4 heatproof plastic or
    glass containers with lids
1/2 c. red wine vinegar

2 c. sugar
1 t. celery seed
1 t. dry mustard
3/4 t. red pepper flakes
1/8 t. garlic salt

Pack pickle slices into containers; set aside. Combine remaining
ingredients in a saucepan over medium-high heat; bring to a boil.
Remove from heat; let cool. Ladle equal amounts of vinegar mixture
into each container; let cool. Add lids. Refrigerate for 2 weeks before
serving, if possible, to allow flavors to blend. May be kept refrigerated
for 8 weeks. Makes about 12 servings.

The leaves had a wonderful frolic,
They danced to the wind's loud song.
They whirled, and they floated and scampered,
They circled and flew along.

– Anonymous

Crabmeat Party Spread

Pearl Teiserskas
Brookfield, IL

I received this recipe from a friend back in 1975. Originally I took it to holiday parties, now my family & friends make this for any occasion when they all get together. There are never any leftovers.

1-1/2 c. cream cheese, softened
2 T. mayonnaise-style salad
   dressing
1/2 c. onion, minced
1 clove garlic, minced

juice of 1/2 lemon
3/4 c. chili sauce
1 lb. imitation crabmeat, diced
crackers or celery sticks

In a bowl, combine cream cheese, salad dressing, onion, garlic and lemon juice. Blend well and spread on a serving platter. Top with chili sauce; sprinkle with crabmeat. Serve with crackers or celery sticks. Makes 10 servings.

Blanching makes fresh veggies crisp and bright...super for dipping. Bring a large pot of salted water to a rolling boil, add trimmed veggies and boil for 3 to 4 minutes, just until they begin to soften. Immediately remove veggies to a bowl of ice water. Cool, drain and pat dry.

Hot Shrimp & Artichoke Dip

Char Frojen
Missoula, MT

Sure to be a hit at your next get-together!

16-oz. container sour cream
1 c. mayonnaise
8-oz. pkg. cream cheese,
   softened
2 6-oz. cans medium shrimp,
   drained

4-oz. can sliced black olives,
   drained
4-oz. jar marinated artichokes,
   drained and shredded
assorted crackers

In a bowl, blend together sour cream, mayonnaise and cream cheese.
Stir in shrimp, olives and artichokes; transfer to a lightly greased
8"x8" glass baking pan. Bake, uncovered, at 350 degrees for
30 minutes. Serve warm with crackers. Makes about 4 cups.

Shrimp Dip à la Lory

Lory Howard
Jackson, CA

A great tailgate recipe...so easy, so good!

6-oz. can medium shrimp,
   drained
1 c. mayonnaise
1 c. shredded Cheddar cheese

1 T. onion, grated
1/8 t. Worcestershire sauce
1/8 t. salt
assorted crackers

Blend all ingredients except crackers in a bowl. Cover and chill until
serving time. Serve with crackers. Makes 6 to 8 servings.

A good rule of thumb for appetizers...allow 6 to 8 servings
per person if dinner will follow. Plan for 12 to 15 per person
if it's an appetizer-only gathering.

Not Just Any Cheese Ball

JoAnn Kurtz
Castaic, CA

This recipe was given to me by a co-worker 15 years ago. I've used it for parties of all kinds and even given it as a hostess gift.

2 8-oz. pkgs. cream cheese,
  softened
1-1/2 T. ranch salad dressing
  mix
1/2 c. celery, finely chopped

3 T. dried, minced onion
1/2 t. granulated garlic,
  or more to taste
1 c. salted peanuts, chopped
snack crackers

In a bowl, mix all ingredients except peanuts and crackers; form into a ball. Wrap in plastic wrap and refrigerate. At serving time, roll cheese ball in chopped peanuts. Serve with crackers. Makes 12 servings.

Spoon dips and spreads into pretty crocks or vintage blue canning jars...they're ideal as hostess gifts. Add a box of crisp crackers and tie on a spreader with a pretty ribbon... sure to be appreciated!

Mediterranean Stuffed Mushrooms

Joyceann Dreibelbis
Wooster, OH

These delicious mushrooms can be stuffed in advance. Prep time is only 30 minutes! For best results, use mushrooms with caps that are about two inches in diameter.

16 mushrooms, stems removed
1 T. olive oil
1/4 c. sun-dried tomatoes in oil, drained and finely chopped
1/2 c. panko dry bread crumbs
1 green onion, thinly sliced
1/2 c. cream cheese, softened
1/2 c. shredded 3-cheese blend
1 T. fresh basil, chopped

Finely chop enough mushroom stems to measure 1/4 cup. Discard any remaining stems. Heat oil in a skillet over medium-high heat. Add chopped stems and tomatoes; cook and stir for 2 to 4 minutes. Add bread crumbs and onion; cook and stir for one minute. Remove from heat; let cool for 10 minutes. Set aside 1/4 cup crumb mixture for topping. In a bowl, mix cream cheese, shredded cheese and basil until blended. Stir in remaining crumb mixture; spoon into mushroom caps, adding about one tablespoon of mixture to each. Arrange mushroom caps on an aluminum foil-lined rimmed baking sheet; sprinkle with reserved crumb mixture. Bake at 400 degrees for 15 to 20 minutes, until heated through. Makes 16 mushrooms.

Make a party tray of savory bite-size appetizer tarts...guests will never suspect how easy it is! Bake frozen mini phyllo shells according to package directions, then spoon in a favorite creamy dip or spread.

Marcie's Autumn Tea

Leona Krivda
Belle Vernon, PA

*My oldest daughter makes this refreshing chilled tea in the fall
and it is always a hit. We hope you will enjoy it also.*

5 tea bags
1/2 c. sugar
5 c. boiling water
5 c. unsweetened apple juice

2 c. cranberry juice cocktail
1/3 c. lemon juice
1/4 t. pumpkin pie spice
ice cubes

Combine tea bags and sugar in a heat-proof one-gallon pitcher. Add
boiling water; let stand for 8 minutes. Discard tea bags. Add juices
and spice; stir well until sugar is dissolved. Chill; serve over ice.
Makes about 3 quarts.

Big, colorful ice cubes for a party punch bowl...
arrange fresh cranberries or thin slices of citrus in
muffin tins, fill with water and freeze.

Harvest Moon Punch

Sandy Ward
Anderson, IN

*This refreshing punch is super-simple to stir up
and will serve a thirsty crowd.*

2 qts. apple cider
1 c. lemon juice

1/2 c. sugar
2 ltrs. ginger ale, chilled

In a punch bowl or large pitcher, combine cider, lemon juice and sugar. Stir until sugar dissolves. Cover and chill. Add ginger ale just before serving. Makes about one gallon.

When I was young, my parents and I would go to my aunt's & uncle's house for Thanksgiving dinner. An elderly neighbor couple and a bachelor neighbor were also invited to share the day. Usually there were 12 to 16 people sitting down to the table. My aunt is a fantastic cook and this was her day to indulge her love of cooking. Besides two roast turkeys, two kinds of stuffing, homemade pickles, pickled beets, applesauce and cranberry relish, there were usually a dozen different pies, cakes, tartlets and cheesecake. Needless to say, we would return for the next two days to finish up all the delicious food. These days, Thanksgiving is a much smaller affair. Even though now it's just my parents, my fiancé and me, I have fond memories of those large dinners with all that wonderful food.

–Lisa Cunningham, Boothbay, ME

Hot Caramel Apple Cider

Jessica Shrout
Flintstone, MD

This slow-cooker beverage is great on cool fall days. A sweet pick-me-up that everyone will love...it's so easy to whip up and go about your day!

3 qts. apple cider or apple juice
6 4-inch cinnamon sticks
1/2 c. caramel ice cream topping

Garnish: whipped cream, additional caramel topping

Pour apple juice or cider into a slow cooker; add cinnamon sticks. Cover and cook on high setting for about 4 hours. Cinnamon sticks will soften and uncurl. Just before serving, stir in 1/2 cup caramel topping. Serve in mugs, topped with a dollop of whipped cream and a drizzle of caramel topping. Serves 12.

Autumn is the perfect time of year to hit all the best craft shows, flea markets and tag sales. Call your best girlfriends, pack a basket of snacks and a thermos of spiced cider, and head out for a day of shopping fun.

QUICK

Sandwiches &

Soups

Buffalo Chicken Cheesesteak Sandwiches

Becky Drees
Pittsfield, MA

A favorite football game meal at our house.

1 T. butter, sliced
1 sweet onion, thinly sliced
1 lb. boneless, skinless chicken
   breasts, thinly sliced
salt and pepper to taste

1/2 c. favorite buffalo wing
   sauce
8 slices provolone cheese
4 sub sandwich rolls, split

Melt butter in a large skillet over medium-high heat. Add onion; sauté until golden, about 3 minutes. Season chicken slices with salt and pepper; add to skillet and sauté until no longer pink. Stir in sauce. With a spatula, separate chicken mixture in skillet into 4 portions; top each with 2 cheese slices. Remove skillet from heat; cover and let stand until cheese melts, about 5 minutes. Scoop each cheese-topped section onto a roll; wrap rolls tightly in aluminum foil. Place rolls on a baking sheet. Bake at 250 degrees for 10 minutes, or until warmed through. Unwrap carefully and serve. Makes 4 servings.

Slip children's drawings between two pieces of clear self-adhesive plastic for placemats that are both practical and playful.

Easy Meatball Hoagies

Donna Wilson
Maryville, TN

*Really quick & easy! I love meatball subs and this is
a great recipe to make at home.*

12-oz. pkg. frozen meatballs
24-oz. jar spaghetti sauce
2 T. butter, softened
1/2 t. garlic powder

4 hoagie rolls, split
Garnish: sliced mozzarella
   cheese

In a saucepan over medium-low heat, combine meatballs and sauce.
Cover and cook for about 15 minutes, stirring occasionally, until
meatballs are cooked. Meanwhile, blend butter and garlic powder in a
small bowl. Partially open rolls; spread cut sides with butter mixture.
Place rolls on a baking sheet. Bake, uncovered, at 350 degrees for
10 minutes, or until toasted. To serve, divide meatballs and sauce
among rolls; top with a slice of cheese. Bake 8 to 10 minutes. Serves 4.

Take the kids to a neighborhood garden center for fall fun...
all-you-can-carry pumpkins, shiny gourds, corn shocks for the
porch posts and maybe even a cup of cool cider. While you're
there, pick out some daffodil bulbs to plant in October.

Mom's Pizza Subs

Debra Stephens
Owasso, OK

This recipe was created by my mother. When I was little, we had one small pizza joint in town. We loved their pizza subs, but they didn't stay in business long. When they closed, Mom studied the ingredients and we made our own at home.

16-oz. pkg. ground pork
    sausage
6-oz. can tomato paste
1/4 c. water
1 t. garlic powder

1 t. dried oregano
8 hamburger buns, split
8 slices provolone cheese
40 pepperoni slices

Brown sausage in a skillet over medium heat; drain. Stir in tomato paste, water and seasonings. Simmer for 5 minutes, or until thickened. Spoon sausage mixture onto bottoms of buns; top each with 5 pepperoni slices and one cheese slice. Add tops of buns; wrap each bun in aluminum foil. Place buns on a baking sheet. Bake at 350 degrees for 10 minutes, or until cheese melts. Unwrap carefully and serve. Makes 8 servings.

Try something new for brown-bag lunches...roll any combination of cheese, deli meat and veggies in a tortilla. Even a kid-friendly peanut butter & jelly wrap tastes terrific!

QUICK
Sandwiches & Soups

Mothers' Club Bar-B-Q

Sandy J. Ward
Brimfield, IL

When I was growing up in a small town in the 60s, our school had no cafeteria. It was a real treat when our Mothers' Club sold these sandwiches once a month as a fundraiser. For our family, my mother tweaked it into a recipe using just one pound of hamburger. Now my own daughter requests this every year for her birthday.

1 lb. ground beef	1 T. mustard
1 onion, chopped	1 t. garlic, minced
1/2 c. barbecue sauce	1 t. vinegar
1/3 c. brown sugar, packed	salt and pepper to taste
1/4 c. catsup	4 to 6 hamburger buns, split

Brown beef and onion in a skillet over medium heat; drain. Stir in remaining ingredients except buns; reduce heat to medium-low. Simmer for about 30 minutes, stirring occasionally. If making several batches, mixture may be kept in a slow cooker on low setting for up to 2 hours. Serve on buns. Makes 4 to 6 servings.

Autumn means shopping for new back-to-school clothing. Preserve the memories in children's outgrown clothing by making a simple lap quilt. Cut large squares and stitch together, then layer with thin batting and a fabric backing. So sweet!

Halloween Sloppy Joes

Jessica Kraus
Delaware, OH

A staple at my house for Halloween night. This recipe is so simple and I always have everything I need on hand. I never use canned Sloppy Joe sauce anymore!

1 lb. ground beef
1 onion, chopped
1 c. catsup
1/4 c. water

2 T. brown sugar, packed
1 T. cider vinegar
1 t. Worcestershire sauce
6 hamburger buns, split

Brown beef and onion in a skillet over medium heat; drain. Stir in remaining ingredients except buns; reduce heat to medium-low. Simmer for 25 minutes, stirring occasionally. To serve, spoon onto buns. Makes 6 servings.

When I was a child, my grandmother and mother always made my costumes for Halloween. So when I became a mother, I knew I wanted my children to have homemade costumes too. Of course, I did not take into account the fact that my grandmother was a master seamstress and I could barely sew on a button! Nevertheless, I did my best and made my boys everything from clowns to scarecrows to Frosty the Snowman. My youngest son even won our local costume parade contest when he was just a year old! They're too old to dress up for Halloween anymore, but the memories of making those costumes, then seeing them so excited to put them on, will be with me forever. I hope that my kids keep those memories too, and maybe will carry on the tradition of Halloween costumes, not from a box, but from the heart.

–Hollie Moots, Marysville, OH

Cheese Frenchies

Brenda Schlosser
Brighton, CO

Back in the 60s and 70s, a restaurant chain called King's Food Host served these delicious crunchy-gooey sandwiches. The restaurants are no longer around, but these are just as good, if not better! Perfect comfort food on a cold day with a hot bowl of tomato soup.

6 slices white bread
3 T. mayonnaise
6 slices American cheese
1 egg
1/2 c. milk

3/4 c. all-purpose flour
1 t. salt
1 c. corn flake cereal, crushed
oil for deep frying

Spread bread slices with mayonnaise on one side. Add 2 slices cheese to each of 3 slices; close sandwiches with remaining bread. Cut sandwiches into triangles; trim off crusts, if desired. Whisk together egg, milk, flour and salt in a shallow dish; place crushed cereal in a separate dish. Dip each triangle into egg mixture; coat with cereal. Add one inch oil to a skillet over medium-high heat; heat to 375 degrees. Add triangles; deep-fry until golden on both sides. Place on paper towels to drain. Serves 3.

How do you know when the oil is hot enough for deep-frying? Drop a cube of bread into the hot oil. If it sizzles and turns golden in 60 seconds, the oil is ready to go.

State Fair Italian Sausages

Tamela James
Grove City, OH

This recipe is inspired by our family's many trips to the Ohio State Fair. We love the Italian sausages sold at the fair, but we don't care for the grilled onions and peppers, so we improvised with our own toppings. The contrast of the hot spicy sausages with the cold crisp lettuce is delicious.

6 to 8 Italian pork sausage links
1/2 head lettuce, shredded
zesty Italian salad dressing
    to taste

6 to 8 hot dog buns, split
mustard to taste

In a large saucepan, cover sausages with water. Bring to a boil over high heat; boil for 10 to 15 minutes. Drain sausages well; grill over medium heat until browned. Shortly before serving time, place lettuce in a bowl; add just enough dressing to coat lettuce well. To serve, place sausages on buns; garnish with mustard and top with lettuce mixture. Makes 6 to 8 servings.

A fireside cookout can be as near as your own backyard! Gather family & friends and enjoy the crisp fall air. Play touch football, toast marshmallows, tell ghost stories, jump into a pile of leaves...be a kid again!

Easy Reuben Stromboli

Jo Ann
Gooseberry Patch

I love the Easy Stromboli recipe in one of our previous cookbooks.
This is a whole flavorful new twist on that recipe!

1 loaf frozen bread dough,
   thawed
8-oz. bottle Thousand Island
   salad dressing, divided
1/4 lb. deli corned beef, chopped

14-1/2 oz. can sauerkraut,
   well drained
1/4 lb. sliced Swiss cheese
1 egg white, beaten
Optional: caraway seed

On a lightly floured surface, roll out dough into a 15-inch by 12-inch
rectangle. Spread 1/3 to 1/2 cup salad dressing down the center of
rectangle. Layer corned beef, sauerkraut and cheese down the center.
Roll up dough, starting on one long edge; pinch ends to seal. Place
seam-side down on a lightly greased baking sheet. Brush with egg
white; sprinkle with caraway seed, if desired. Bake at 350 degrees for
30 to 35 minutes, until golden and cheese is melted. Slice; serve
warm with remaining salad dressing. Makes 8 servings.

Whip up this super-simple veggie dip! Blend one cup cottage
cheese, 1/4 cup plain Greek yogurt, one tablespoon minced
onion, one teaspoon dried parsley and 1/4 teaspoon dill weed.
Serve with bite-size fresh vegetables...a great go-with
for sandwich suppers.

Sloppy Joe Pocket Pies

Mel Chencharick
Julian, PA

*Need something quick to take for the kids to eat after
the game? They'll love these yummy little pockets!*

2 lbs. ground beef chuck
1 onion, chopped
16-oz. can Sloppy Joe sauce
1-1/2 t. garlic powder

6 9-inch pie crusts
1 c. shredded Cheddar cheese
1 egg yolk, lightly beaten

In a large skillet, brown beef and onion over medium-high heat; drain.
Stir in sauce and garlic powder. Reduce heat to low; simmer for
20 minutes. Remove from heat; cool slightly. Meanwhile, on a lightly
floured surface, unroll pie crusts. With a 5-inch round cutter, cut
5 circles from each crust, re-rolling dough as necessary. Spoon
2 tablespoons beef mixture into the center of each circle; top with
1-1/2 teaspoons cheese. Lightly brush edges of circles with egg yolk;
fold over to enclose filling. Crimp edges with a fork to seal. Place pies
on lightly greased baking sheets. Bake at 400 degrees for 20 minutes,
or until golden. Best if served immediately. Makes 2-1/2 dozen.

Sloppy Jane Sandwiches

Joyceann Dreibelbis
Wooster, OH

*This simple slow-cooker recipe is easily doubled for
a tailgating party with friends.*

16-oz. pkg. hot dogs,
   sliced 3/4-inch thick
28-oz. can baked beans
1/3 c. chili sauce

1 t. dried, minced onion
1 t. mustard
6 to 8 hot dog buns,
   split and toasted

In a slow cooker, stir together all ingredients except buns. Cover and
cook on low setting for 2 to 3 hours. To serve, spoon into buns.
Serves 6 to 8.

QUICK
Sandwiches & Soups

Auntie B's Hamburger BBQ

*Bethi Hendrickson
Danville, PA*

My Aunt Barb used to make this recipe all the time when I was a kid. Now I make it for my family. It can be made ahead or even frozen for busy evenings. It is a family favorite!

1 lb. ground beef	2 T. water
Optional: 1/2 c. onion, chopped	1 T. white vinegar
1/2 c. catsup	1 T. mustard
3 to 4 T. brown sugar, packed	8 hamburger buns, split
2 T. Worcestershire sauce	Optional: 8 slices cheese

In a skillet over medium heat, brown beef with onion, if using; drain. In a small bowl, combine remaining ingredients except buns and cheese. Whisk until smooth; pour over beef mixture. Reduce heat to low; simmer for 15 to 20 minutes, stirring occasionally. Serve on hamburger buns, topped with cheese, if desired. Makes 8 servings.

Throw a pumpkin painting party. Provide acrylic paints, brushes and plenty of pumpkins...invite kids to bring their imagination and an old shirt to wear as a smock. Parents are sure to join in too!

My Famous Shredded Chicken

Vickie Zettler
Springfield, OH

I grew up in a family where my mother and grandmother made everything from scratch. Later, as a single mother raising two sons with "hollow legs," I sometimes had to invent recipes that produced not only quality but quantity. I've been making this for years, and the other day one of my sons called to ask me for the recipe. He's 43 years old now... I was so happy!

40-oz. pkg. frozen boneless,
  skinless chicken tenderloins
10-3/4 oz. can cream of
  mushroom soup
10-3/4 oz. can cream of
  chicken soup

10-3/4 oz. can cream of
  celery soup
salt and pepper to taste
8 to 10 sandwich buns, or
  cooked rice or noodles

Place chicken in a slow cooker, separating pieces. Top with soups; season with salt and pepper. Cover and cook on low setting for 8 to 10 hours, until chicken is very tender. Uncover; shred chicken with 2 forks and stir into soup mixture. Continue cooking, uncovered, for about 30 minutes, until gravy is thick. Serve chicken mixture spooned onto buns or ladled over rice or noodles. Makes 8 to 10 servings.

Give any sandwich a goblin face...the kids will love 'em!
Arrange olive slices for eyes, a banana pepper nose,
carrot crinkle ears and parsley hair.

Ultimate Grilled Cheese Sandwiches

Gladys Kielar
Whitehouse, OH

*You'll never burn the grilled cheese again! This way is
so much easier and more delicious. Now all of the sandwiches
come out crisp and ready at the same time. You will love these.*

8 slices white bread
8 slices American cheese
8 t. margarine, softened

4 t. grated Parmesan cheese,
   divided

Assemble bread and cheese to make 4 sandwiches, enclosing 2 slices
cheese in each. Spread outsides of sandwiches with margarine; place
on an ungreased baking sheet. Bake, uncovered, at 400 degrees for
8 minutes. Sprinkle with half of the Parmesan cheese. Flip
sandwiches; sprinkle with remaining Parmesan. Return to oven
for 6 to 8 minutes, until golden. Makes 4 servings.

Save the plastic liners when you toss out empty
cereal boxes. They make terrific wrappers for sandwiches
that will go into lunchboxes.

Becki's Turkey Salad

Rebecca Etling
Blairsville, PA

A wonderful way to use up leftover turkey! The ingredients are a surprising combination and taste delicious.

4 c. cooked turkey or chicken,
   cubed
1 c. celery, chopped
3/4 c. sweetened dried
   cranberries

3/4 c. low-fat mayonnaise
2 green onions, chopped
1 t. Italian seasoning
1 t. paprika
1/2 t. pepper

Combine all ingredients in a bowl; mix with a fork until well blended. Cover and refrigerate for one hour to allow flavors to blend. May be served with bread as a sandwich or spooned onto lettuce as a salad. Makes 6 to 8 servings.

Hot Turkey Sandwiches

Irene Robinson
Cincinnati, OH

Tired of Thanksgiving leftovers? Turn them into something new and tasty in a jiffy with these simple open-faced sandwiches.

4 slices white bread, toasted
8 thick slices deli roast turkey

3 c. prepared stuffing
1 c. turkey gravy

Place each slice of toast on a microwave-safe plate. Divide turkey, stuffing and gravy among toast slices. Microwave, uncovered, on high for 30 to 40 seconds, until heated through. Makes 4 servings.

To freshen a loaf of bread that's beginning to go stale, tuck a stalk of celery into the bread bag overnight.

Thanksgiving Sandwich

Cynthia Johnson
Verona, WI

The creamy spread in this recipe is very versatile...serve it with crackers for a tasty snack or on hot toast for breakfast.

4 English muffins, split
  and toasted

8 slices deli roast turkey
Garnish: fresh spinach

Spread each English muffin half with desired amount of Orange Cream Cheese Spread. Layer 4 muffin halves each with 2 slices turkey and desired amount of spinach; top with remaining muffin halves. Makes 4 servings.

Orange Cream Cheese Spread:

8-oz. pkg. cream cheese,
  softened
1/4 c. orange marmalade

1/2 c. sweetened dried
  cranberries
1/4 c. chopped walnuts

Combine all ingredients in a bowl; mix well. Cover and refrigerate for 30 minutes before serving. Keep refrigerated.

Thanksgiving is so family-centered...why not have a post-holiday potluck with friends, the weekend after Turkey Day? Everyone can bring their favorite "leftover" concoctions and relax together.

Greek Patty Pockets

Louise Greer
Cartersville, GA

These are the tastiest hot pockets you will ever eat...all the flavors and juices cook right into the bread. My favorite will always be Greek, but Mexican is a close second. Make 'em by the dozens, as they will keep in the freezer for several months. I guarantee these will be a hit for just about any kind of fall activities you enjoy.

1 lb. ground beef, chicken
   or turkey
1/2 c. onion, finely chopped
1 T. salt
1/2 T. pepper
garlic powder and ground
   coriander to taste

6 pita rounds
Garnish: crumbled feta cheese,
   sliced black olives,
   cucumbers, lettuce and
   tomatoes, Greek salad
   dressing

Combine meat, onion and seasonings. Mix well and form into 6 patties. Slice open each pita round; place a patty inside and press closed. Wrap packets tightly in aluminum foil; freeze. To serve, place wrapped packets on a baking sheet. Bake at 350 degrees for about 25 minutes, until hot and meat is cooked through. Serve with desired toppings on the side. Makes 6 servings.

Mexican Patty Pockets:

Prepare, wrap, freeze and bake as above, using ground cumin instead of coriander and folded 8-inch corn tortillas instead of pitas. Serve with shredded Cheddar cheese, sliced black olives, lettuce and tomatoes, sour cream and salsa.

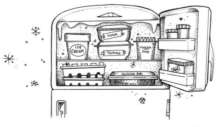

No more freezer mysteries! After wrapping, be sure to label and date food packages. A permanent ink marker works well.

◯ QUICK ◯
Sandwiches & Soups

Laurel Pizza Burgers

Debby Hardisky
New Castle, PA

This recipe was given to me by Donna Gentile, my best friend for many years. Our children attended elementary school together and loved these mini pizzas that were served in the cafeteria. All the kids couldn't wait to get one!

1 lb. ground beef
1/2 lb. bologna, ground or very
    finely chopped
1-1/2 c. pasteurized process
    cheese spread, shredded

1-1/2 c. spaghetti sauce
1 t. dried parsley
1/4 t. dried oregano
8 sandwich buns, split

Brown beef in a skillet over medium heat; drain. Stir in remaining ingredients except buns. Simmer over low heat for about 10 minutes, until cheese melts. Separate buns and arrange, cut-side up, on an ungreased baking sheet. Spoon beef mixture onto buns. Bake, uncovered, at 350 degrees for about 20 minutes, until golden. Makes 8 servings of 2 mini pizzas each.

Show your spirit...dress up a garden scarecrow
in a hometown football jersey. Go team!

Taco Sloppy Joes

Gina Wiberg
Harris, MN

I'm happy to share this recipe that our family loves. I used to make it for my family, and now our grown kids make it for their friends.

1 lb. ground beef
1/2 c. onion, chopped
10-3/4 oz. can tomato soup
2/3 c. catsup
1-1/4 oz. pkg. taco
    seasoning mix

2 T. mustard
4 to 6 hamburger buns, split
Garnish: American or
    Cheddar cheese slices
Optional: sour cream

Brown beef and onion in a skillet over medium heat; drain. Stir in soup, catsup, seasoning mix and mustard. Reduce heat to low; simmer for about 10 minutes. Add a little water if too thick. To serve, spoon onto buns. Top with cheese and sour cream, if desired. Makes 4 to 6 servings.

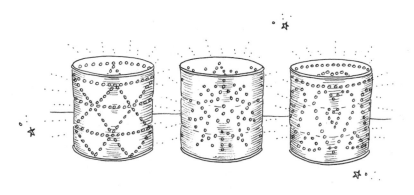

Pierced tin lanterns are so pretty twinkling on the dinner table... perfect for casual entertaining. Fill an empty tin can with water, freeze solid, then tap a design of holes all around with awl and hammer. After the ice has melted, set a votive candle inside.

Cheesy Quesadillas

Shannon Reents
Loudonville, OH

My family loves these when we're watching football on TV.
You may wish to make some without the peppers
for those who prefer milder flavors.

16-oz. pkg. shredded Pepper
   Jack cheese
1 c. fresh parsley, chopped

5 jalapeño peppers, seeded
   and chopped
16 8-inch flour tortillas

Combine cheese, parsley and peppers in a bowl. For each quesadilla, spoon a portion of cheese mixture into the center of a tortilla. Fold over; press the edges together. Spray a large skillet with non-stick vegetable spray; heat over medium heat. Cook quesadillas, one to 2 at a time, until golden on both sides and cheese is melted. Quesadillas may also be toasted in a toaster oven. Keep warm until serving time, or reheat in toaster oven for 5 minutes. For best results, do not reheat in a microwave. Makes 16 servings.

Whip up a zippy Tex-Mex side dish pronto! Prepare instant rice, using chicken broth instead of water. Stir in a generous dollop of spicy salsa, top with shredded cheese and cover with a lid for a few minutes, until the cheese is melted.

Chili Con Carne

Catherine Matthews
Wise, VA

A hearty, warm and spicy meal for a chilly fall evening. Top it
with your favorite shredded cheese and serve with saltines.

2 lbs. ground beef
1 onion, diced
2 14-1/2 oz. cans diced
    tomatoes
2 15-1/2 oz. cans dark or
    light kidney beans

2 T. chili powder
1 T. ground cumin
2 T. salt
1 T. pepper

Brown beef and onion in a large skillet over medium heat; drain. Add
undrained tomatoes and beans; mix well and stir in seasonings. Bring
to a boil. Reduce heat to low and simmer for 30 minutes, stirring
occasionally. Add a little water if a thinner consistency is desired.
Makes 8 servings.

Host a chili cook-off! Ask neighbors to bring a pot of their
"secret recipe" chili to share, then have a friendly judging for
the best. You can even hand out wooden spoons,
oven mitts and aprons as prizes!

Pop's Harvest Chili

Odell Underwood
Mount Hope, WV

This flavorful chili is perfect for autumn...it warms the soul and brings the family together. Serve with warm fresh-baked cornbread.

1 lb. ground beef
1/2 lb. ground pork sausage
1/4 c. green onions, chopped
1-oz. pkg. chili seasoning mix
1/2 c. yellow, red or orange
  pepper, diced

1 c. sliced mushrooms
15-1/2 oz. can Great Northern
  or pinto beans
14-1/2 oz. can lima beans
14-1/2 oz. can Italian-seasoned
  diced tomatoes

In a heavy Dutch oven over medium heat, combine beef, sausage and green onions. Sauté until browned; drain. Stir in seasoning mix, pepper, mushrooms and undrained beans and tomatoes. Simmer over low heat until vegetables are soft, about 10 minutes. Add enough water to cover ingredients, or to desired consistency. Simmer for 20 to 30 minutes, stirring occasionally. Serves 6 to 8.

October is crisp days and cool nights, a time to curl up around the dancing flames and sink into a good book.

–John Sinor

Autumn Chili Soup

Debra Collins
Gaylesville, AL

*This is one of my family's favorite chili dishes during
football season. Serve with corn chips.*

1 lb. ground beef
14-1/2 oz. can can diced
  tomatoes
15-1/2 oz. can kidney beans,
  drained and rinsed

15-oz. can corn, drained
10-oz. can diced tomatoes and
  green chiles, drained
2 c. water
1-oz. pkg. taco seasoning mix

Brown beef in a large stockpot over medium heat; drain. Stir in
undrained tomatoes and remaining ingredients; bring to a boil. Reduce
heat to low. Simmer, uncovered, for 15 to 20 minutes, stirring
occasionally. Makes 6 servings.

This is my favorite time of the year. We always had a big
Louisiana hayride with as many adults as children coming along,
singing songs and just visiting. Then after the hayride we'd all
go to someone's house for a bowl of homemade chili. We still
do this today on Halloween for all our grandchildren.
Fall fun doesn't get any better!

–Nan Calcagno, Grosse Tete, LA

◯ QUICK ◯
Sandwiches & Soups

Sent-to-Bed Tomato Soup

Margaret Welder
Madrid, IA

This soup, served with a toasted cheese sandwich, was one of my mother's favorite quick suppers. It got its name one night when I complained about having it for supper and my father sent me to bed with NO supper! I'm 75 now and I still remember that so well. I have made this soup many times for my family, and my husband still thinks it is the best.

3 T. butter
1 stalk celery, diced
1/4 c. onion, minced
2 c. canned diced tomatoes
   with juice
1/4 t. baking soda

1 t. sugar
1 T. all-purpose flour
2-1/2 c. whole milk, divided
2-1/2 t. salt, or to taste
1/4 t. pepper
Optional: minced fresh parsley

Melt butter in a saucepan over medium heat. Add celery and onion; sauté until soft. Add tomatoes with juice; bring to a boil. Add baking soda and sugar; stir down the foam. In a jar with a tight lid, shake together flour and one cup milk; add to mixture in saucepan. Stir in remaining milk, salt and pepper; return to a boil. Cook, stirring often, for about 2 minutes, until thickened. Serve soup sprinkled with parsley, if desired. Makes 6 servings.

Try something new...grilled cheese croutons! Make grilled cheese sandwiches as usual, then slice them into small squares. Toss into a bowl of creamy tomato soup...yum!

Ham & Corn Chowder

Molly Ebert
Columbus, IN

This is a simple yet rich and comforting soup to share on a rainy day...a delicious way to use some of that leftover holiday ham.

2 T. butter
1/2 c. onion, finely chopped
3 T. all-purpose flour
14-1/2 oz. can chicken broth
2 c. potatoes, peeled and diced

2 15-oz. cans corn
2 c. half-and-half
1-1/2 c. cooked ham, diced
2 T. fresh parsley, snipped

Melt butter in a large saucepan over medium heat. Add onion and cook until tender, stirring frequently. Add flour; stir to make a paste. Slowly whisk in broth, stirring until smooth; add potatoes. Cover and cook for 10 minutes, or until potatoes are just tender. Stir in undrained corn and half-and-half. Reduce heat to low. Simmer, uncovered, for 6 to 8 minutes. Stir in ham and parsley; heat through but do not allow to boil. Makes 8 servings.

Just for fun, serve up soft pretzels instead of dinner rolls... so easy, the kids can do it! Twist strips of refrigerated bread stick dough into pretzel shapes and place on an ungreased baking sheet. Brush with beaten egg white, sprinkle with coarse salt and bake as the package directs.

Simple Sweet Corn Soup

*Karen Hibbert
Abergele, Wales*

Fantastic for children for a warming lunchtime dish. If you prefer your onions less crunchy, sauté them in a little butter before adding to the soup. Shredded chicken can be added for a heartier soup.

2 c. chicken broth
1/2 t. garlic powder
1/4 t. dry mustard
salt and pepper to taste
1 c. frozen corn
14-3/4 oz. can creamed corn

2 green onions, chopped,
   or 2 T. dried, chopped onion
Optional: leftover mashed
   potatoes
saltine crackers

In a large saucepan over medium heat, stir together broth and seasonings. Add frozen corn, creamed corn and onions; stir again. Cook for several minutes, until corn is thawed. If a thicker soup is desired, stir in mashed potatoes to desired consistency. Bring to a boil. Reduce heat to medium-low; simmer for 20 minutes. Serve with crackers. Makes 4 servings.

When we were young, my brother Carl, sister Sue and I would go along when my parents helped my grandparents make hay. We were too little to help, but I remember fondly that Grandma would lay a blanket out in the back of the pickup. She would have a jug of lemonade, snacks and coloring books to keep us busy. In between loads of hay, we kids would nap and play outside in the small creek or near the barn. Whenever Grandpa and Dad brought in another load, we had to hop back into the truck bed and stay there until they were gone. Grandma and Mom would unload the hay into the loft. As soon as they headed out for another load, we would explore some more, catching bugs, butterflies and the occasional minnow. This is one of my favorite childhood memories.

–Sandy Groezinger, Stockton, IL

Homestyle Chicken Noodle Soup

Nancy Wise
Little Rock, AR

Simple to make...sure to make you feel better in a jiffy!
Chicken thighs are extra flavorful and budget-friendly too.
Use low-sodium broth, if you like.

1 T. oil
1 c. onion, chopped
2 c. celery, sliced
2 c. carrots, peeled and sliced
8 c. chicken broth

1-1/2 lbs. chicken thighs
7-oz. pkg. fine egg noodles,
  uncooked
salt and pepper to taste

Heat oil in a soup pot over medium heat; add vegetables. Sauté until onion is translucent, about 5 minutes; drain. Add broth to pot along with chicken, removing skin from chicken pieces, if desired. Increase heat to medium-high; bring to a boil. Reduce heat to medium-low and simmer for 30 to 45 minutes, until chicken is very tender. Remove chicken to a plate, reserving broth; let cool. Shred or dice chicken, discarding bones; set aside. Return to a boil; stir in noodles and simmer for 8 minutes. Add chicken, salt and pepper; heat through. Makes 8 servings.

For the most flavorful chicken soup, use bone-in, skin-on chicken. Skin and bones are easily removed after the chicken is cooked. Chill the soup overnight and skim off the fat before rewarming and serving your delicious soup.

Wild Rice Soup

Leona Krivda
Belle Vernon, PA

We all love this soup and it is so easy. I make it quite often, from late fall throughout winter. It's a great make-ahead, since the flavor is even better when refrigerated overnight before serving.

6-oz. pkg. long-grain &
  wild rice mix
1 T. onion, minced
2 10-3/4 oz. cans cream of
  potato soup
6 c. milk

2 c. shredded Cheddar or
  American cheese
1 T. fresh parsley, chopped
pepper to taste
1/3 to 1/2 c. crumbled bacon
  or bacon bits

Prepare rice according to package directions; transfer to a soup pot. Stir in remaining ingredients except bacon; add bacon and stir again. Simmer over medium-low heat for about 30 minutes. Cool soup to room temperature; cover and refrigerate until the next day. Shortly before serving time, reheat soup over low heat, adding a little milk if too thick. Makes 6 to 8 servings.

Start a delicious soup supper tradition on Halloween night. Soup stays simmering hot while you hand out treats, and it isn't too filling, so everyone has more room to nibble on goodies!

Cream of Potato Soup

Vickie
Gooseberry Patch

Simple and comforting. When I want a smoother texture, I use an immersion blender to purée it right in the saucepan.

1 T. butter
1/2 c. green onions, sliced
2 c. chicken broth
1-1/2 lbs. new yellow potatoes, cubed

salt and pepper to taste
1-1/2 c. heavy cream
Garnish: additional sliced green onions

Melt butter in a large saucepan over medium-low heat. Add green onions; cook for one minute. Add broth, potatoes and seasonings; bring to a boil over high heat. Reduce heat to low. Cover and simmer until potatoes are tender, 15 to 20 minutes. Stir in cream; heat through without boiling. Garnish soup with additional onions. Makes 4 servings.

Zucchini Bisque

Gloria Larue-Schantz
Breiningsville, PA

This recipe is delicious...our family loves it.

2 c. zucchini, chopped
1 c. water
1/2 c. tomato juice
1 T. onion, chopped

1 cube chicken bouillon
1/8 t. dried basil
8-oz. pkg. cream cheese, cubed

In a saucepan over medium heat, combine all ingredients except cream cheese. Bring to a boil; reduce heat to low. Cover and simmer for 20 minutes, or until zucchini is tender. Pour soup into a blender; add cream cheese and blend until smooth. Return to saucepan; gently heat through. Makes 4 servings.

Kitchen scissors make quick work
of slicing green onions.

Lori's Green Tomato Soup

Lori Rosenberg
University Heights, OH

I made this soup last fall for the first time. When I shared it with neighbors, they gave it a thumbs-up and then went home to their own gardens in search of any lingering tomatoes to use up!

2 T. olive oil
8 slices bacon
1-1/2 c. green onions, chopped
1 T. garlic, minced
1 bay leaf
1 t. salt

1/2 t. pepper
4 to 5 c. green tomatoes, chopped
1 c. chicken broth
2 c. water

Heat oil in a large pot over medium-high heat. Add bacon; cook until nearly crisp. Add green onions, garlic and bay leaf; cook until tender. Drain; stir in salt, pepper and tomatoes. Add broth and water. Bring to a boil; reduce heat to low. Partially cover and simmer for 35 minutes. Add more salt and pepper, if needed. Discard bay leaf before serving. Serves 4.

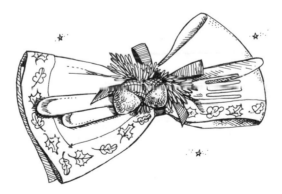

Dress up fabric napkins in no time. Roll each napkin, tie with ribbon in russet or rich brown, and tuck a pair of acorns under the ribbon.

Mexican Soup

Carole Clark
Sterling Heights, MI

This is really the best meatless soup ever and it just takes a few minutes to put together. Make it as spicy or as mild as you like by adjusting the amounts of jalapeños and their juice.

32-oz. container chicken or
   vegetable broth
2 14-1/2 oz. cans Mexican
   stewed tomatoes, chopped
1 c. cooked rice
1/4 c. fresh cilantro, chopped

6 canned chopped jalapeños,
   drained
Optional: 3 T. jalapeño juice
Garnish: shredded Cheddar
   cheese, sour cream,
   crushed tortilla chips

Add broth and tomatoes with juice to a soup pot over medium heat. Bring to a boil; reduce heat to low. Stir in rice, cilantro, jalapeños and jalapeño juice, if using. Simmer for about 10 minutes. Ladle into bowls; garnish as desired. Serves 4.

Mom's Taco Soup

Carol McClurg
Otsego, MN

I created this slow-cooker recipe in a quest to find foods that I could enjoy with my food allergies, and that my family also liked.

1-1/2 to 2 lbs. boneless,
   skinless chicken breasts
   or tenderloins
2 to 3 c. chicken broth
24-oz. jar salsa

15-oz. can black beans
15-oz. can pinto beans
Garnish: shredded Cheddar
   cheese, sour cream,
   corn chips

Place chicken in a slow cooker; stir in broth, salsa and undrained beans. Cover and cook on low setting for 8 to 10 hours, until chicken is very tender. Shred chicken with 2 forks right in the slow cooker; stir. Serve soup with desired toppings. Serves 6 to 8.

Sandwiches & Soups

Spinach Tortellini Soup

Pamela Bowser
Fowler, OH

This is a family favorite passed on from one member to another.
It makes a nice meatless dish for a gathering and goes a
long way. It freezes well to keep on hand for a busy day.

16-oz. pkg. frozen cheese
    tortellini, uncooked
1 onion, chopped
2 cloves garlic, chopped
1/4 c. olive oil
28-oz. can crushed tomatoes
28-oz. can diced tomatoes

10-oz. pkg. frozen spinach,
    thawed and squeezed dry
48-oz. can chicken broth
1 t. dried basil
salt and pepper to taste
1/2 c. grated Romano cheese

Prepare tortellini according to package directions; drain. Meanwhile, in a soup pot over medium heat, sauté onion and garlic in oil until transparent. Drain; add tomatoes with juice, spinach and broth. Reduce heat to low; simmer for about 20 minutes. Add cooked tortellini, seasonings and cheese. Simmer for 5 to 10 minutes, until heated through. Makes 25 to 30 servings.

If you like toasted pumpkin seeds, try toasting winter squash seeds too! Rinse seeds and pat dry, toss with olive oil to coat, spread on a baking sheet and sprinkle with salt. Bake at 350 degrees for 10 to 15 minutes, until crisp. Enjoy as a snack or sprinkle on hot soup for a crunchy garnish.

Beef, Barley & Spinach Soup

Alice Hardin
Antioch, CA

*I love flavorful hearty soups...so good for you
and so easy to make!*

3/4 lb. lean ground beef
1 c. onion, chopped
14-1/2 oz. can diced tomatoes
1-1/2 c. carrots, peeled and
   thinly sliced
1/2 c. quick-cooking barley,
   uncooked
4 c. water

1-1/2 t. beef bouillon granules
1-1/2 t. dried thyme
1 t. dried oregano
1/2 t. garlic powder
1/8 t. salt
1/4 t. pepper
6-oz. pkg. fresh baby spinach

In a soup pot over medium heat, brown beef with onion, stirring to
break up beef; drain. Stir in tomatoes with juice and remaining
ingredients except spinach; bring to a boil over high heat. Reduce heat
to low. Cover and simmer for 12 to 15 minutes, until barley and
carrots are tender, stirring occasionally. Stir in spinach; simmer
for several more minutes, until spinach starts to wilt. Makes 4 to
5 servings.

Ladle individual portions of leftover soup into small
freezer bags...seal, label and freeze. Then, when you need
a quick-fix lunch or dinner, simply transfer soup to
a microwave-safe bowl and reheat.

QUICK
Sandwiches & Soups

Pumpkin Chowder

Sandy Westendorp
Grand Rapids, MI

*This blend of everyday ingredients is
anything but ordinary.*

1/2 lb. bacon, diced
2 c. onion, chopped
2 t. curry powder
2 T. all-purpose flour
1-lb. pie pumpkin, peeled,
   seeded and chopped

2 potatoes, peeled and cubed
4 c. chicken broth
1 c. half-and-half
salt and pepper to taste
Garnish: toasted pumpkin
   seeds, sliced green onions

Brown bacon in a stockpot over medium heat for 5 minutes; add
onion. Sauté for 10 minutes; add curry powder and flour, stirring
until smooth and creamy, about 5 minutes. Add pumpkin, potatoes
and broth; simmer until pumpkin and potatoes are tender, about
15 minutes. Pour in half-and-half; season with salt and pepper.
Simmer for 5 minutes; do not boil. Spoon into soup bowls; garnish
with pumpkin seeds and green onions. Serves 6.

For a quick & easy table runner, choose fabric printed with
autumn leaves and Indian corn in glowing gold, orange and
brown. Simply pink the edges...all done!

Curry Butternut & Apple Soup

Carla Slajchert
Tampa, FL

*This soup is always a favorite of my family's when
the temperatures start to drop.*

1 butternut squash, halved
   and seeded
2 t. butter, divided
salt and pepper to taste
2 Granny Smith apples, peeled,
   halved and cored

2 c. chicken broth
1 t. garlic powder
1 t. onion powder
1 t. curry powder
1/2 c. sour cream
1 T. lime juice

Place squash halves cut-side up on a baking sheet. Add one teaspoon
butter to each half; season with salt and pepper. Place apples next to
squash on pan. Bake at 400 degrees for 30 to 45 minutes, until
fork-tender. Scoop out squash pulp with a spoon. In a large saucepan,
combine squash pulp, apples, broth and seasonings. Bring to a simmer
over medium heat. Simmer for about 10 minutes, until heated through.
Meanwhile, stir together sour cream and lime juice; set aside. Purée
soup in batches in a blender until smooth; reheat soup, if desired.
Serve in soup bowls, topped with dollops of sour cream mixture.
Makes 4 to 6 servings.

When puréeing hot soup, be sure to remove the stopper
from the lid of your blender so steam pressure doesn't
build up inside. Cover the hole in the lid with a folded
kitchen towel to prevent a mess before blending.

100

QUICK
Sandwiches & Soups

Best-Ever Brocco-flower Soup

Sandy Coffey
Cincinnati, OH

Great for game day or for warming up after raking leaves.

3 c. broccoli, chopped
2 c. cauliflower, chopped
4 c. chicken broth
2 c. milk, divided

2 c. cooked chicken, diced
1 t. salt
6 T. cornstarch
1 c. shredded Cheddar cheese

In a large saucepan over medium-high heat, cook broccoli and cauliflower in broth until tender. Do not drain. Reduce heat to low; add 1-1/2 cups milk, chicken and salt. In a small bowl, stir cornstarch into remaining milk; mix until smooth and stir into mixture in saucepan. Cover and cook over low heat, stirring frequently, until soup is hot and thickened. Stir in cheese until melted. Makes 6 servings.

November 15 is National Clean-Out-Your-Refrigerator Day... cook up a big pot of "surprise soup" with whatever you find in the fridge! Perfect for a fall day, and the fridge will be ready for Thanksgiving groceries.

Down-East Fish Chowder

Lynda Robson
Boston, MA

Mom used to make her chowder on cold, wet days...
a bowl of it always warmed us right up!

3 to 4 slices bacon
1 c. onion, chopped
3 to 4 potatoes, peeled
  and cubed
1/2 t. garlic powder
1/2 t. dried oregano

1/2 t. paprika
2 12-oz. cans evaporated milk
1 lb. cod or other white fish,
  cut into chunks
salt and pepper to taste
oyster crackers

In a Dutch oven over medium-high heat, cook bacon until crisp.
Remove bacon to a paper towel, reserving drippings in pan. Add
onion, potatoes and seasonings to drippings; cook and stir until onion
is tender. Stir in evaporated milk; bring just to a boil. Reduce heat to
low; cover and simmer for 20 minutes, stirring occasionally. Add fish;
cover and simmer an additional 10 minutes, until fish flakes easily
with a fork and potatoes are tender. Season with salt and pepper;
garnish with crisp bacon. Serve with oyster crackers. Serves 6.

Eat-it-all bread bowls make a hearty soup extra special. Cut the
tops off round bread loaves and hollow out, then rub with olive
oil and garlic. Slip into the oven for 10 minutes at 400 degrees,
until crusty and golden. Ladle in soup and serve right away.

Nana's Clam Chowder

Chelsea Oliver
Arlington, TN

I love clam chowder and this recipe is my favorite! My Nana makes it for me throughout the year so that I always have some of this wonderful soup whenever I want. It freezes and reheats very well.

3 slices bacon, diced
1 onion, diced
2 6-1/2 oz. cans chopped clams
12-oz. can evaporated milk
2 10-3/4 oz. cans cream of
   potato soup
2 T. lemon juice
1 T. pepper, or to taste

In a stockpot over medium heat, cook onion with bacon until onion is tender; drain. Stir in clams with juice and remaining ingredients. Bring to a boil; reduce heat to medium-low. Simmer for 10 to 15 minutes, stirring occasionally. Serves 6 to 8.

Keep the pantry stocked with canned vegetables, creamy soups, rice mixes, pasta and other handy meal-makers. If you pick up two or three items whenever they're on sale, you'll have a full pantry in no time at all.

Navy Bean Soup

MaryAlice Dobbert
King George, VA

This hearty, satisfying fall soup is ready in less than an hour,
yet tastes like it simmered all day. Add a loaf of crusty
French bread and this is total comfort food.

1 onion, chopped
1/2 c. butter, sliced
6 c. water
3 cubes chicken bouillon
4 c. cooked ham, shredded
1 c. instant mashed potato
   flakes

4 16-oz. cans navy beans
1 t. onion powder
1 t. garlic powder
Optional: chopped green chiles,
   fresh parsley to taste

In a Dutch oven over medium heat, sauté onion in butter until lightly
golden. Stir in water and bouillon cubes; add ham and bring to a boil.
Reduce heat to low; simmer for 15 minutes. Stir in instant potatoes;
add beans with liquid and remaining ingredients. Return to a boil,
stirring constantly; reduce heat to low and simmer for 30 minutes.
Makes 6 to 8 servings.

Dried beans are inexpensive and come in lots of varieties.
Instead of soaking, dried beans can be slow-cooked overnight
on low. Cover with water and add a teaspoon of baking soda.
In the morning, simply drain and they're ready to use.

Italian Bean & Pasta Soup

Mel Chencharick
Julian, PA

This recipe is a winner...very tasty! Get some of your friends together and have a soup & salad bar. You make the soup and have each person bring some fixin's for a salad. The ladies of our church do this and it's always a fun time for all.

2 ham hocks
12 c. water
1 onion, chopped
1 c. celery, chopped
1 c. carrots, peeled and chopped

15.8-oz. can diced tomatoes
2 16-oz. cans navy beans, drained
2 T. dried Italian seasoning
2 c. ditalini pasta, uncooked

In a large Dutch oven over high heat, combine ham hocks, water, onion, celery and carrots. Bring to a boil. Reduce heat to low and simmer, uncovered for one hour. Remove ham hocks and allow to cool. Remove meat from ham hocks, discarding skin, bones and fat. Return meat to Dutch oven; stir in tomatoes with liquid and remaining ingredients. Bring to a boil; reduce heat and simmer until pasta is tender, about 10 minutes. Serve immediately. Makes 10 to 12 servings.

Do you have a favorite soup recipe that you don't serve often due to lack of time? Try making it in a slow cooker instead! A recipe that simmers for 2 hours on the stovetop can generally cook all day on the low setting without overcooking.

Tea Room Squash Soup

Charmie Fisher
Fontana, CA

This recipe was given to me many years ago by a friend. It is such a rich and satisfying soup...perfect on a chilly autumn evening with some crusty bread! Make it lower in calories by substituting reduced-fat cheese and whole milk instead of half-and-half.

6 to 8 crookneck yellow
    squash, sliced
2 onions, chopped
1 t. garlic powder
1/2 c. butter

1/4 t. baking soda
16-oz. pkg. pasteurized process
    cheese spread, cubed
2 c. half-and-half
salt to taste

Combine squash and onions in a large saucepan; cover with water. Cook over medium heat until vegetables are fork-tender. Drain most of the liquid. Working in batches, purée mixture in a food processor until smooth; transfer to a large saucepan. Add remaining ingredients. Heat through over medium-low heat, until cheese is melted. Serve soup in small bowls. Makes 8 servings.

For a fruity cream cheese spread, combine one 8-ounce package of softened cream cheese with 1/4 cup apricot preserves. Stir until smooth. So delicious on warm slices of quick bread!

30-Minute MEALS

Ghostly Shepherd's Pie

Donna Wilson
Maryville, TN

*We have enjoyed making this cute dinner idea ever since
my older kids were little. Great for Halloween!*

1 lb. ground beef
1 onion, diced
16-oz. pkg. frozen mixed
   vegetables, divided
14-1/2 oz. can diced tomatoes
12-oz. jar beef gravy
1-1/2 c. water

2 T. butter
1/2 t. garlic powder
1/2 c. milk
2-1/4 c. instant mashed potato
   flakes
1/4 c. grated Parmesan cheese
1 egg, beaten

Brown beef and onion in a skillet over medium heat; drain. Set aside
12 peas from the mixed vegetables for the ghosts' eyes. Add
remaining mixed vegetables, tomatoes with juice and gravy to skillet.
Cook over medium heat until vegetables are tender. Meanwhile, in a
saucepan over medium heat, bring water to a boil; stir in butter and
garlic powder. Remove from heat. Stir in milk, potato flakes, Parmesan
cheese and egg. Spoon beef mixture into a lightly greased 8"x8" baking
pan. With a spoon, make 6 mounds of potato mixture on top to
resemble ghosts. Place 2 peas on each mound to resemble eyes. Bake,
uncovered, at 375 degrees for 20 minutes, or until heated through.
Serves 6.

Plan a harvest scavenger hunt for the whole family. Send them
out with a list of fall finds...a golden oak leaf, a red maple leaf,
a pumpkin, a scarecrow, a red apple and a hay bale, just to
name a few. It's not only lots of fun, it's a great way to get
outside and enjoy the fabulous fall weather!

Oktoberfest Pie

Amy Hunt
Traphill, NC

A wonderful easy meal to share after a day at the pumpkin patch.
Add some pickled beets and hot rolls on the side...your family
may just take you out for dessert!

14-oz. pkg. Kielbasa turkey
   sausage, cut into
   1/2-inch pieces
14-oz. can sauerkraut, drained
1 c. shredded Swiss cheese

3/4 c. low-fat biscuit baking mix
1/2 c. skim milk
1/2 c. non-alcoholic beer
2 eggs, beaten

Spray a 9" glass pie plate with non-stick vegetable spray. Layer
Kielbasa, sauerkraut and cheese in pie plate; set aside. In a bowl, stir
together remaining ingredients until well blended; pour over cheese.
Bake, uncovered, at 400 degrees for about 35 minutes. Let stand
several minutes; cut into wedges. Makes 6 servings.

Crunching through orange and yellow leaves on the walk
home from school...watching the Indian corn, pumpkins and
scarecrows going up on the neighbors' front porches...making a
nest under the apple tree in the backyard with a blanket and
good book to read so we could dream and soak up the chilly
fall air until we were called in for a hearty dinner of pork
chops, sweet potatoes and apple cobbler. These are my
favorite memories of autumn.

–Sheri Kohl, Wentzville, MO

One-Pot Beefy Macaroni

Robyn Binns
Crescent, IA

*This hearty dish is perfect for weeknights when you don't want
to spend the rest of the evening cleaning up the kitchen.
Everything is cooked in one pot...even the pasta!*

2 lbs. ground beef
1 onion, chopped
3 cloves garlic, chopped
3 c. water
2 14-1/2 oz. cans diced
   tomatoes

2 15-oz. cans tomato sauce
2 t. soy sauce
1 T. Italian seasoning
salt and pepper to taste
2 c. elbow macaroni,
   uncooked

Brown beef in a stockpot over medium heat; drain. Add onion and
garlic; cook for 3 to 5 minutes. Stir in water, tomatoes with juice,
tomato sauce, soy sauce and seasonings. Cook for 15 minutes, stirring
occasionally. Add uncooked macaroni. Cover and cook for 20 to
30 minutes, stirring several times. Remove from heat. Let stand,
covered, for 15 minutes. Makes 6 to 8 servings.

Need a few new ideas for family meals? Host a recipe swap!
Invite friends to bring a favorite casserole along with enough
recipe cards for each guest. While everyone enjoys a delicious
potluck, collect the recipe cards, staple together and
hand out when it's time to depart.

Leea's Quick Spaghetti

Leea Mercer
League City, TX

My kids love this...it's delicious and very budget-friendly too!

7-oz. pkg. spaghetti, uncooked
1 lb. ground beef
1/2 c. onion, diced
salt and pepper to taste
2 8-oz. cans tomato sauce

6-oz. can tomato paste
3 cloves garlic, minced
2 to 3 T. dried basil
1 to 2 t. dried oregano

Cook spaghetti according to package directions; drain. Meanwhile, brown beef and onion in a skillet over medium heat; drain. Add salt and pepper; stir in tomato sauce, tomato paste, garlic and seasonings. If too thick, add a little water. Reduce heat to low. Simmer for 20 to 30 minutes, stirring occasionally. Serve sauce over spaghetti. Serves 4.

Garden-Fresh Garlic Chive Bread

Gladys Kielar
Whitehouse, OH

A loaf of hot, buttery garlic bread makes any dish a meal.

1/2 c. butter, softened
1/4 c. grated Parmesan cheese
2 T. fresh chives, chopped

1 clove garlic, minced
1 loaf French bread, sliced
   1-inch thick

In a small bowl, blend butter, Parmesan cheese, chives and garlic. Spread on one side of each bread slice. Reassemble loaf; wrap in a large piece of heavy-duty aluminum foil. Seal edges, forming a packet; place on a baking sheet. Bake at 350 degrees for 20 to 25 minutes, until heated through. Makes 10 to 12 servings.

Whip up a simple rustic centerpiece... fill an old-fashioned colander with colorful apples and pears. They're perfect for snacking too.

Taco-Filled Peppers

Shannon Reents
Loudonville, OH

My family loves stuffed peppers and Mexican food,
so I came up with this two-in-one dish for them.

1 lb. ground beef
1-oz. pkg. taco seasoning mix
1 c. salsa
15-1/2 oz. can kidney beans,
    drained
4 peppers, tops removed
1 tomato, chopped
1/2 c. shredded Cheddar cheese
1/2 c. sour cream

Brown beef in a skillet over medium heat; drain. Stir in seasoning
mix, salsa and beans; bring to a boil. Simmer for 5 minutes.
Meanwhile, add peppers to a large saucepan of boiling water. Cook
peppers for 3 to 5 minutes; rinse in cold water and drain well. Spoon
1/2 cup beef mixture into each pepper; arrange peppers in an
ungreased 9"x9" baking pan. Cover and bake at 350 degrees for
10 to 12 minutes. Top with tomato and cheese; serve with sour
cream. Makes 4 servings.

Make your own taco seasoning mix. In a jar, combine 3/4 cup
dried, minced onion, 1/4 cup each salt and chili powder,
2 tablespoons each cornstarch, red pepper flakes, ground cumin
and dried, minced garlic and one tablespoon dried oregano.
Four tablespoons of mix equals a 1-1/4 ounce envelope.

Idaho Tacos

LaShelle Brown
Mulvane, KS

This is a tasty quick & easy meal to toss together on a busy day.
If time is short, you can bake the potatoes in the microwave while
you are making the beef mixture to go on top.

4 russet potatoes, baked
1 lb. ground beef
1-1/4 oz. pkg. taco seasoning
   mix

1/2 c. water
1 c. shredded Cheddar cheese
Garnish: sliced green onions
Optional: salsa

With a sharp knife, cut an X in the top of each warm potato; fluff pulp with a fork and set aside. Brown beef in a skillet over medium heat; drain. Stir in seasoning mix and water; bring to a boil. Simmer over low heat for 5 to 7 minutes, stirring occasionally. To serve, top potatoes with beef mixture, cheese, green onions and salsa, if desired. Makes 4 servings.

Some of my fondest autumn memories are from the late 1950s when our elementary school had the most fabulous Halloween carnivals. They took place on a Saturday afternoon and all the kids wore their costumes. Sponsored by the PTA, all our mothers worked at the carnival and transformed the schoolyard from a sea of concrete into a playground of all types of game booths. They converted one of the classroom bungalows into a country store with canned goods and scout crafts for sale. The "older" junior high school kids came and danced to the beat of Ted Raden (every kid took lessons at his dance studio). I remember bringing home all kinds of junk I'd won, as well as goldfish carried in a plastic bag filled with water. Those were the best childhood memories!

– Debbie Muer, Encino, CA

Mini Turkey Pot Pies

Cathy Hillier
Salt Lake City, UT

My kids love to help me make these little pot pies over Thanksgiving weekend with leftovers from the big Turkey Day meal.

1-1/2 c. cooked turkey, cubed
10-3/4 oz. can cream of chicken
  soup
1-1/2 c. frozen mixed
  vegetables, thawed

1/2 c. cooked potato, diced
12-oz. tube refrigerated
  biscuits
1/2 c. shredded Cheddar cheese

Combine chicken, soup, vegetables and potatoes in a saucepan. Simmer over medium-low heat for 5 minutes. Meanwhile, spray 10 muffin cups with non-stick vegetable spray. Flatten biscuits slightly; press into the bottoms and up the sides of muffin cups. Divide chicken mixture among cups; gently press down. Top with cheese. Bake at 350 degrees for 15 minutes, or until golden and cheese is melted. Cool muffin tin on a wire rack for 5 minutes before removing. Serves 4 to 6, one to 2 mini pot pies each.

Hosting dinner on Thanksgiving? Ask everyone to bring a baby photo. Have a contest...the first person to guess who's who gets a prize!

Barb's Chili Beans

Barbara Imler
Noblesville, IN

I created this recipe as a substitute for refried beans, but it can be served with any kind of meal, not just Mexican food. It's zingy-ier and more tasty than ordinary canned refried beans...healthier too.

1 onion, chopped
1 green pepper, chopped
1 T. butter or oil
2 15-1/2 oz. cans chili beans
10-oz. can diced tomatoes with
    green chiles, drained

1 clove garlic, minced
2 t. chili powder
1/4 t. red pepper flakes
1/2 t. salt

In a skillet over medium heat, sauté onion and green pepper in butter or oil for 5 minutes. Stir in undrained chili beans and remaining ingredients. Reduce heat to low. Simmer until thickened, about 30 minutes, stirring occasionally. Serves 4 to 6.

If you've added a bit too much hot chili seasoning,
it's easy to cool it off...simply stir in a spoonful each of
lemon juice and sugar.

Chicken Lo Mein

Stacy Lane
Millsboro, DE

*I first learned this recipe in my home economics class in high school.
I took it home, revamped it a little, and we've been enjoying for over ten
years now! You can use any meat and vegetables you have on hand.
I often share the recipe with first-time cooks and newlyweds, since it's
so easy to make and easy on the budget.*

1 T. oil
2 boneless, skinless chicken
   breasts, sliced
1 to 2 c. chopped broccoli,
   carrots, cabbage, celery
   and/or mushrooms
4 3-oz. pkgs. low-sodium
   chicken-flavored ramen
   noodles

4 c. water
1 T. low-sodium soy sauce
2 t. cornstarch
1 t. garlic powder
1 t. dried parsley
Optional: onion powder
   to taste

Heat oil in a large saucepan over medium heat. Add chicken; sauté
until golden. Add vegetables to saucepan; break up ramen noodles
and add to saucepan. In a separate saucepan, bring water to a boil.
Stir in remaining ingredients, adding contents of seasoning packets to
taste; add to chicken mixture. Cover and cook over medium-high heat
for about 10 minutes, until vegetables are tender. Serves 5.

A notepad on the fridge is handy for a running grocery list...
no more running to the store at the last minute
before starting dinner!

Cashew Nut Chicken

LaShelle Brown
Mulvane, KS

Your family will love this easy, delicious recipe. The longer the chicken marinates, the better it will taste, so feel free to tuck it in the fridge the night before.

4 boneless, skinless chicken
    breasts, cut into 1-inch cubes
soy sauce to taste
1/2 to 1 bunch green onions,
    chopped

2 T. oil
1/2 c. cashew halves or pieces
cooked rice

Place chicken in a glass dish; add soy sauce to taste. Cover and let stand at least 15 minutes to overnight (refrigerate if more than one hour). Heat oil in a wok or skillet over medium-high heat. Drain chicken and add along with green onions; cook and stir until chicken is almost done. Add cashews; continue cooking for several minutes, until cashews soften. To serve, spoon over cooked rice. Makes 4 servings.

Stir-frying is a terrific way to make a quick and tasty dinner. Slice veggies into equal-size cubes or slices before you start cooking...they'll all be done to perfection at the same time.

Speedy Chicken-Broccoli Alfredo

Sheri West
York, SC

I came up with this recipe one night when I was short on time. My two teenagers were super hungry and needed to leave the house again quickly for the homecoming football game and the marching band that would perform at the game. It was a success!

16-oz. pkg. rotini pasta, uncooked
1 bunch broccoli, cut into flowerets
3 boneless, skinless chicken breasts, sliced
1 to 2 T. olive oil
10-3/4 oz. can reduced-fat cream of chicken soup
16-oz. jar roasted garlic Parmesan Alfredo sauce
1 c. shredded Italian-blend cheese
salt and pepper to taste

Cook pasta according to package directions, adding broccoli to cooking pot; drain. Meanwhile, heat oil in a large skillet over medium heat. Add chicken; cook until chicken juices run clear. Drain; stir in soup, sauce and cheese. Add pasta mixture; stir gently until coated with sauce. Makes 8 servings.

Olive oil stays freshest when refrigerated...pour a little into a small squeeze bottle to keep in the cupboard for everyday use.

30-Minute
◐ Meals ◐

Pork Cacciatore

Gladys Brehm
Quakertown, PA

This recipe was handed down in my family. It's quick and delicious.

1 T. olive oil
1 onion, chopped
4-oz. can sliced mushrooms, drained
1 clove garlic, minced
10-oz. can diced tomatoes

1 lb. boneless pork loin, cut into bite-size pieces
1 t. Italian seasoning
1/2 t. salt
1/2 t. sugar
cooked white or brown rice

Heat oil in a skillet over medium heat. Add onion, mushrooms and garlic, sauté for 3 minutes, or until slightly softened. Stir in tomatoes with juice, pork, seasonings and sugar. Cover and simmer for 10 minutes, or until pork is no longer pink in the center. To serve, spoon pork mixture over cooked rice. Serves 4 to 5.

Apple picking can be a fun family outing! The kids will be amazed to see all the different kinds of apples and so many are just the right size for little ones. Take a picnic and make a day of it, with fresh-picked apples for dessert.

Oven-Barbecued Pork Chops

Sue Neely
Greenville, IL

Need some comfort food? Try this recipe for barbecue indoors.
I like to serve it with warm cornbread and vinegary coleslaw.

3 t. canola oil, divided
4 to 6 bone-in pork chops,
   3/4-inch thick
1/4 t. salt
1/4 t. pepper

1 onion, chopped
1 clove garlic, chopped
1/3 c. orange juice
1/2 c. barbecue sauce

Heat 2 teaspoons oil in a large oven-safe skillet over high heat.
Season pork chops with salt and pepper. Add to skillet and cook
until almost golden; transfer to a plate. Add onion and remaining oil
to skillet; cook and stir just until softened. Add garlic; cook and stir
for 30 seconds. Add orange juice; cook until most of the liquid has
evaporated. Stir in barbecue sauce. Return chops to the skillet, turning
to coat with sauce. Place skillet in the oven. Bake, uncovered, at
400 degrees for 5 to 10 minutes, until chops are barely pink in the
center. Serve chops topped with some of the sauce from the skillet.
Serves 4.

Keep a few packages of frozen ravioli tucked in the freezer
for speedy meals anytime. Quickly cooked and topped with
your favorite sauce, they're terrific as either a side dish
or a meatless main.

30-Minute 🍴 Meals 🍴

Sausage, Red Beans & Rice

Diane Cohen
Breinigsville, PA

Looking to lighten up? This recipe is also good with turkey sausage and light cheese.

14-oz. pkg. smoked pork
   sausage, cut into bite-size
   pieces
10-oz. can diced tomatoes with
   green chiles
15-1/2 oz. can kidney beans,
   drained and rinsed

2 t. chili powder
2 c. water
2 c. instant rice, uncooked
1-1/2 c. pasteurized process
   cheese spread, cubed

Brown sausage in a non-stick skillet over medium-high heat for 5 minutes, stirring occasionally. Drain. Stir in undrained tomatoes, beans, chili powder and water; bring to a boil. Stir in uncooked rice and cheese. Reduce heat to low. Cover and simmer for 5 to 7 minutes, until water is absorbed. Stir until cheese is completely melted. Serves 6.

Bold Beans

Kathy Collins
Brookfield, CT

The first time I made this recipe, I wasn't sure if my family would like it...these beans do have a little kick to them. Now it's the only kind of beans they want me to make!

16-oz. pkg. bacon, chopped
14-oz. pkg. chili-cheese smoked
   pork sausage, sliced
   1/2-inch thick

1 onion, chopped
1 green pepper, chopped
4 22-oz. cans barbecue style
   beans

In a large saucepan over medium heat, cook bacon until crisp; drain. Add sausage, onion and pepper; cook until vegetables are tender. Stir beans into sausage mixture. Simmer over low heat for 30 minutes, stirring occasionally. Makes 15 to 18 servings.

Beefy Spinach Biscuit Bake

Tamatha Knauber
Lancaster, NY

Delicious...a real all-in-one meal.

2 7-oz. tubes refrigerated
  buttermilk biscuits
1-1/2 lbs. ground beef
1/2 c. onion, chopped
10-oz. pkg. frozen chopped
  spinach, thawed and drained
4-oz. can sliced mushrooms,
  drained

1 c. crumbled feta cheese or
  shredded Monterey Jack
  cheese
1/4 c. grated Parmesan cheese
1-1/2 t. garlic powder
salt and pepper to taste
2 T. butter, melted

Press and flatten biscuits into the bottom and sides of a greased
11"x7" baking pan; set aside. Brown beef and onion in a skillet over
medium heat; drain. Combine spinach and mushrooms in a bowl;
mix well. Stir in cheeses, seasonings and beef mixture. Spoon into
prepared crust. Drizzle with melted butter. Bake, uncovered, at
375 degrees for 25 to 30 minutes, until bubbly and crust is lightly
golden. Makes 6 servings.

Pinching pennies at the grocery store? Give store brands a try
for canned veggies, soups and other pantry staples. You'll find
they usually taste just as good as famous-label items...in fact,
often they're made by the same companies.

Beef Turnovers

Trisha Cooper
Spanish Fork, UT

My family loves this recipe...I double it to make sure there's enough!
For individual turnovers, cut out 6-inch circles of pie crust.

1 lb. ground beef, browned and
    drained
2 stalks celery, finely chopped
1 onion, chopped
2 cubes beef bouillon

1/8 t. pepper
1 T. soy sauce
3 T. cornstarch
1 c. cold water
2 9-inch pie crusts

Brown beef in a skillet over medium heat; drain. Add celery, onion, bouillon, pepper, soy sauce and enough water to cover completely. Simmer for 10 minutes, stirring occasionally. Dissolve cornstarch in one cup water; add to skillet and simmer until thickened. Drain, reserving gravy from skillet. On a lightly floured surface, roll out one pie crust into a 9-inch circle; place on a baking sheet. Spoon half of beef mixture onto circle; fold in half and press edges with a fork. Score or pierce 3 to 4 times to vent steam. Repeat with remaining pie crust and beef mixture. Bake at 425 degrees until bubbly and golden, about 15 minutes. Serve reserved gravy in a gravy boat alongside turnovers. Serves 4.

Fill vintage jelly jars with candy corn and set a tealight inside each one. Their sweet glow will make the prettiest place settings.

Holiday Turkey Quesadillas

Kelly Gray
Hedgesville, WV

*A quick-fix meal to enjoy the day after Thanksgiving or Christmas.
It was inspired by my children's love of spicy Mexican food
and my love of sweet & simple recipes.*

4 8-inch flour tortillas
2 c. cooked turkey, shredded
1-1/2 c. whole-berry
　cranberry sauce
2 c. shredded Mexican-blend
　cheese

4 t. garlic salt, or to taste
2 t. pepper
2 t. dried tarragon
Optional: salsa verde,
　sour cream

Spray a 13"x9" baking pan generously with non-stick vegetable spray. Place 2 tortillas side-by-side in the pan. Layer turkey, sauce, cheese and seasonings equally over the tortillas. Spray remaining tortillas on both sides; place on top of ingredients in pan. Bake, uncovered, at 350 degrees for 30 to 35 minutes. Serve topped with salsa verde and sour cream, if desired. Makes 6 servings.

Bundle everyone up in their merriest mittens, hats and coats and go outdoors! While everyone's home for Thanksgiving, it's the perfect time to take photos for this year's Christmas cards.

Thanksgiving Meatballs

Stephanie Nicholson
Ontario, Canada

Family gatherings were a special time in our home. We always celebrated with family dinners, but when I moved away after high school I didn't always make it home for Thanksgiving. This recipe came in handy when I was feeling nostalgic for that big turkey dinner!

6-oz. pkg. turkey stuffing mix
1 lb. ground turkey

1 egg, beaten
salt and pepper to taste

Prepare stuffing mix according to package directions; let cool. In a large bowl, combine turkey, egg and stuffing; season with salt and pepper. Form into 2-inch meatballs. Place in an ungreased 13"x9" baking pan. Bake, uncovered, at 350 degrees for 12 to 15 minutes, turning after 7 minutes. To serve, dip in Cranberry Spice Sauce or toss to coat. Makes one to 2 dozen meatballs.

Cranberry Spice Sauce:

1 c. water
1 c. brown sugar, packed
12-oz. pkg. fresh cranberries
zest of 1/2 orange

1/4 c. orange juice
1/2 t. allspice
1/2 t. cinnamon

In a saucepan over medium-high heat, bring water and brown sugar to a boil. Add remaining ingredients; reduce heat to low. Simmer until cranberries just start to pop and gently fall apart. Cover and chill slightly before serving. Makes 2-1/2 cups sauce.

Delicious autumn! My very soul is wedded to it.

–George Eliot

Sweet-and-Sour Pork Chops

Cheryl Culver
Perkins, OK

Sweet-and-sour foods are a favorite with some of my family and so I like to make this dish especially for them. It is very good and so easy to make. Sure makes my family happy!

20-oz. can pineapple chunks, drained and juice reserved
1/2 c. catsup
1 T. brown sugar, packed
1 T. cider vinegar
3 carrots, peeled and sliced 1/4-inch thick

1 green pepper, cut into chunks
2 T. oil
4 to 6 pork loin chops, 1-inch thick

In a large saucepan, combine reserved pineapple juice, catsup, brown sugar and vinegar. Cook over medium heat for 5 minutes, until hot and brown sugar dissolves. Add pineapple chunks, carrots and green pepper; remove from heat. In a large skillet, heat oil over medium heat; add pork chops and cook until golden on both sides. Arrange chops in a lightly greased shallow 13"x9" baking pan; spread pineapple mixture over top. Cover with aluminum foil. Bake at 350 degrees for 25 to 35 minutes, until chops are no longer pink inside and vegetables are crisp-tender. Makes 4 to 6 servings.

A baked sweet potato is a delectable fast-fix fall side. Simply pierce the potato several times, then bake until tender, about 45 minutes at 400 degrees. Top with butter and a dusting of cinnamon-sugar.

Potato Doughnuts, page 216

Apple Cider Syrup, page 22

Bacon & Cheese Muffins, page 28

Harvest Moon Punch, page 65

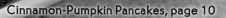

Cinnamon-Pumpkin Pancakes, page 10

Slopppy Jane Sandwiches, page 76

Speedy Little Devils, page 181

Easy Meatball Hoagies, page 69

Monterey Mushroom Squares, page 48

Jack-o'-Lantern Jumble, page 36

Navy Bean Soup, page 104

Roasted Veggies & Penne Pasta, page 149

Easy Corn Fritters, page 165

Poppy Seed Cake, page201

Easy Chicken Manicotti, page 148

Garden-Fresh Garlic Chive Bread, page 111

Pumpkin Chowder, page 99

Nanny's Peanut Butter Goblins, page 180

Slow-Cooker Scalloped Potatoes, page 167

Hot Cherry Pepper Chicken, page 143

Beefy Spinach Biscuit Bake, page 122

Taffy Apple Pizza, page 193

Harvard Beet Spice Cake,
page 200

Hearty Sausage & Egg Bake, page 9

Peach Cobbler Muffins, page 13

Mom's Everything Waffles, page 22

Shrimp-Stuffed Tomato Poppers, page 46

Raspberry Punch, page 52

Cheesy Macaroni Skillet, page 134

Cheese-Stuffed Biscuits, page 94

Baked Ham in Peach Sauce, page 130

Roast Chicken Dijon, page 150

Lemony Blackberry Crisp, page 196

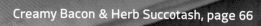
Creamy Bacon & Herb Succotash, page 66

Picnic Salad Skewers, page 37

Cabbage Tomato Slaw, page 71

Cow-Country Beans, page 64

Chicken-Fried Steak, page 129

Green Bean Bundles,
page 81

Sour Cherry Pie, page 197

Summer Sparkle, page 53

Mom's Raisin Bread, page 111

Cream of Zucchini Soup, page 97

Raspberry Pretzel Salad, page 89

Mom's Hot Bacon Dressing,
page 158

Comfort Food Classics

Chicken-Fried Steak

Donna Deeds
Marysville, TN

Authentic chicken-fried steak is crunchy outside,
tender inside and served with plenty of creamy gravy!

2-1/4 t. salt, divided
1-3/4 t. pepper, divided
6 4-oz. beef cube steaks
1 sleeve saltine crackers,
   crushed
1-1/4 c. all-purpose flour,
   divided

1/2 t. baking powder
1/2 t. cayenne pepper
4-3/4 c. milk, divided
2 eggs, beaten
3-1/2 c. peanut oil
mashed potatoes

Sprinkle 1/4 teaspoon each salt and pepper over steaks. Set aside. Combine cracker crumbs, one cup flour, baking powder, one teaspoon salt, 1/2 teaspoon pepper and cayenne pepper. Whisk together 3/4 cup milk and eggs. Dredge steaks in cracker crumb mixture; dip in milk mixture and dredge in cracker mixture again. Pour oil into a 12" skillet and heat to 360 degrees. Fry steaks, in batches, 10 minutes. Turn and fry each batch 4 to 5 more minutes or until golden. Remove to a wire rack on a jelly-roll pan. Keep steaks warm in a 225-degree oven. Carefully drain hot oil, reserving cooked bits and one tablespoon drippings in skillet. Whisk together remaining flour, salt, pepper and milk. Pour mixture into reserved drippings in skillet; cook over medium-high heat, whisking constantly, 10 to 12 minutes or until thickened. Serve gravy with steaks and mashed potatoes. Serves 6.

Nobody likes lumpy gravy! If the gravy has lumps, pour it through a mesh tea strainer just before serving time.

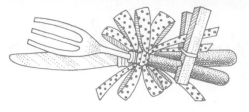

Baked Ham in Peach Sauce
JoAnna Nicoline-Haughey
Berwyn, PA

*This ham with its fruity sauce is equally scrumptious served hot
at a holiday dinner or cold at a summer picnic.*

5-lb. fully-cooked ham
1 t. whole cloves
2 16-oz. cans sliced peaches,
   drained

10-oz. jar apricot preserves
1 c. dry sherry or apple juice
1 t. orange zest
1/2 t. allspice

Place ham in an ungreased 13"x9" baking pan. Score surface of ham
in a diamond pattern; insert cloves. Combine remaining ingredients in
a blender or food processor. Process until smooth and pour over ham.
Cover ham with aluminum foil. Bake at 325 degrees for 30 minutes,
basting occasionally with sauce. Uncover and bake for an additional
30 minutes; continue to baste. Remove ham to a serving platter; slice
and serve with sauce from pan. May be served hot or cold. Makes
10 servings.

Don't overlook Grandma's ironstone pitcher & bowl set when
setting out a dinner buffet! Fill the pitcher with refreshing
ice water and lemon slices...put the bowl to work serving up
a party-size portion of your favorite salad or side.

Best-Ever Country Ribs

Jill Nikunen
Kalispell, MT

With just 3 ingredients, this is the easiest BBQ rib recipe ever! We like to serve it with twice-baked potatoes and a crisp green salad for an easy everyday meal that's anything but ordinary.

1 onion, cut into wedges
3 lbs. boneless country-style
   pork ribs, cut into 2-inch
   cubes

18-oz. bottle barbecue sauce

Place onion wedges in the bottom of a lightly greased slow cooker. Place ribs on top of onion. Cover and cook on high for one hour. Stir; pour barbecue sauce over ribs. Cover; reduce heat and cook on low for an additional 4 hours, until ribs are tender. Serves 4 to 6.

Give a new white tablecloth a warm vintage look with tea-dyeing. Fill a large pot with water, bring to a boil and steep 8 to 10 teabags. Add the prewashed, damp tablecloth to the pot and simmer for at least 30 minutes, until it's the tint you like. Rinse, dry and enjoy.

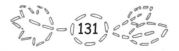

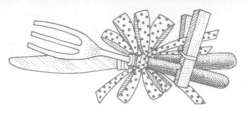

Country Noodle Dish

Christine Waterbury
Sheboygan, WI

Serve with a crisp tossed salad and piping-hot garlic bread.

1 lb. ground beef or turkey
1 onion, chopped
Optional: 2 T. green pepper,
  chopped
11-oz. can corn, drained

2 10-3/4 oz. cans tomato soup
8-oz. pkg. medium egg noodles,
  cooked
1/2 to 3/4 c. water
salt and pepper to taste

In a skillet over medium heat, brown meat with onion and green pepper, if using. Drain; stir in corn. Stir in soup, cooked noodles and water to desired consistency. Add salt and pepper to taste. Heat through and serve. Makes 4 to 6 servings.

Look for colorful old-fashioned cut flowers like zinnias and dwarf sunflowers at farmers' markets and even your neighborhood supermarket. Arrange a generous bunch in a tall stoneware crock for a cheery centerpiece.

Comfort Food Classics

Baked Potatoes & Chicken Sauce
Karie Rittenour
Delaware, OH

A few simple ingredients turn baked potatoes into
a filling, comforting meal.

4 baking potatoes
1 to 2 t. oil
2 5-oz. cans chicken, drained
   and flaked
1 c. sour cream

1/2 c. mayonnaise
4 t. milk
1/2 t. seasoned salt
1/4 t. pepper
Optional: fresh parsley, chopped

Pierce skins of potatoes several times with a fork; rub oil lightly
over potatoes. Bake at 350 degrees for about one hour, until tender.
Combine remaining ingredients in a small saucepan over low heat.
Heat through, stirring occasionally, until hot and bubbly. Slice baked
potatoes in half lengthwise; place each potato on a plate. Spoon
chicken mixture over potatoes. Garnish with a sprinkle of parsley, if
desired. Makes 4 servings.

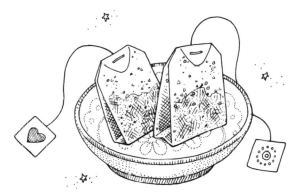

Tiny china plates called butter pats can often be found at
tag sales. Use them as whimsical teabag holders...little girls
would love to play with them as doll dishes too. So sweet!

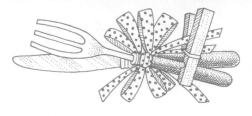

Cheesy Macaroni Skillet

Donna Scheletsky
Baden, PA

*Even if you're just arriving home from work, you can serve your family
this stovetop casserole...it's easy & quick to fix. They'll love it!*

2 c. elbow macaroni, uncooked
1/2 lb. bacon, diced
14-1/2 oz. can diced tomatoes

8-oz. can tomato sauce
1 c. shredded Cheddar cheese

Cook macaroni according to package directions; drain. Fry bacon in a
large skillet until crisp. Drain, leaving about one tablespoon drippings
in skillet. Add tomatoes with juice, tomato sauce and cooked macaroni.
Sizmmer over low heat until hot and bubbly, about 20 minutes. Add
cheese; place lid on skillet and let stand until cheese is melted, about
5 minutes. Serves 4.

When making a favorite casserole, it's easy to make a double
batch. After baking, let the extra casserole cool and tuck
it in the freezer...ready to share with a new mother,
carry to a potluck or reheat on a busy night at home.

Comfort Food Classics

Grandma's Ham Potpie

Eva Drummond
Timberville, VA

My grandma used to make the very best country ham potpie...not the crust-topped casserole, but rather a kind of Pennsylvania Dutch dish with noodle dumplings. She made her own dough from scratch. Now I use ready-made frozen dumplings. It is quick & easy to feed a crowd with this recipe. My grandchildren request this a lot.

2 10-oz. pkgs. cooked
  ham, cubed
6 qts. water
6 potatoes, peeled
  and diced

2 12-oz. pkgs. frozen potpie
  dumplings or frozen
  homestyle egg noodles
salt and pepper to taste
Garnish: chopped onion

Combine ham and water in a large saucepan. Simmer over medium heat for 30 minutes. Add potatoes and cook for an additional 15 minutes. Increase heat so water is boiling and add frozen dumplings or noodles, one at a time. Stir in salt and pepper to taste. Reduce heat and simmer for 15 minutes. Stir frequently to avoid sticking to pan. If mixture gets too thick, add a little hot water. Garnish servings with chopped onion. Serves 8 to 10.

Tie ruffled vintage aprons onto the backs of kitchen chairs for a sweet welcome to a country-style supper.

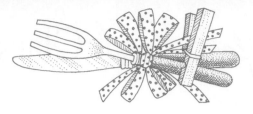

Poor Man's Meal

JoAnne Fajack
Youngstown, OH

This recipe brings back a lot of memories for me. It was made by my dad when the Second World War was going on. Times were hard...food was hard to get and many things weren't available at all. Dad grew the potatoes in our garden as well as the onions and parsley. We would eat it with bread that the lady next door had baked in an outdoor oven. This will feed around 6 people very well.

1 T. oil
1-lb. pkg. hot dogs, sliced
   1/2-inch thick
1 onion, chopped
salt, pepper, Italian seasoning
   and dried parsley to taste

6 to 8 potatoes, peeled and
   sliced 1/2-inch thick
paprika to taste

Place oil in a frying pan over medium heat. Add hot dogs and onion; cook until lightly browned. Add water to cover and bring to a boil. Add seasonings to taste. Reduce heat and simmer for about 20 minutes. Add potatoes and enough paprika to give the whole mixture a red color. Cook until potatoes are tender, adding a little more water if needed. Add additional seasonings to taste. Serves 6.

Embellish a small notebook with seed packet clippings...
oh-so useful for making shopping lists or keeping schedules.
Tie up a stack with rick rack or ribbon for gift giving.

Comfort Food Classics

Becky's BBQ Beef for a Crowd

Becky Hall
Belton, MO

This is a very flexible recipe...just the thing for a take-it-easy cookout. It holds well in a slow cooker, freezes well and reheats well in the microwave. I've used this recipe for large groups, cooking 12 to 15 pounds of meat at a time, doubling the other ingredients and increasing the baking time to 6 hours. The smoke flavoring adds so much, so don't omit it!

5 to 6-lb. beef chuck roast
1/2 to 1 t. salt
1/2 to 1 t. pepper
2 14-1/2 oz. cans stewed or
   crushed tomatoes

2 onions, chopped
3 T. sugar
2 T. smoke-flavored cooking
   sauce
Optional: vinegar to taste

Place roast in an ungreased large roasting pan; sprinkle with salt and pepper to taste. Mix remaining ingredients. If mixture is too sweet, add vinegar, about one teaspoon at a time. Pour over roast. Cover and bake at 325 degrees for 4 hours, basting occasionally. Makes 10 to 12 servings.

Thrifty country cooks were used to putting away fresh meat in large amounts for later use. Why not do as they did and save money on meals? Stock up at supermarket sales on large packages of ground beef, chuck steak, chicken or pork chops, then repackage into recipe-size portions before freezing.

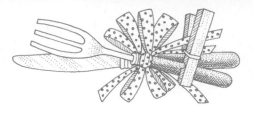

Tuna & Noodle Casserole

Marcie Graham
Sulphur, LA

Everybody's favorite comfort food.

8-oz. pkg. wide egg noodles,
  cooked
2 6-oz. cans tuna, drained
10-3/4 oz. can cream of
  mushroom soup
1 c. milk

1 c. shredded Cheddar cheese
1 tomato, sliced
salt and pepper to taste
3/4 c. to 1 c. seasoned dry
  bread crumbs

Mix cooked noodles with tuna, soup, milk and cheese. Transfer to a buttered 9"x9" baking pan. Arrange tomato slices on top; sprinkle with salt and pepper. Top with bread crumbs. Bake, uncovered, for 15 minutes at 375 degrees, until hot and bubbly. Serves 6.

First aid for old casserole dishes with baked-on food spatters! Mix equal amounts of cream of tartar and white vinegar into a paste. Spread onto the dish and let stand for 30 minutes to an hour. The spatters will wash off easily.

Comfort Food Classics

Grandma Great's Chicken Casserole

Judy Taylor
Butler, MO

This hearty casserole was my mother-in-law's special dish. Whether it's a family gathering or church social, everyone loves it!

4 to 5 boneless, skinless
   chicken breasts
1 green pepper, chopped
2 onions, chopped
1/2 c. oil
4-oz. can sliced mushrooms,
   drained

Optional: 2-oz. jar sliced
   pimentos, drained
8-oz. pkg. pasteurized process
   cheese spread, shredded
16-oz. pkg. thin spaghetti,
   cooked

Place chicken in a large saucepan; add water to cover. Simmer over medium heat until tender, about 30 minutes. Remove chicken and cool. Drain saucepan, reserving 2 cups broth. In the same pan, cook pepper and onions in oil; drain. Stir in reserved broth, mushrooms and pimentos, if desired; bring to a simmer. Chop chicken and add along with cheese and spaghetti. Transfer to a lightly greased 2-quart casserole dish. Cover and bake at 350 degrees for 30 minutes. Uncover; continue baking until lightly golden on top and liquid is absorbed, 20 to 30 minutes. Makes 6 to 8 servings.

Blue Willow is a classic vintage china pattern, so soothing to the eye...why not start a collection of pieces from tag sales and thrift shops? Whether they're fine porcelain or treasures from the 5 & dime, your mix & match finds are sure to blend together.

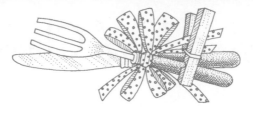

Aunt B's Chicken Tetrazzini

Bryna Dunlap
Muskogee, OK

This makes two large trays of cheesy, chickeny pasta...perfect for any church gathering when a covered dish is requested.

8 c. chicken broth
2 yellow onions, chopped
2 green peppers, chopped
16-oz. pkg. angel hair pasta, uncooked
2 lbs. boneless, skinless chicken breasts, cooked
2 4-oz. cans sliced mushrooms, drained

2 c. butter
1-1/2 c. all-purpose flour
4 c. milk
6 c. pasteurized process cheese spread, cubed
Garnish: bread crumbs

In a large stockpot over medium heat, simmer broth, onions and peppers until boiling. Add pasta and cook as directed; do not drain. Add chicken and mushrooms; set aside. In a medium saucepan over medium-low heat, combine butter, flour, milk and cheese. Cook and stir until thickened; add to broth mixture and combine well. Pour into two lightly greased deep 13"x9" baking pans and top with bread crumbs. Bake, uncovered, at 350 degrees for 30 minutes, or until hot and bubbly. Makes about 12 servings.

Don't pass up large, old-fashioned enamelware stockpots at tag sales. They're just the right size for family-size portions of stew, soup and other favorites...and, indispensible for simmering chicken & noodles.

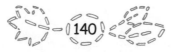

Comfort Food Classics

Skillet Turkey Stroganoff

Tammy Woodall
Glasgow, KY

With ground turkey and whole-wheat noodles, this is a yummy, healthy take on beef stroganoff. Use lowfat sour cream if you like.

1 lb. ground turkey, browned
   and drained
10-3/4 oz. can cream of
   mushroom soup

1 c. sour cream
1/2 c. milk
cooked whole-wheat egg
   noodles

Combine all ingredients except noodles in a skillet over medium heat. Cook until thickened, stirring occasionally, about 15 minutes. Serve spooned over cooked noodles. Serves 4.

You're sure to find lots of sweet old-fashioned picture books in small-town thrift stores. Keep them piled in a basket for wee visitors to enjoy.

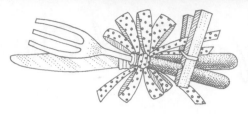

Tomato Beef Stew

Michelle Sheridan
Athens, AL

Ladle over fluffy biscuits...yum!

4 lbs. stew beef, cubed
16-oz. pkg. frozen mixed
   vegetables
29-oz. can tomato sauce

1/4 c. onion, chopped
1-1/2 oz. pkg. beef stew
   seasoning mix
1 T. Worcestershire sauce

Combine all ingredients in a slow cooker; stir well. Cover and cook on low setting for 9 to 10 hours, or on high setting for 4 to 5 hours. Makes 10 to 12 servings.

Make a double recipe of your favorite comfort food and invite neighbors over for supper...what a great way to get to know them better. Keep it simple with a tossed salad, warm bakery bread and brownies for dessert...it's all about food and fellowship!

Comfort Food Classics

Paprika Beef & Noodles

Joan White
Malvern, PA

Choose sweet Hungarian paprika for the most robust flavor.

2 to 2-1/2 lbs. boneless beef
   chuck roast, cubed
2 onions, chopped
3 T. butter
8-oz. can tomato sauce
2 t. Worcestershire sauce
2 t. sugar
2 t. paprika

1-1/2 t. caraway seed
1 t. dill weed
1/8 t. garlic powder
1 to 2 t. salt
1/4 t. pepper
8-oz. container sour cream
cooked egg noodles

In a Dutch oven over medium-high heat, cook beef and onions in butter until meat is browned. Add sauces, sugar and seasonings; bring to a boil. Reduce heat to low; cover and simmer for 1-3/4 to 2 hours, or until beef is tender. Remove from heat; stir in sour cream. Serve over cooked noodles. Serves 4 to 6.

Every farmhouse kitchen should have a wooden tasting spoon by the stovetop! With a spoon at each end and a groove in the handle, the design allows hot food to cool slightly before being sampled by the cook. If you're lucky, you may find a hand-carved example at a craft fair.

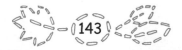

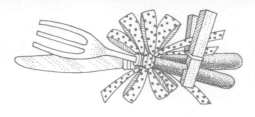

Brown Sugar Ham

Melissa Dawn
Kennewick, WA

For the prettiest presentation, score the ham in a diamond pattern before brushing on the sweet & savory glaze.

4 to 5-lb. fully cooked ham
1 c. brown sugar, packed
1/2 c. spicy mustard

1/3 c. honey
1 T. dried rosemary
1 T. ground cumin

Place ham in an ungreased large roaster pan. Mix together remaining ingredients and spread over ham. Bake, covered, at 375 degrees for 35 to 40 minutes. Uncover and bake for an additional 10 to 15 minutes. Let stand briefly before slicing. Serves 8 to 10.

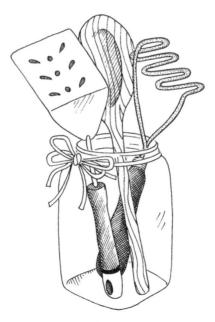

Fill a large canning jar or an enamelware pitcher with vintage red-handled kitchen utensils...instant nostalgia!

Comfort Food Classics

Cheryl's Country-Style Ribs

Cheryl Tesar
DeWitt, NE

A family favorite...so delicious, there are rarely any leftovers!
I like to serve it with golden cornbread, a pot of
baked beans and sweet baked apples.

7 to 8 lbs. country-style pork
   ribs, sliced into serving-size
   portions

salt to taste
2 onions, sliced
1/2 c. brown sugar, packed

Place ribs in an ungreased large roaster pan; sprinkle lightly with salt.
Top ribs with onion slices, brown sugar and 3/4 of Barbecue Sauce.
Cover and bake at 350 degrees for 2 hours. Uncover and add
remaining sauce. Increase oven to 400 degrees; bake for an additional
30 minutes. Makes 12 to 15 servings.

Barbecue Sauce:

2 c. catsup
1 c. water
1/2 c. sugar
1/2 c. vinegar
1/2 c. Worcestershire sauce

2 T. smoke-flavored cooking
   sauce
1 t. garlic powder
1 t. salt

Combine all ingredients and mix well. Keep refrigerated.

Relax and serve your next
dinner party family-style...
set large platters of food
right on the table so guests
can help themselves.

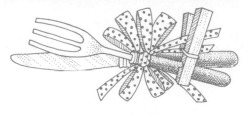

Roast Chicken & Vegetables

Beckie Butcher
Elgin, IL

This is my own creation from about 10 years ago, when I discovered my true love of cooking. Every time I serve this, I get rave reviews from some of the best cooks in my family...it's quite an ego booster!

3 to 4-lb. roasting chicken
salt and pepper to taste
1 onion, chopped

2 carrots, peeled and chopped
3 stalks celery, chopped
1 tomato, sliced

Place chicken in an ungreased roasting pan. Sprinkle with salt and pepper to taste. Fill loosely with Sage Stuffing, allowing room for stuffing to expand. Place onion, carrots and celery around chicken; add enough water to cover vegetables. Cover; bake at 350 degrees for one hour. Add tomato; cover again and bake for 30 additional minutes. Uncover to allow browning; bake for a final 30 minutes, until juices run clear. Place chicken on a platter and carve. Serve stuffing and vegetables separately. Serves 4 to 6.

Sage Stuffing:

14-oz. pkg. sage-flavored
    stuffing mix
2 to 2-1/2 c. boiling water
1 egg, beaten

1 onion, chopped
1 stalk celery, chopped
Optional: dried sage to taste

Place stuffing mix in a large bowl. Add water to desired consistency; toss to moisten. Stir in remaining ingredients until well blended.

Turn leftover bread stuffing into a tasty side dish, or toss in some browned sausage to make it a main dish. Simply spoon stuffing into green peppers or squash halves and bake at 350 degrees until heated through and tender.

Comfort Food Classics

Delicious Drumsticks

Renae Scheiderer
Beallsville, OH

*This is a good recipe that was given to me when I was first married
and just learning how to cook. I still enjoy fixing it!*

1/2 c. all-purpose flour
1/2 t. paprika
1 t. salt

1/4 t. pepper
1/4 c. butter, melted and cooled
1-1/2 lbs. chicken drumsticks

Mix flour and seasonings in a shallow bowl; place melted butter in a
separate shallow bowl. Dip drumsticks into butter; roll in flour mixture
to coat. Arrange in an ungreased 8"x8" baking pan. Bake, uncovered,
at 425 degrees until done, about 50 minutes. Makes 4 to 6 servings.

Keep a large shaker of seasoned flour close at hand for
sprinkling on pork chops and chicken before frying.
A good mix is one cup flour, 1/4 cup seasoned salt
and one tablespoon pepper.

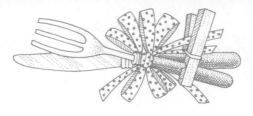

Country Chicken & Dumplin's

Jennifer Jones
McDonough, GA

My mother-in-law always made this for me when I came to visit.
It always warmed me up and made me feel so cozy.
It's great with fried okra!

4 to 5-lb. chicken
2 14-1/2 oz. cans chicken broth
3 c. water
10-3/4 oz. can cream of chicken
  soup

2 10-oz. tubes refrigerated
  biscuits, quartered
salt and pepper to taste

Place chicken in a large pot; add broth and water. Bring to a boil; reduce heat and simmer for about 45 minutes, until chicken is done. Remove chicken from pot, reserving broth; let chicken cool for 30 minutes. Add soup to reserved broth in pot; stir to mix over medium heat. Pull chicken from bones and return to the pot. Add biscuit pieces. Simmer for 15 minutes, or until dumplings have puffed up, stirring occasionally. Add salt and pepper to taste. Serves 5.

A soup tureen adds old-fashioned flair to any dinner table
or buffet. Warm it up before ladling in homemade chicken
& dumplings or beef stew and it will stay hot longer.
Just fill with hot water, let stand for a few minutes,
pour out the water and it's ready!

Comfort Food Classics

Homestyle Beef Stew

Sophia Graves
Okeechobee, FL

This recipe has such wonderful memories for me. My mom would only make this on the coldest of winter days. We never knew when that would be, but I knew when I walked up to the house that Mom had something good cooking in the kitchen by the steam on the windows. When I opened the front door, the aroma would just envelope me... I could hardly wait until dinner!

2 to 3-lb. beef roast, cut into
    bite-size pieces
salt and pepper to taste
1 c. all-purpose flour
1/2 c. olive oil, divided
5 c. beef broth
5 cloves garlic

9 new redskin potatoes,
    quartered
1 lb. baby carrots
1/2 to 1 lb. mushrooms,
    quartered
1/2 to 1 c. pearl onions
10-oz. pkg. frozen peas

Sprinkle beef with salt and pepper; coat with flour. Spray a large pot with non-stick vegetable spray. Working in two batches, brown beef in oil over medium heat; remove beef from pot and set aside. Add broth to pot, scraping up all the browned bits in the bottom. Return meat to pot; add garlic and additional salt and pepper to taste. Bring to a boil for 15 minutes. Reduce heat, cover and simmer. After one hour, stir and cover again. Check meat for doneness after 2 hours; add potatoes, carrots, mushrooms and onions. Cover, increase heat to medium and cook for 30 minutes more, or until vegetables are tender. Remove from heat; discard garlic and stir in peas. Cover; let stand for about 20 minutes until peas are heated through. Makes 8 to 10 servings.

Quick & easy farmhouse napkin
rings! Glue a charm or button
to a little grapevine ring
and slip in a cloth napkin.

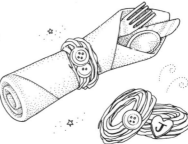

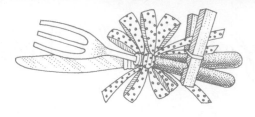

Roast Chicken Dijon

Kendall Hale
Lynn, MA

*This recipe is so simple and scrumptious...we love it! Sometimes
I'll make extra sauce to toss with redskin potatoes and
tuck them around the chicken for a meal-in-one.*

3 to 4-lb. roasting chicken
1/4 c. Dijon mustard
2 T. lemon juice

1 T. olive oil
salt and pepper to taste

Place chicken on a rack in an ungreased roasting pan. Mix mustard,
lemon juice and oil in a small bowl. Brush mixture over chicken;
sprinkle with salt and pepper. Bake, uncovered, at 425 degrees for
40 minutes, or until chicken juices run clear when pierced with a fork.
Let stand for several minutes before slicing. Serves 4 to 6.

Don't toss the bones from a roast chicken! Turn it into
delicious broth...it's oh-so-simple with a slow cooker.
Combine the bones with a big handful of chopped onion,
carrots and celery. Add 6 cups water, cover and cook on
low setting for 8 to 10 hours. Strain, refrigerate and skim fat,
then freeze in one-cup portions. They'll be ready to use
in your favorite recipes.

Comfort Food Classics

Brunswick Chicken Bake

Jill Valentine
Jackson, TN

My husband loves a big kettle of down-home Brunswick stew, so when I found this casserole-style recipe, I knew he'd like it too. For a really traditional dish, sometimes I'll substitute a package of frozen sliced okra for one of the packages of succotash.

2 T. oil
2-1/2 lbs. chicken
1 onion, chopped
2 T. all-purpose flour
.9-oz. pkg. Italian salad
    dressing mix

14-1/2 oz. can diced tomatoes
    with green peppers and
    onions
1 bay leaf
2 10-oz. pkgs. frozen
    succotash, thawed

Heat oil in a large skillet over medium-high heat. Brown chicken on all sides, about 15 minutes. Drain, reserving 2 tablespoons drippings in skillet. Arrange chicken in an ungreased 13"x9" baking pan and set aside. Add onion to skillet; sauté until tender. Stir in flour and salad dressing mix. Add tomatoes and bay leaf; cook and stir until bubbly. Stir in succotash and heat through. Pour skillet mixture over chicken; cover with aluminum foil. Bake at 350 degrees for one hour, until chicken juices run clear when pierced with a fork. Discard bay leaf before serving. Serves 4.

A toy-size little red wagon filled with seasonal flowers makes a nostalgic, farmhouse centerpiece.

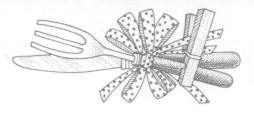

Chicken & Dumplings

Julie Kline
Kewanna, IN

Our farm family enjoys this after a long day of harvest or beef cattle chores. It's a hearty meal paired with coleslaw and a dish of fruit.

2 c. cooked chicken, chopped
8 c. chicken broth
1 c. potatoes, peeled and diced
1 c. celery, chopped
1/2 c. carrots, peeled and diced

1/4 c. onion, minced
1 c. frozen peas
1/4 t. dried parsley
pepper to taste

Combine chicken, broth, potatoes, celery, carrots and onion in a Dutch oven. Bring to a boil over medium heat while preparing Potpie Dumplings. Drop dumplings into boiling broth. Cover and cook for 15 minutes over medium heat. Stir in frozen peas, parsley and pepper to taste. Cook for about 2 minutes, until peas are cooked through, and serve. Makes 6 to 8 servings.

Potpie Dumplings:

2 c. all-purpose flour
2 t. salt
2 T. butter, chilled

2 eggs, beaten
1/4 c. water

Combine flour and salt. Cut in butter with a pastry blender or 2 forks. Stir in eggs and water until combined. Knead on a floured surface for 2 minutes. Roll out thinly on a floured surface; cut into one-inch squares.

Throw an apron party! Invite your best girlfriends to tie on their frilliest vintage aprons and join you in the kitchen to whip up a favorite dish together. It's a fun way to catch up with everyone.

Comfort Food Classics

Schinken Nudeln

Christine Middleton
Nicholson, PA

German ham and noodles...delicious with or without catsup.

2 T. olive oil
2 T. butter
1 onion, finely chopped
1/2 lb. cooked ham, cut into
   bite-size cubes
Optional: 1/4 lb. bacon, chopped
16-oz. pkg. spaghetti, cooked

salt and pepper to taste
1/4 t. dried oregano
1/4 t. dried basil
1/2 t. dried parsley
2 eggs, beaten
Optional: catsup

Heat oil and butter in a large skillet. Sauté onion until transparent; add ham and bacon, if using. Cook until meat is done; quickly stir in seasonings. Transfer ham mixture to a separate dish. Add cooked spaghetti to skillet; top with ham mixture. Fry until spaghetti turns golden on bottom. Stir from bottom, mixing everything together; fry until heated through. Just before serving, pour in eggs; stir over low heat to mix and cook eggs, 3 to 5 minutes. Serve with catsup, if desired. Makes 6 servings.

If you're short on table space, an old-fashioned wooden ironing board makes a sturdy sideboard. Just adjust it to a convenient height, add a pretty table runner and set out the food... come & get it!

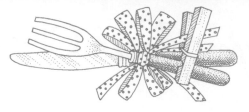

Honey & Brown Sugar Meatloaf
Lea Ann Burwell
Charles Town, WV

My father-in-law raises honeybees and shares the honey with us. One day I experimented with it and this has become my husband's favorite meatloaf recipe. It is simply delicious. He also likes to use the leftovers to make hot meatloaf sandwiches the next day...yum!

2-1/2 lbs. ground beef
1 sleeve saltine crackers,
   crushed
1 egg, beaten

2 c. catsup, divided
1/2 c. honey
1/2 c. brown sugar, packed

Mix ground beef, cracker crumbs, egg and 1/2 cup catsup in a large bowl until thoroughly mixed. Shape into a loaf and place in an ungreased 13"x9" baking pan. Spread 1/2 cup catsup on top of loaf. Bake at 350 degrees for one hour and 15 minutes. Mix honey, brown sugar and remaining catsup together with a whisk. Remove meatloaf from oven and pour glaze over the top. Place meatloaf under the broiler until glaze starts to bubble. Let cool slightly before slicing. Serves 6 to 8.

Often, for the tastiest country cooking, no fancy tools are needed...dig right in and mix that meatloaf with your hands!

Flat Meatballs & Gravy

Susan Harford
Pleasanton, CA

My husband's mother, Arlene Harford, used to make this recipe for her children. David has in turn made it for our three girls, Jennifer, Liz and Stephanie. It continues to be a family favorite.

2 lbs. ground beef round
1 egg, beaten
1/2 c. milk
1 T. all-purpose flour
1 t. salt
1/2 t. pepper

Optional: 1 onion, diced
2 T. butter
10-3/4 oz. can cream of
   mushroom soup
cooked rice

Mix all ingredients except butter, soup and rice together in a large bowl; set aside. Melt butter in a frying pan over medium heat. Scoop beef mixture into frying pan with an ice cream scoop; use spoon to shape into flattened meatballs. Brown over medium heat, turning several times. Remove meatballs to an ungreased 2-quart casserole dish; reserve drippings in pan. Stir soup into drippings; pour over meatballs. Bake, uncovered, at 350 degrees for 30 minutes. Serve over cooked rice. Serves 8.

Don't have enough dining-table chairs for when everyone gets together? Pick up mismatched tag-sale chairs for a song... paint them in a country color like barn red or robin's egg blue. Stencil on stars, hearts or even family members' names for a sweet personal touch.

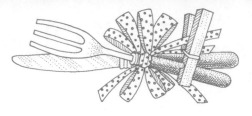

Easy Baked Chicken

Patti Walker
Mocksville, NC

This is a yummy quick meal for hurried evenings when I'm running the children back & forth from tennis matches or football practice. I like to put this dish in to bake while I run out to do carpool...when we get home, it's ready to serve! I round out the meal with steamed green beans.

6 frozen boneless, skinless
    chicken breasts
10-3/4 oz. can cream of
    mushroom soup
10-3/4 oz. can cream of
    onion soup

1/2 c. milk
2 T. margarine, diced
cooked egg noodles

Arrange frozen chicken in a single layer in a lightly greased 13"x9" baking pan. Mix soups and milk together; spread mixture over chicken, covering chicken well. Dot chicken with margarine. Cover baking pan with aluminum foil so that it is sealed well. Bake at 350 degrees for one to 1-1/2 hours, until cooked through. Serve chicken over egg noodles; spoon sauce from pan over all. Serves 4 to 6.

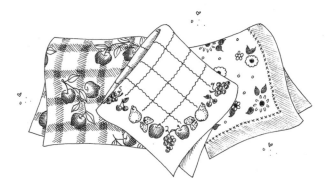

A simple trick to add down-home flavor to a roasting chicken.
Cover it with several thick slices of hickory-smoked
country bacon before popping it into the oven.

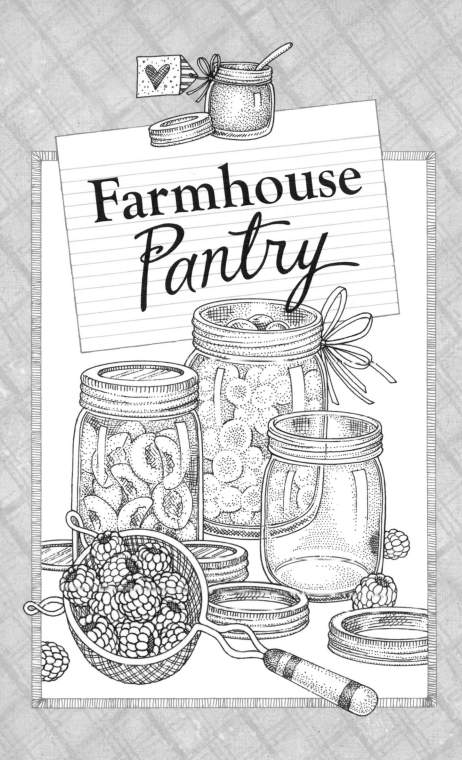

Farmhouse Pantry

Mom's Hot Bacon Dressing

Jacqueline Kurtz
Wernersville, PA

My mom used to make this all the time to drizzle over fresh endive...
it's a country classic. This dressing is very good added to
homemade hot potato salad too.

4 slices bacon
2 T. sugar
2 T. all-purpose flour
1 egg, beaten

2 T. cider vinegar
1/4 c. water
3/4 c. milk

In a skillet over medium heat, cook bacon until crisp. Remove bacon and drain, reserving drippings in skillet. In a small bowl, mix sugar, flour, egg and vinegar until smooth. Stir in water and milk and add to drippings. Crumble bacon and return to skillet. Cook over medium-low heat until thickened. More water or milk may be added until dressing reaches desired consistency. Serve warm. Makes 4 servings.

When frying bacon, it's easy to prepare a few extra slices to tuck into the fridge. Combine with juicy slices of sun-ripened tomato, frilly lettuce and creamy mayonnaise for a fresh BLT sandwich...tomorrow's lunch is ready in a jiffy!

Farmhouse *Pantry*

Sweet-and-Sour Dressing

Lori Graham
Pittsfield, PA

A friend shared this recipe for an easy, light dressing. It's tasty on taco salads as well as on tossed green salads.

6 T. cider vinegar
1 c. brown sugar, packed
1 T. sugar

1/4 c. oil
1/4 t. garlic salt

In a small saucepan over low heat, cook and stir all ingredients until sugars are dissolved. Cool; pour into a covered container. May be kept refrigerated for up to 2 weeks. Makes 10 servings.

Line the inside of a kitchen cabinet door with self-stick cork tiles. It'll be a handy place to tack favorite recipes, take-out menus, frequently called phone numbers and more! Just for fun, attach button-box buttons to thumbtacks with glue.

Spicy Hot Dog & Burger Sauce

Judith Zechman
Butler, PA

*Try this tasty sauce at your next school fundraiser
or neighborhood cookout...it's sure to be a hit!*

1 lb. ground beef, browned
   and drained
8-oz. can tomato sauce
2 c. water
1-1/2 T. Worcestershire sauce
1 T. prepared horseradish
1 t. hot pepper sauce

1 T. dried, minced onion
1 T. chili powder
1 t. dried oregano
1 t. cayenne pepper
1/8 t. nutmeg
1/8 t. salt

Combine all ingredients in a large saucepan. Cover and simmer over low heat for 30 minutes, stirring occasionally. May also be prepared in a slow cooker; cover and cook on low setting for several hours. Serve immediately or keep refrigerated. Makes about 5 cups.

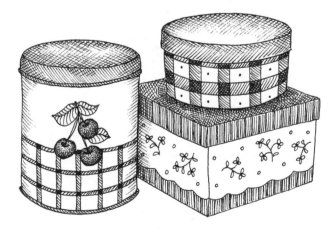

Corral mail, recipe clippings and family photographs
in style...cover hatboxes with pretty vintage wallpaper.

Farmhouse *Pantry*

Margaret's Chili Sauce

Brenda Conkling
Marquette Heights, IL

My mother-in-law gave me this recipe...it's wonderful when you have lots of tomatoes ripening in the garden! I like to serve some of it immediately and then freeze the rest so we can enjoy the flavor of fresh tomatoes throughout the year.

16 lbs. tomatoes, peeled
   and chopped
1 onion, chopped
1 green pepper, chopped
1/2 c. cider vinegar
1 c. brown sugar, packed

1 c. sugar
2 t. allspice
2 t. cinnamon
salt and pepper to taste
5 to 6 1-pint plastic freezer
   containers

Place tomatoes, onion and green pepper in a large Dutch oven. Add vinegar, sugars and spices; bring to a boil over medium-high heat. Reduce heat to a low simmer. Cook for 1-1/2 to 2 hours, stirring often, until cooked down and thickened. Add salt and pepper to taste. Remove from heat; cool slightly and spoon into containers. Place in freezer. Makes 5 to 6 containers.

Tin cans with colorful, vintage-style labels make clever holders for potted plants.

Savory Steak Butter

Cathy Clemons
Narrows, VA

Dad always loved extra-juicy steaks and chops...no dry meat for him! This saucy butter was just the thing and it also added a little zing to the flavor of the meat. Lately I've found the new chipotle-flavored hot pepper sauce is tasty in this too.

1/2 c. butter, softened
2 T. steak sauce
1 T. Worcestershire sauce
1 t. smoke-flavored cooking
    sauce

1/8 t. hot pepper sauce
1 clove garlic, crushed
1/2 t. seasoned salt

In a small bowl, beat together butter and remaining ingredients until well blended. Shape into a log; wrap in plastic wrap and refrigerate. At serving time, slice to serve on grilled steaks or chops. If desired, plastic-wrapped log may be wrapped in aluminum foil and frozen for up to 6 months; no need to thaw before using. Makes about 1/2 cup.

Nostalgic food advertisements from vintage ladies' magazines can be found at most flea markets. Choose one or several to frame for a whimsical wall decoration.

Farmhouse *Pantry*

All-Purpose Meat Marinade

Caroline Stoltzfus
Sarasota, FL

This versatile marinade is delicious with beef, pork, chicken and even fish. We especially enjoy it for marinating cubed meats for grilled kabobs.

1/2 c. oil	1 T. Dijon mustard
1/4 c. soy sauce	1 T. dried parsley
1/4 c. red wine vinegar	1 clove garlic, pressed
1/8 c. lemon juice	1/2 t. salt
1 T. Worcestershire sauce	1/2 t. pepper

Whisk all ingredients together. Keep refrigerated in a covered container. To use, place 4 to 6 pieces of chicken, beef, pork or fish in a plastic freezer bag or container and add marinade. Refrigerate or freeze until ready to prepare. Grill meat, brushing occasionally with marinade. Discard any excess marinade that has been used. Makes about one cup.

Fill uniquely shaped bottles from Grandma's pantry with herb vinegars...you can even tuck in a fresh sprig of herbs or herb blossoms. They'll sparkle on a windowsill.

Great Chicken BBQ Sauce

Kim Faulkner
Delaware, OH

Why use ordinary bottled barbecue sauce? This yummy sauce can easily be stirred up with ingredients you probably already have in the pantry!

1 c. catsup
1/4 c. Worcestershire sauce
1/4 c. brown sugar, packed
2 T. cider vinegar

2 t. salt
1 t. dry mustard
1/2 t. garlic powder

Mix all ingredients together in a small saucepan. Simmer over very low heat for one hour, stirring occasionally. Use to baste chicken pieces while grilling. Makes about 1-1/2 cups.

Fill Mason jars with your own special savory sauce to give as a take-home gift. Tie on a recipe card and a BBQ brush with a bit of jute...cookout guests will love it!

Farmhouse *Pantry*

Banana Pepper Mustard

Sharon Demers
Dolores, CO

This year our garden was bursting with banana peppers! A good friend shared this recipe with me...from now on, I will be sure to plant banana peppers every year. This mustard has a sweet-hot taste that's especially delicious with soft pretzels.

32-oz. jar mustard
32-oz. bottle cider vinegar,
   divided
6 c. sugar
40 to 50 banana peppers,
   seeded and finely chopped

9 T. cornstarch
8 to 10 1-pint canning jars and
   lids, sterilized

Combine mustard, 3 cups vinegar, sugar and peppers in a Dutch oven. Bring to a boil over medium heat, stirring constantly. Mix cornstarch with remaining vinegar; slowly stir into mustard mixture. Cook and stir until thickened. Remove from heat and pour into hot sterilized jars, leaving 1/2-inch headspace. Wipe rims; secure with lids and rings. Process for 10 minutes in a boiling water bath. Set jars on a towel to cool; check for seals. Makes 8 to 10 jars.

A cabin with plenty of food is better than a hungry castle.
–Irish Saying

Rosemary Crumb Coating

Margaret Welder
Madrid, IA

This recipe came from my sister-in-law. It is a scrumptious way to cook chicken or pork chops...and much healthier than frying!

1-1/2 c. dry bread crumbs
1/2 c. all-purpose flour
2 T. salt
1 T. dried rosemary

1 T. paprika
1/4 t. onion powder
3 T. oil

Combine all ingredients; toss to mix. May be kept refrigerated indefinitely in a covered container. To use, moisten chicken pieces or pork chops with water; roll in crumbs. Place on a baking sheet lined with aluminum foil that has been sprayed with non-stick vegetable spray. Bake at 350 degrees for 25 to 35 minutes, until done. Discard any excess crumbs that were used to coat the meat. Makes about 2 cups.

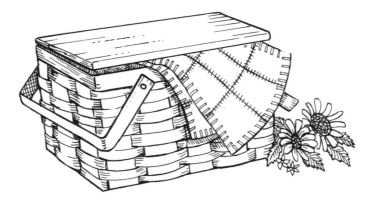

Thrift shops always have heaps of gently used baskets. Keep several on hand and you'll be ready to put together a gift at a moment's notice. Tuck in a loaf of fresh-baked bread or a dozen cookies wrapped up in a tea towel...oh-so thoughtful!

Farmhouse *Pantry*

Stacie's Spaghetti Sauce

Stacie Allison
Fredericksburg, VA

This is the recipe my mother used back in the days before you could buy spaghetti sauce in a jar at any grocery. It is still my favorite and so easy to make. Serve over your favorite pasta.

1 onion, chopped
1 green pepper, chopped
1 T. olive oil
1 lb. ground beef
28-oz. can chopped tomatoes
15-oz. can tomato sauce
6-oz. can tomato paste
1 T. Worcestershire sauce
1 t. garlic powder
salt and pepper to taste

In a large skillet or stockpot over medium heat, sauté onion and green pepper in oil until tender. Add ground beef and cook until browned; drain. Stir in remaining ingredients. Reduce heat to low; cover and simmer for at least one hour, stirring occasionally. Makes 4 to 6 servings.

A tall old-fashioned milk can is perfect for holding umbrellas inside the back door.

Grandma Ginny's Hot Dog Sauce
Wendy Chapman
Barboursville, WV

This yummy recipe was handed down to me from my grandma. It's a "must" at any family picnic! This sauce freezes well in small containers to be reheated later in the microwave.

2-1/2 lbs. lean ground beef
1 onion, chopped
2 c. water

24-oz. bottle catsup
2-1/2 T. chili powder
1 t. ground cumin

Combine ground beef, onion and water in a large saucepan. Bring hamburger to a boil over medium heat and stir to crumble meat. When meat is browned, add remaining ingredients; stir together. Simmer on low heat for 2-1/2 hours, stirring occasionally. Makes 8 to 10 cups.

Share your favorite tried & true recipes with a new bride who's just learning to cook. Jot down recipes on individual cards, along with your special touches or hints for success. Slip the cards into the pages of a mini photo album and tie with a homespun ribbon. She'll think of you whenever she uses it!

Farmhouse *Pantry*

Dad's Sweet Mustard

Kathy Majeske
Denver, PA

This recipe has been in my dad's family for several generations. Dad loves to make it at Christmastime to go along with homemade pork sausage from a small hometown meat market. This mustard has a little zing to it...just the way we like it!

1 c. dry mustard
1 c. sugar

3 T. all-purpose flour
1 c. cider vinegar

Mix together mustard, sugar and flour in a bowl; set aside. Heat vinegar until hot, without boiling; add to dry ingredients. Pour into a blender; process until mixed. Store in a covered jar in the refrigerator. Makes about 3 cups.

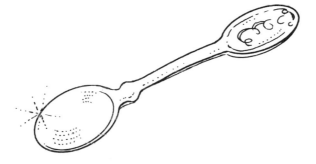

Silver-plated baby spoons are ideal for serving up dollops of mayonnaise, preserves, chutney and other condiments. Polish up Bobby and Janie's almost-forgotten little spoons or scoop up vintage finds at a tag sale.

Charlotte's Hot Endive Dressing

Melody Chencharick
Julian, PA

This was a special favorite of my father's...baked ham served with Mom's hot endive dressing. It is delicious spooned over mashed potatoes! She always prepared this in her trusty old cast-iron skillet.

1/3 c. cider vinegar
3/4 c. water
1 lb. bacon
2 eggs, beaten

1 c. sugar
2 T. cornstarch
2 T. mustard
1 head endive, chopped

Combine vinegar and water; set aside. In a skillet over medium heat, cook bacon until crisp. Remove bacon from skillet, reserving drippings. Crumble bacon into bits and set aside. Add eggs to drippings in skillet over low heat; cook and stir until scrambled. Add vinegar mixture to skillet; stir until well blended. Mix together sugar, cornstarch and mustard; add to skillet. Add endive and cook until softened, about 5 minutes. Serves 4 to 6.

Don't pass up a pretty sugar bowl just because it has lost its lid...turn it into a sweet flower vase. Slip a block of floral foam inside and arrange short-stemmed marigolds or zinnias in the foam.

Farmhouse *Pantry*

Jo's Poppy Seed Dressing

Marion Sundberg
Ramona, CA

My Aunt Jo made this dressing whenever we went to her house or she came to ours. It is scrumptious on any kind of salad. For a lighter dressing, substitute one cup of plain yogurt for one cup of the mayonnaise.

2 c. mayonnaise
2/3 c. white vinegar
1 c. sugar

2 to 3 T. poppy seed
2 t. mustard

Combine all ingredients and whisk together until smooth. Keep refrigerated in a covered container. Makes 12 servings.

Half-pint glass milk bottles make fun containers for serving salad dressings. Fill each bottle with a different variety of dressing and set them around the table, or place bottles in a wire milk carrier...so clever!

Bread & Butter Pickles

Rhonda Hauenstein
Tell City, IN

When I was growing up, we canned everything we grew in our family garden. Canning pickles was such fun! I liked slicing the pickles, so that was my "job." Now my daughter, Erika, and I can pickles every summer for my parents.

4 lbs. pickling cucumbers, sliced
3 to 4 onions, sliced
2 green peppers, sliced into
   strips
1/2 c. canning salt
3 c. cider vinegar

5 c. sugar
1-1/2 t. turmeric
1-1/2 t. celery seed
2 T. mustard seed
6 1-quart canning jars and
   lids, sterilized

Combine cucumbers, onions, green peppers and salt in a large bowl or crock. Add ice water and ice to cover; let stand for 3 hours. Drain; place in a large kettle and set aside. Combine vinegar, sugar and spices; stir well and pour over cucumber mixture. Bring to a boil over medium-high heat. Reduce heat and continue cooking until cucumbers turn a deep yellow color. Remove from heat and fill hot sterilized jars, leaving 1/2-inch headspace. Wipe rims; secure with lids and rings. Process for 20 minutes in a boiling water bath. Set jars on a towel to cool; check for seals. Makes 6 jars.

Trying your hand at pickle making? Don't get into a pickle! For best results, ask for a pickling variety of cucumbers at the farmers' market rather than using regular salad cukes from the supermarket.

Farmhouse *Pantry*

Picnic Sweet Pickles

Ruie Richardson
Marinette, WI

This is such an easy way to have your own "homemade" pickles!
Add some red pepper flakes or tuck in some whole peeled
garlic cloves to suit your own taste.

32-oz. jar whole dill pickles,
   drained
2 c. sugar
1/4 c. white vinegar

1/4 c. water
5 whole cloves
2 to 3 1-inch cinnamon sticks

Rinse pickles well. Trim off ends of pickles, slice into chunks and return to jar; set aside. Mix remaining ingredients in a saucepan over medium heat. Simmer for 5 minutes; do not boil. Pour mixture over pickles in jar; seal jar. Let stand at room temperature for 24 hours before refrigerating. Makes one quart.

Wouldn't family members love a jar of pickles made from Mom's tried & true recipe? Dress up the jar with a nostalgic label. Color photocopy her handwritten recipe on cardstock and cut out with decorative-edged scissors. Glue to the jar and tie rick rack around the lid...so thoughtful!

Farmhouse Beet Relish

Kelly Masten
Hudson, NY

This relish is served every year at the local Evangelist church's Dutch Supper. It is absolutely delicious...they ALWAYS sell out well before the last seating! I was finally able to talk one of the senior members into sharing the recipe with me. It can be served as a side dish, spooned onto your favorite hoagie or used as a hot dog relish...no matter how you serve it, it is sure to be a hit!

4 c. beets, cooked, peeled and
   chopped
4 c. onions, chopped
1 T. salt
1 T. prepared horseradish

1-1/2 c. sugar
3 c. white vinegar
3 to 4 1/2-pint canning jars
   and lids, sterilized

In a large heavy saucepan, combine all ingredients. Bring to a boil over medium heat. Turn heat to medium-low and simmer for 10 minutes, stirring until sugar dissolves. Remove from heat. Ladle relish, while boiling hot, into hot sterilized jars, leaving 1/8" headspace. Wipe rims; secure with lids and rings. Allow to cool completely. Store in refrigerator until ready to use, up to 4 weeks. If desired, for longer shelf-life, process jars for 15 to 20 minutes in a boiling water bath immediately after applying lids. Set jars on a towel to cool; check for seals. Makes 3 to 4 jars.

Show off ruby-red beet relish in Mom's antique cut-glass compote. When washing cut glass, add a little white vinegar to the rinse water...the glass will really shine!

Farmhouse *Pantry*

Refrigerator Pickles

Kay Barg
Sandy, UT

Super simple...a great recipe for first-time pickle makers.

3 c. cucumbers, peeled and
    sliced
1 onion, thinly sliced
3/4 c. sugar

2/3 c. white vinegar
1/2 t. celery seed
1/2 t. mustard seed
1/4 t. salt

Mix cucumbers and onion in a glass or plastic bowl; set aside. Stir remaining ingredients together in a microwave-safe container. Microwave on high for 3 minutes, stirring after 2 minutes. Pour over cucumber mixture. Cover and refrigerate for 24 hours before serving, to blend flavors. Keep refrigerated. Makes one quart.

A small drawer from an old end table or dresser makes a useful key keeper to hang near the back door. Paint the drawer as you like or découpage with clippings. Add cup hooks inside to hold keys and a hanging wire on the back... an easy organizer!

Gooseberry Conserve

Angie Stone
Argillite, KY

Serve with roast chicken or turkey...yummy!

3 lbs. gooseberries, stems
   removed
3 lbs. sugar
16-oz. pkg. raisins

juice and zest of 3 oranges
2 c. nuts, chopped or broken
4 1-pint canning jars and lids,
   sterilized

Combine all ingredients except nuts in a large heavy saucepan. Bring to a boil over medium heat, stirring until sugar dissolves. Reduce heat and cook until thick, stirring frequently. Mix in nuts. Spoon into hot sterilized jars, leaving 1/4-inch headspace. Wipe rims; secure with lids and rings. Process in a boiling water bath for 10 minutes; set jars on a towel to cool. Check for seals. Makes 4 jars.

A butter dish makes a delightful mini windowsill garden. Turn over the lid, set it on the butter dish, fill with soil and plant with a tiny, low-growing herb like thyme or chamomile.

Farmhouse *Pantry*

Candy Apple Jelly

Linda Vogt
Las Vegas, NV

*My friends & family love this sparkling red jelly so much that they
return the empty jars to remind me to make some more for them!*

4 c. apple juice or cider
1/2 c. red cinnamon candies
1-3/4 oz. pkg. fruit pectin

4-1/2 c. sugar
3 1-pint canning lids and jars,
   sterilized

Combine apple juice or cider, candies and pectin in a large heavy
saucepan. Bring to a full boil over high heat, stirring constantly. Stir in
sugar and return to a full boil. Boil for 2 minutes, stirring constantly.
Remove from heat. Skim off foam and and any unmelted candies.
Pour hot liquid into hot sterilized jars, leaving 1/4-inch headspace.
Wipe rims; secure with lids and rings. Process in a boiling water bath
for 5 minutes; set jars on a towel to cool. Check for seals. Makes
3 jars.

Add a spatterware finish to a decorative thrift-store wooden
bowl. Paint the outside of the bowl with acrylic craft paint
and let dry. Dip the bristles of a dry toothbrush into a
contrasting color of paint. Blot on a paper towel to remove
excess paint, then pull your thumb across the bristles
to spatter the paint...quick & easy speckles!

Cranberry-Tomato Chutney

Debi DeVore
Dover, OH

The tangy flavor of this quick-to-make chutney perfectly complements roast pork. For a delightful appetizer to serve with crackers, spoon some chutney over a block of cream cheese.

5 c. cranberries
28-oz. can crushed tomatoes
1 c. golden raisins
3/4 c. sugar
1 t. salt
3/4 t. ground ginger

Combine all ingredients in a large heavy saucepan over medium heat. Bring to a boil. Reduce heat; cover and simmer for 20 to 25 minutes, stirring occasionally, until cranberries and raisins are tender. Transfer to a covered container; cool. Refrigerate for 2 to 3 days before serving. Keep refrigerated. Makes 6 cups.

Old-fashioned canning jars in all sizes are easy to find at tag sales and flea markets...use them for vases, tumblers and kitchen storage.

Jezebel Raisin Sauce

Ellen Folkman
Crystal Beach, FL

This sauce is absolutely delicious with baked ham. I found this recipe before I was married and have been using it for nearly 20 years. It's very easy to make...I hope you'll give it a try!

1 c. sugar
1/2 c. water
8-oz. jar currant jelly
1 c. raisins, chopped
2 T. vinegar
1 T. Worcestershire sauce

1/2 t. salt
1/8 t. pepper
1/4 t. cinnamon
1/8 t. ground cloves
1/8 t. ground ginger

Combine sugar and water in a large saucepan over medium heat. Bring to a boil; boil for 2 minutes, stirring until sugar dissolves. Add remaining ingredients; reduce heat to medium and cook until blended. Serve hot. Refrigerate any leftovers; reheat before serving. Makes 2 cups.

A primitive painted three-legged milking stool makes a delightful plant stand.

Oregon Jewel Jam

Ellie Brandel
Milwaukie, OR

My husband and I bought a case of peaches from a roadside fruitstand on our honeymoon. This recipe was given to us by the farmer, and now I make it every year and think of our memorable vacation.

4 c. peaches, peeled and
   chopped
7 c. sugar
1/2 c. water
20-oz. can crushed pineapple

juice and zest of 1 lemon
4-oz. jar maraschino cherries,
   drained and finely chopped
6 1/2-pint canning jars and
   lids, sterilized

Mix peaches, sugar, water, pineapple with juice, lemon juice and zest in a large kettle. Cook over low heat for one hour, stirring frequently. Remove from heat; let stand for 5 minutes. Stir in cherries. Spoon into hot sterilized jars, leaving 1/4-inch headspace. Wipe rims; secure with lids and rings. Process in a boiling water bath for 10 minutes; set jars on a towel to cool. Check for seals. Makes 6 jars.

Homemade fruit jam isn't just for spreading on bread.
Stir a spoonful into warm breakfast oatmeal...yum!

Farmhouse *Pantry*

Blueberry-Pecan Relish

Jill Ball
Highland, UT

A jar of this sweet, nutty relish makes a beautiful gift that looks like you spent a lot of time making it...that's your little secret!

16-oz. pkg. frozen blueberries,
   thawed and drained
1 apple, cored, peeled and
   coarsely chopped
1 c. pecans, finely chopped
1/2 c. sugar

2 t. cider vinegar
1 t. allspice
1/2 t. cinnamon
4 t. lemon juice
3 to 4 1-pint canning jars and
   lids, sterilized

In a large heavy saucepan, combine all ingredients except lemon juice. Bring to a boil over medium heat, stirring constantly. Remove from heat; stir in lemon juice. Spoon into hot sterilized jars, leaving 1/8" headspace. Wipe rims; secure with lids and rings. Process jars for 5 minutes in a boiling water bath. Set jars on a towel to cool; check for seals. Relish may also be kept refrigerated, without processing, for 2 to 3 weeks. Makes 3 to 4 jars.

Whip up a chalkboard to hang in the pantry for jotting down shopping lists...no more last-minute runs to the supermarket! Simply paint a baking sheet or shallow pan with chalkboard paint and tie on a piece of chalk.

Fresh Herb Pesto Sauce

Colleen Hinker
Santa Rosa, NM

Classic Italian pesto is made with fresh basil and pine nuts,
but try other tasty combinations too, like rosemary and
pecans or oregano and almonds...delicious!

2 c. fresh herb leaves, coarsely
   chopped
6 cloves garlic, chopped
1 c. chopped nuts

1/2 c. plus 1 T. olive oil, divided
1/2 t. salt
3/4 c. grated Parmesan or
   Romano cheese

Mix herbs, garlic, nuts, 1/2 cup oil and salt in a blender. Process until
smooth, adding a little more oil if needed to make blending easier.
Transfer to a bowl and stir in grated cheese. Refrigerate in an airtight
container or spoon into ice cube trays and freeze for later use. Makes
about 1-1/2 cups.

Some yummy ways to enjoy pesto sauce...serve with meat
or fish. Stir into hot pasta dishes or vegetables. Add to
sour cream or mayonnaise to make a dressing.

Farmhouse *Pantry*

Homemade Tartar Sauce

Barb Stout
Delaware, OH

You can whip up this fresh tartar sauce in a jiffy.

1 c. mayonnaise
2 T. dill pickles, chopped
2 T. green olives with pimentos,
   chopped
1 T. onion, grated

1 T. fresh parsley, chopped
1 T. capers
1 T. lime or lemon juice
1/4 t. garlic salt

Combine all ingredients; mix well. Cover and refrigerate until serving time. Makes about 1-1/2 cups.

Stir up some fish-fry mix the next time Dad heads for a fishing trip. Combine 2 cups yellow cornmeal, 2 tablespoons lemon-pepper seasoning, a tablespoon of garlic salt and a teaspoon of pepper; store in a covered container. To use, coat fish fillets and let stand for several minutes, then deep-fry until golden, 7 to 10 minutes. Serve with lemon wedges and tartar sauce...delectable!

Cranberry-Jalapeño Relish

Gloria Robertson
Midland, TX

We enjoy this relish served as an appetizer...
its zingy flavor really wakes up a turkey dinner too!

1 c. water
1 c. sugar
1/4 t. salt
12-oz. pkg. cranberries
3 jalapeño peppers, seeded
   and chopped

1/4 c. fresh cilantro, chopped
1 apple, cored and grated
8-oz. pkg cream cheese
crackers, tortilla chips

Bring water, sugar and salt to a boil in a large saucepan over medium heat. Add cranberries. Reduce heat; simmer until cranberries pop and sauce thickens, stirring occasionally. Add jalapeños, cilantro and apple; stir gently to mix. Chill and serve spooned over a block of cream cheese. Serve with crackers or tortilla chips. Relish may be stored in freezer containers until needed. Makes 4 cups.

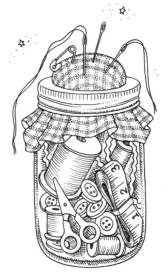

Create a sweet mini sewing kit..it's so handy! You'll need a pint-size Mason jar with a two-part lid. Pad the flat lid piece with cotton batting, cover with a circle of fabric and slide on the jar ring. Fill the jar with needles & thread, tiny scissors and a few spare buttons, screw on the lid and it's ready to use!

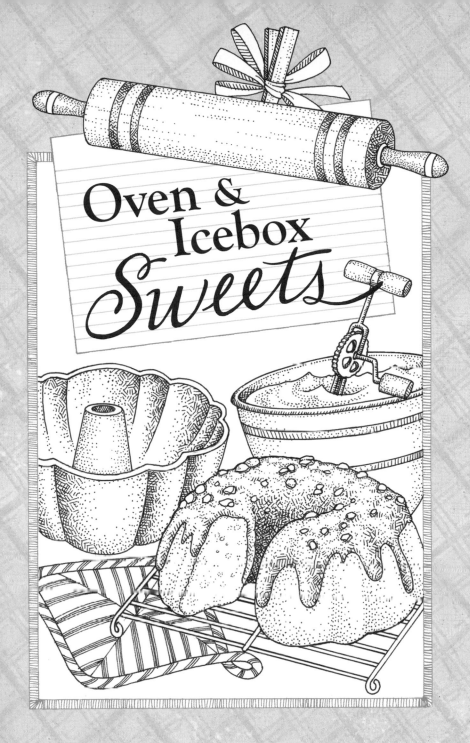

Oven &
Icebox
Sweets

Chocolate Icebox Cake

Joan Trefethen
Fairborn, OH

Surprise...it's pudding! This easy dessert is a family favorite.

3.4-oz. pkg. cook & serve
vanilla pudding
3.4-oz. pkg. cook & serve
chocolate pudding
3 c. milk, divided

2 sleeves graham crackers,
divided
Garnish: whipped cream,
chocolate sprinkles

Prepare pudding mixes separately as packages direct, using 1-1/2 cups milk for each one. Let puddings cool slightly. Line the bottom of an ungreased 13"x9" baking pan with whole crackers. Line sides of pan with halved crackers. Spoon vanilla pudding over crackers. Cover with another layer of whole crackers; spoon chocolate pudding over crackers. Crumble remaining crackers over top. Refrigerate until chilled. At serving time, dollop individual portions with whipped cream; garnish with sprinkles. Serves 8 to 10.

Create charming cupcake stands from tag-sale teacups and saucers. Invert each teacup and glue its saucer on top with epoxy glue. So clever!

Oven & Icebox *Sweets*

Amish Cream Pie

Kristen Cook
Avon Lake, OH

My younger sister and I love to visit Ohio Amish country. We always eat at one of the Amish-owned restaurants. On one trip, we tried this old-fashioned cream pie. It was so delicious, we started making trips just for the pie! We started experimenting in our own kitchens and we finally put together this recipe. We're happy to share it with everyone.

1/3 c. all-purpose flour
1/2 c. butter, melted
1 c. brown sugar, packed
1 pt. whipping cream

9-inch pie crust or graham
cracker crust
Garnish: whipped cream

In a large bowl, blend flour into melted butter. Add brown sugar; mix thoroughly. Add cream and stir until well blended. Pour into crust. Bake at 375 degrees for 50 to 55 minutes, until center is jiggly but not liquid. Cool. Serve with whipped cream. Serves 6 to 8.

Nothing says farm-fresh flavor like dollops of whipped cream
on a homemade dessert. It's easy too. In a chilled bowl,
with chilled beaters, whip one cup of whipping cream
until soft peaks form. Mix in 2 teaspoons sugar and
2 teaspoons vanilla extract.

Old-Fashioned Rice Pudding

Gretchen Hickman
Galva, IL

My grandmother was an excellent country cook...this recipe is hers.

5 c. cooked rice
3 c. evaporated milk
1-1/3 c. brown sugar, packed
6 T. butter, softened

4 t. vanilla extract
1 to 2 t. nutmeg
6 eggs, beaten
1 to 2 c. raisins

Combine all ingredients; pour into a lightly greased slow cooker. Cover and cook on low setting for 4 to 6 hours, or on high setting for one to 2 hours. Stir after first 30 minutes. Serves 4 to 6.

Vanilla-Almond Coffee

Kathy Grashoff
Fort Wayne, IN

A cup of this coffee warms you right up on a chilly day!

1 lb. regular or decaf
  ground coffee

2 T. vanilla extract
2 T. almond extract

Place ground coffee in a large jar with a tight-fitting lid. Add extracts; cover and shake well. Cover and store in refrigerator. Prepare ground coffee as usual. Makes one pound.

Don't hide a pretty glass cake stand in the cupboard! Use it to show off several of Mom's best dessert plates or arrange colorful, seasonal fruit on top.

Graham Cracker Apple Crisp

Evie Prevo
Livermore, CA

This dessert was a sweet tradition at our family's holiday dinners as well as at other times of the year. It's a little different because it uses graham crackers in the topping instead of oats. It is the only kind of apple crisp Mom ever made for us...Grandma made it too.

8 Granny Smith apples, cored, peeled and sliced
1/2 c. water
1-1/4 c. sugar, divided
1 c. graham cracker crumbs

1/2 c. all-purpose flour
1 t. cinnamon
1/8 t. salt
1/2 c. butter, melted

Arrange apple slices in a buttered 11"x7" baking pan. Use more or less apples depending on their size; pan should be nearly full to the top but not heaping. Mix water and 1/2 cup sugar together; sprinkle over apples. Mix remaining sugar, graham cracker crumbs, flour, cinnamon and salt and sprinkle over apples. Drizzle melted butter evenly over topping. Bake at 450 degrees for 10 minutes; lower heat to 350 degrees and bake for an additional 40 minutes. Serves 8 to 10.

Core apples and pears in a jiffy...cut in half,
then use a melon baller to scoop out the core.

Apple Butter Roly-Poly

Lori Zolla
Friedens, PA

*This family recipe was originally made by my maternal grandmother,
Stella. It never lasts long at my house! It's especially
scrumptious made with homemade apple butter.*

2-1/2 c. all-purpose flour
1 t. salt
1 c. shortening
1/4 c. water

4 T. butter, softened and divided
1 c. apple butter, divided
4 t. sugar, divided

In a medium bowl, combine flour and salt. Cut in shortening and mix
with a fork until mixture is fine and crumbly. Sprinkle in water until
all flour is moistened and pastry almost cleans side of bowl, using
more or less water as needed. Divide pastry into two equal portions.
Roll out one portion between 2 sheets of wax paper into an 18-inch
by 8-inch rectangle. Peel off top sheet of wax paper. Spread dough
with 2 tablespoons butter; spread 1/2 cup apple butter over butter,
spreading within one inch of edges. Sprinkle 2 teaspoons sugar on
top of apple butter. Roll pastry up into a log, starting at one of the
short ends. Pinch ends shut; place seam-side down in an ungreased
13"x9" baking pan. Repeat to make a second log. Bake at 425 degrees
for 30 minutes, or until lightly golden. Cool; cut logs into one-inch
slices. Makes 2 logs, 10 servings each.

Serve up fruit crisps or pies
in a yummy new way...layer
spoonfuls in tall parfait glasses,
layered with sweetened whipped
cream and crunchy toasted nuts
or even crushed granola.

Oven & Icebox *Sweets*

The Best Blondies

Elizabeth Cisneros
Chino Hills, CA

*For an extra-special dessert, serve squares topped with
a scoop of butter brickle ice cream...delicious!*

1 c. butter, melted
2 c. brown sugar, packed
2 eggs, beaten
2 t. vanilla extract
2 c. all-purpose flour
1/2 t. baking powder

1/4 t. salt
1 c. chopped pecans
1 c. white chocolate chips
3/4 c. toffee or caramel baking
   bits

Line a 12"x9" baking pan with parchment paper. Spray sides of pan with non-stick vegetable spray and set aside. In a large bowl, mix together butter and brown sugar. Beat in eggs and vanilla until mixture is smooth. Stir in flour, baking powder and salt; mix in pecans, chocolate chips and baking bits. Pour into prepared pan and spread evenly. Bake at 375 degrees for 30 to 40 minutes, until set in the middle. Allow to cool in pan before cutting into squares. Makes one dozen.

If you see a vintage cake pan with its own slide-on lid at a tag sale, snap it up! Not only is it indispensible for toting frosted bar cookies to a party, it also makes a clever lap tray for kids to carry along crayons and coloring books on car trips.

French Silk Chocolate Pie

Linda Mercer
Shelbyville, TN

My grandmother and mother used to make these light, refreshing pies for every family gathering...such sweet memories!

1/2 c. butter
3/4 c. sugar
2 eggs
2 1-oz. sqs. unsweetened
  baking chocolate, melted
  and cooled

8-oz. container frozen whipped
  topping, thawed
9-inch pie crust, baked and
  cooled, or chocolate graham
  cracker crust

In a large bowl, blend together butter and sugar until light and creamy. Add eggs, one at a time; beat for 5 full minutes with an electric mixer on medium speed. Add melted chocolate and blend; fold in whipped topping. Spoon into crust; refrigerate for at least 4 hours. Makes 6 servings.

For an extra-special gift, wrap up a jar of homemade jam in a lacy vintage handkerchief and tie it with a ribbon.

Oven & Icebox *Sweets*

Walnut Fudge Cake

Wendy Lee Paffenroth
Pine Island, NY

*For double fudgy deliciousness, I like to microwave some fudge frosting
in a coffee mug for about 20 seconds and pour it over the cooled cake.
Decorate the top with more crushed walnuts...yum!*

3 eggs, beaten
1/4 c. oil
1/3 c. sour cream
1/2 c. coffee, brewed and cooled

18-1/2 oz. pkg. dark fudge cake
  mix
1/2 c. walnuts, ground
Optional: 1 to 3 T. milk

Mix eggs, oil, sour cream and coffee until well blended. Add dry cake
mix and walnuts. If batter is too thick, stir in a little milk until a good
batter consistency is reached. Pour into a greased Bundt® cake pan.
Bake at 325 degrees for 45 minutes, or until cake pulls away from
sides of pan and springs back to the touch. Cool cake in pan for 30 to
40 minutes before turning out onto a cake plate. Makes 10 to
12 servings.

For blue-ribbon perfect chocolate cakes with no white streaks,
use baking cocoa instead of flour to dust the greased pans.

Betty's Easy Cherry Cobbler

Betty Lou Wright
Hendersonville, TN

This long-time family favorite always puts a smile on my husband's face. I usually double the recipe and bake it in a 13"x9" pan...doesn't that tell you how much he loves it? We like cherries, but feel free to substitute your favorite flavor of fruit filling.

1/2 c. margarine
1 c. sugar
3/4 c. all-purpose flour
2 t. baking powder

1/4 t. salt
3/4 c. milk
21-oz. can cherry pie filling

Place margarine in an 8"x8" glass baking pan; set in a 325-degree oven to melt. Combine sugar, flour, baking powder, salt and milk; mix well with a wire whisk. Pour over melted margarine; do not stir. Spoon pie filling on top of batter; again, do not stir. Bake at 325 degrees for about an hour, until golden. Serve warm. Makes 6 servings.

A whistling teakettle adds cheer to any farmhouse kitchen.
It's easy to remove the hard water and lime build-up in a
barn-sale find. Just pour in 2 cups of white vinegar and
bring to a boil. Simmer for 10 minutes, then rinse well...
it'll be ready to brew up a cup of tea!

Oven & Icebox *Sweets*

Miss Lizzie's Pound Cake

Jody Brandes
Hartfield, VA

This recipe came from a neighbor of my grandfather's back in the 1950's. I've been making it for 45 years and topping it with my mom's caramel frosting. I think you'll love it as much as I do!

1 c. butter, softened	1 c. milk
1/2 c. shortening	1 t. imitation vanilla butter
3 c. sugar	and nut flavoring
1/4 t. salt	3 c. all-purpose flour
6 eggs	

Beat together butter and shortening; gradually add sugar and salt. Add eggs, one at a time, beating well after each addition; set aside. Mix together milk and flavoring; add to butter mixture alternately with flour. Spread into a greased and floured 10" tube pan. Bake at 325 degrees for one hour, until a toothpick inserted in center tests clean. Remove from pan; cool completely before frosting. Serves 8 to 10.

Caramel Frosting:

1-1/2 c. brown sugar, packed	5-oz. can evaporated milk
1/2 c. sugar	1 t. vanilla extract
1/2 c. butter	

In a saucepan over medium heat, combine all ingredients except vanilla. Cook for 15 minutes, stirring constantly. Remove from heat; stir in vanilla. Immediately spread over cooled cake.

Eggs work best in baking recipes when they're brought to room temperature first. If time is short, just slip the eggs carefully into a bowl of lukewarm water and let stand for 15 minutes...they'll warm right up.

Lemony Blackberry Crisp

Pat Gilmer
West Linn, OR

The perfect reward for an afternoon spent picking blackberries!

5 c. fresh or frozen blackberries
1/4 c. sugar
2 T. cornstarch
3 T. lemon juice
25 vanilla wafers, crushed
1/2 c. old-fashioned oats,
   uncooked

1/2 c. light brown sugar,
   packed
1/4 c. all-purpose flour
1/2 t. cinnamon
1/2 c. butter, melted
Garnish: vanilla ice cream

Place blackberries in a cast-iron Dutch oven; sprinkle with sugar and set aside. In a cup, stir together cornstarch and lemon juice; add to berries and mix gently. In a bowl, combine vanilla wafer crumbs, oats, brown sugar, flour and cinnamon. Add butter; stir until crumbly. Sprinkle crumb mixture over berries. Bake, uncovered, at 400 degrees for 25 to 30 minutes, until bubbly and lightly golden. Serve warm, topped with a scoop of ice cream. Makes 4 to 6 servings.

Fresh-picked berries are a special country pleasure.
Store them in a colander in the refrigerator to let
cold air circulate around them. There's no need to
wash them until you're ready to use them.

Oven & Icebox *Sweets*

Sour Cherry Pie

Sharon Demers
Dolores, CO

When I was a little girl my father would sing to me, "Can you bake a cherry pie, Sharon girl, Sharon girl?" My reply would always be a giggle and then a big "Nooo!" Well, I can finally make a cherry pie and only wish that my dad were still with us so I could serve him a big piece.

2 9-inch pie crusts
4 c. sour cherries, pitted and
   1/2 c. juice reserved
1 c. sugar
1 T. all-purpose flour

2-1/2 T. cornstarch
juice and zest of one lime
2 T. butter, diced
1 egg, beaten
2 T. whipping cream

Roll out one crust; place in a 9" pie plate. Wrap with plastic wrap and chill. Roll out remaining crust 1/8-inch thick. Cut as many one-inch-wide strips as possible to make a lattice; cut any leftover crust into leaf shapes with a cookie cutter. Place lattice strips and leaves on a parchment paper-lined baking sheet; cover with plastic wrap and chill. Combine cherries and juice in a large bowl. Sprinkle with sugar, flour, cornstarch, lime juice and zest. Toss well and pour into pie crust; dot with butter. Weave lattice strips over filling. Arrange leaves in a decorative pattern on lattice. Whisk together egg and cream; brush over lattice and edges of crust. Bake at 400 degrees for about 50 minutes, until crust is golden and juices in center of pie are bubbly. Cool slightly before cutting. Makes 6 to 8 servings.

An intricate lattice pie crust is glorious, but there's an easier way! Simply lay half the lattice strips across the pie filling in one direction, then lay the remaining strips at right angles. No weaving required!

Thrifty Bread Pudding

Missie Brown
Delaware, OH

I started to make a bread pudding one night and realized I was out of white sugar. So...I substituted brown sugar and my husband liked it even better! Sprinkle the top with your favorite nuts.

7 hamburger buns, torn into
   bite-size cubes
1/4 c. butter, melted
3/4 c. raisins
2 t. cinnamon

5 eggs, beaten
1-1/2 c. brown sugar, packed
3 c. milk
1 t. vanilla extract
1 t. nutmeg

Combine bread cubes, melted butter, raisins and cinnamon in an ungreased 2-quart casserole dish; set aside. In a separate bowl, stir eggs and brown sugar together until sugar is dissolved. Add milk and vanilla; mix together thoroughly and pour over bread mixture. Sprinkle nutmeg over the top. Bake at 350 degrees for about 35 minutes, or until a knife inserted into center comes out clean. Serves 4 to 6.

Who doesn't remember penny candy from the corner store?
Fill antique apothecary jars with a variety of candies...
butterscotch drops, licorice whips, root beer barrels, caramels,
jawbreakers, peppermints and lemon drops. Set out several
filled jars and let everyone choose their favorite for
a sweet trip down memory lane.

Oven & Icebox *Sweets*

Sweet Fritters

Betty Gretch
Owendale, MI

A country farm recipe that has been handed down for generations. We couldn't wait for the fritters to get done...they filled the kitchen with such a sweet aroma. We ate them up as soon they were made. Enjoy them like we did, still warm from the fryer.

2 eggs, beaten
1/2 c. milk
1 c. all-purpose flour
1 t. baking powder
1 t. lard, melted

Optional: 1/2 c. apple, cored,
  peeled and finely diced
oil for deep frying
Garnish: powdered sugar

In a large bowl, whisk together eggs and milk. Stir in flour, baking powder and salt; mix in lard. Add diced apple, if desired. Heat several inches of oil to 375 degrees in a deep fryer. Drop batter into fryer by tablespoonfuls, a few at a time; fry until golden. Cool slightly and dust with powdered sugar; serve warm. Makes 2 dozen.

Sugar Cookie Dough

Bake up an oversized skillet cookie! Pat your favorite sugar cookie dough into the bottom of a cast-iron skillet. Bake at 350 degrees for 40 to 45 minutes, until golden on top and slightly browned on the edges. Cookie will continue to bake for a few minutes out of the oven. Turn onto a wire rack to cool slightly and cut into wedges. Yummy!

Harvard Beet Spice Cake

Betty Wachowiak
Waukegan, IL

Your friends will love trying this sweet, spicy cake...
make them guess what the "secret ingredient" is!

16-oz. jar Harvard beets
1/2 c. butter, softened
1-1/4 c. sugar
2 eggs, beaten
2-1/4 c. all-purpose flour
4 t. baking soda

1-1/2 t. allspice
1 t. cinnamon
1/4 t. ground cloves
1 c. chopped walnuts
Garnish: powdered sugar

Process beets in a blender until smooth; set aside. In a large bowl, beat butter with sugar until light and fluffy. Add eggs; beat well and set aside. Sift together flour, baking soda and spices. Add flour mixture to butter mixture alternately with puréed beets, mixing well after each addition. Fold in walnuts. Turn batter into a greased and lightly floured 9-cup Bundt® pan. Bake at 350 degrees for 55 minutes, or until cake tests done. Cool cake in pan on a wire rack for 30 minutes. Turn cake out of pan onto a cake plate. Sift powdered sugar over cake. Makes 8 to 10 servings.

A sweet addition to your baking cupboard...a heart-shaped cake pan for cakes that say "I love you."

Oven & Icebox *Sweets*

Pineapple Upside-Down Cake

Cathy Clemons
Narrows, VA

An old favorite with a little twist. This doubly fresh-tasting cake has always been a hit at my office. Some like to say it's a good way to get your Vitamin C...really it's just an excuse to eat another slice!

6 T. butter
1 c. brown sugar, packed
20-oz. can pineapple slices,
   drained
8 to 10 maraschino cherries

18-1/2 oz. pkg. yellow cake mix
3 eggs, beaten
1/3 c. oil
20-oz. can crushed pineapple
Garnish: whipped cream

Melt butter in a 13"x9" baking pan in a 350-degree oven. Remove pan from oven; sprinkle brown sugar over butter. Arrange pineapple slices decoratively in pan; fill in spaces with cherries and set aside. In a large bowl, combine dry cake mix, eggs, oil and crushed pineapple with its juice. Beat with an electric mixer on high speed for 2 minutes. Pour batter over pineapple slices. Bake at 350 degrees for 40 minutes, or until cake tests done. Remove from oven; allow to cool 10 to 15 minutes in pan. Place a serving platter onto pan and very carefully invert cake onto platter. Serve warm or at room temperature, topped with whipped cream. Makes 16 servings.

Toss a few slices of apple in the cookie jar
to keep cookies soft and fresh.

Orange Icebox Cookies

Janice Curtin
Anna, IL

*My mother, Eunice, was an excellent cookie baker. This recipe is from
way back in the 1950's. She always made a tin of cookies for my
kids once a week when they were growing up.*

1 c. shortening
1/2 c. sugar
1/2 c. brown sugar, packed
1 egg, beaten
2-3/4 c. all-purpose flour

1/2 t. baking soda
1/2 t. salt
2 T. orange juice
1 T. orange zest
1/2 c. chopped nuts

Mix together shortening, sugars and egg in a large bowl; set aside. Sift
together flour, baking soda and salt; gradually add to sugar mixture.
Stir in orange juice, zest and nuts. Divide dough in half; roll each
half into a 2-inch-thick log and refrigerate overnight. Slice 1/4-inch
thick. Place on ungreased baking sheets. Bake at 350 degrees for
9 to 11 minutes. Makes 5 to 6 dozen.

Big potato chip tins make roomy containers for storing
cookie cutters. You may even find one from a long-gone
but fondly remembered hometown chip maker.

Oven & Icebox *Sweets*

Country Raisin Gingersnaps

Michelle Greeley
Hayes, VA

*My great-grandmother, Stella Carver, made these cookies in the
1930's. She was the cook at a logging camp in Michigan.*

3/4 c. shortening
1 c. sugar
1 egg, beaten
1/2 c. molasses
3-1/2 c. all-purpose flour
2 t. baking soda

1 t. salt
1 t. ground ginger
1/4 t. ground cloves
1/2 t. cinnamon
1-1/2 c. raisins, chopped
Garnish: sugar

In a large bowl, beat shortening with an electric mixer on high speed
until creamy. Gradually beat in sugar until fluffy. Add egg; beat until
blended. Reduce mixer to medium speed; beat in molasses and set
aside. Sift flour, baking soda, salt and spices; gradually add to
shortening mixture. Fold in raisins. Turn dough out onto a sheet of
aluminum foil. Wrap and refrigerate for one to 2 hours. Form into
one-inch balls and roll in sugar; place on greased baking sheets.
Bake at 375 degrees for 10 to 12 minutes, until tops of cookies are
crackled. Let stand for 2 minutes before removing cookies from
baking sheets. Makes about 3-1/2 dozen.

Treat everyone to fresh-baked
cookies & icy cold milk...
served up in pint-size
vintage milk bottles!

Wash-Day Peach Pie

Jennifer Bryant
Bowling Green, KY

Nanny tells me that this pie got its name because it was so simple farmwives could make it on the days they did the laundry...the old-fashioned way! It's more like a cobbler than a pie...yummy made with pears instead of peaches too.

1 c. self-rising flour
1 c. sugar
1 c. milk
15-oz. can sliced peaches,
   drained

1/4 c. butter, sliced
Garnish: vanilla ice cream or
   whipped topping

Stir together flour and sugar; add milk and stir until smooth. Pour batter into a greased 1-1/2 quart casserole dish; spoon peaches over top. Place butter in center. Bake at 350 degrees for one hour, or until golden. Serve warm, topped with ice cream or whipped topping. Makes 8 servings.

Hang up an old-fashioned mini washboard where family messages, calendars and to-do lists can easily be found. Fabric yo-yo's hot-glued to button magnets will hold everything in place and add a dash of whimsy.

Telephone Cookies

Julie Gavin
San Antonio, TX

We've been making these scrumptious no-bakes for nearly 50 years now. They came about through my grandma's telephone eavesdropping. She shared a party line with her neighbors as they lived out in the country. One day when Grandma wanted to use the phone, she picked up the receiver and heard the neighbor lady giving out a recipe. She quickly wrote down the ingredients and directions, but never caught the name of the recipe. We love these cookies...kids love to make them too!

2 c. powdered sugar, divided
2 T. butter, softened
1 c. creamy peanut butter

1-1/2 c. crispy rice cereal
3 T. milk
1 c. sweetened flaked coconut

Combine one cup powdered sugar, butter, peanut butter and cereal in a large bowl. Mix with your hands and form into walnut-size balls. Place in a plastic freezer container; freeze. To make frosting, combine remaining powdered sugar and milk until smooth. Dip frozen cookies into frosting and roll in coconut. Keep stored in the freezer in a sealed container. Makes 6 dozen.

A one-gallon glass apothecary jar makes a great cookie jar. Personalize it by using a glass paint pen to add a message like "Grandma's Special Cookies" and hearts or swirls just for fun.

Grandma & Katie's
Frozen Dessert

Jennifer Brown
Garden Grove, CA

This used to be my birthday cake every year...I loved it! To this day every time we make this dessert, I think of all those birthday parties in the backyard.

1/2 c. creamy peanut butter
1/2 c. light corn syrup
2 c. crispy rice cereal
2 c. chocolate-flavored crispy
  rice cereal

1/2 gal. vanilla ice cream,
  softened
1/2 to 1 c. Spanish peanuts
Garnish: chocolate syrup

Blend together peanut butter and corn syrup in a large bowl. Add cereals; stir until coated. Press into the bottom of a ungreased 13"x9" baking pan. Spread ice cream over cereal mixture; sprinkle with peanuts. Swirl chocolate syrup over top. Cover with aluminum foil; freeze at least 4 hours before serving. Cut into squares to serve. Makes 15 to 18 servings.

A retro tin breadbox makes a convenient
cubby for favorite cookbooks.

Oven & Icebox *Sweets*

Sweet Vanilla Pudding

Elizabeth Cisneros
Chino Hills, CA

There's nothing more comforting than a bowl
of warm homemade pudding!

1/4 c. sugar	2 egg yolks, beaten
2 T. cornstarch	1 T. butter
1/8 t. salt	2 t. vanilla extract
2 c. milk	1/4 t. nutmeg

In a small saucepan, combine sugar, cornstarch and salt. Stir in milk; cook and stir over medium heat until thickened. Reduce heat to low; continue cooking and stirring for 2 minutes. Place egg yolks in a small bowl. Add a small amount of hot milk mixture to yolks; stir and return all of yolk mixture to pan, stirring constantly. Bring to a gentle boil; cook and stir one minute longer. Remove from heat; add butter, vanilla and nutmeg. Let cool in pan for 15 minutes, stirring every 5 minutes. Transfer to dessert bowls; cover and refrigerate. May be served slightly warm or cold. Serves 4.

A double boiler is a "must" for melting chocolate without scorching. To be sure the water in the bottom pan doesn't boil down too low, drop in a glass marble when you fill the pan. The marble will rattle when it's time to add more water.

Martha's Shredded Apple Pie

Patti Walker
Mocksville, NC

Every year at Christmastime, my Grandmother Martha would make the best apple pies. The first time my boyfriend tasted her pie, he said he would definitely marry me if I could cook as well as she did. I guess I passed the test, because we have been married over 15 years! This is a family heirloom recipe that my Granny (great-grandmother) first made...don't tell my grandmother I shared it!

8 Granny Smith apples, cored, peeled and shredded
1/4 t. lemon juice
1-1/2 t. apple pie spice
2 9-inch pie crusts
1/2 c. butter, melted
2 c. sugar
3 eggs, beaten
nutmeg to taste

Place apples in a large bowl; toss with lemon juice and spice. Pierce unbaked crusts lightly with a fork; fill with apples. Mix melted butter, sugar and eggs; pour mixture evenly over apples. Dust the top of each pie with a dash of nutmeg. Bake at 350 degrees for 45 minutes to an hour. Allow to cool (if you can wait!) before slicing. Makes 2 pies, 8 servings each.

An apple pie without some cheese
Is like a kiss without a squeeze.
–Old saying

Oven & Icebox *Sweets*

Grandma's Custard Pie

Teena Hippensteel
Fort Wayne, IN

This is a recipe that my grandma made on the farm and handed down to my mom and me. We love this pie...Grandma still does too! If you wish, you can use two, 8-inch pie crusts to make two shallower pies.

4 eggs, beaten
1/2 c. sugar
1/4 t. salt
1 t. vanilla extract

2-1/2 c. milk
nutmeg to taste
9-inch deep-dish pie crust

Whisk eggs, sugar, salt and vanilla together; beat well and set aside. In a medium saucepan over medium-low heat, heat milk just until bubbles form around the edge. Stir in egg mixture; pour into crust. Sprinkle nutmeg on top. Bake at 475 degrees for 5 minutes. Reduce heat to 425 degrees and continue to bake for 15 to 20 minutes, until top is golden. Let cool before slicing. Serves 6 to 8.

If you love to bake, keep a small vintage coffee grinder on hand for grinding whole spices. The extra-fresh flavor of freshly ground cinnamon, cloves and nutmeg can't be beat.

Coconut Fridge Cake

Jennifer Holcomb
Port Angeles, WA

Whenever I make this cake, I smile! This yummy recipe was given to me by one of my most favorite people in the whole world...my sister-in-law, Barb. Not only is it the yummiest cake ever, it makes me think of Barb and how lucky we are to have her in our family.

18-1/2 oz. pkg. white cake mix
16-oz. container frozen whipped
  topping, thawed
8-oz. container sour cream
1 c. sweetened flaked coconut
1 c. sugar

Prepare cake mix according to package directions, baking in two, 9" round baking pans. Cool; slice each layer horizontally in half to make 4 layers. To make frosting, mix remaining ingredients together well. Frost and stack layers on a cake plate; frost top and sides of cake with remaining frosting. Cover and refrigerate cake for one to 3 days before serving, as flavor improves with age. Serves 8 to 10.

Invite friends & family to an old-fashioned ice cream social!
Set up tubs of ice cream and lots of toppings...fluffy whipped
cream, peanuts, bananas, maraschino cherries, hot fudge
sauce and butterscotch topping. Give a prize for
the most creative sundae!

Oven & Icebox *Sweets*

Rainy Day Cookies

Mary Gentry
Pikeville, KY

*A couple of these chocolate and nut-filled cookies
will cheer you up on even the gloomiest day!*

1 c. butter, softened
1/4 c. sugar
3/4 c. brown sugar, packed
1 t. vanilla extract
3.4-oz. pkg. instant vanilla
    pudding mix

2 eggs, beaten
2-1/4 c. self-rising flour
12-oz. pkg. semi-sweet
    chocolate chips
8-oz. pkg. black walnuts,
    chopped

Combine butter, sugars, vanilla and dry pudding mix in a bowl; beat until smooth and creamy. Beat in eggs; add flour gradually. A little more butter may be added if batter seems too dry. Stir in chocolate chips and nuts until batter is stiff. Drop by rounded teaspoonfuls, 2 inches apart, on ungreased baking sheets. Bake at 375 degrees for 8 to 10 minutes. Makes 2 dozen.

Teacups & saucers can be had for a song at tag sales. Start a
collection with a single theme...all cups with pink roses,
blue forget-me-nots or whatever strikes your fancy.
They'll be a fun topic of conversation at any tea party!

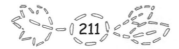

Cherry Pie Supreme

Debbie Manning
Wayland, IA

My son loves cheesecake and my husband loves cherry pie.
So I combined the two to create this delectable dessert.

21-oz. can cherry pie filling,
　divided
9-inch pie crust
4 3-oz. pkgs. cream cheese,
　softened

1/2 c. sugar
2 eggs, beaten
1/2 t. vanilla extract
Garnish: 1 c. frozen whipped
　topping, thawed

Spread half of pie filling in bottom of crust; set aside remaining filling.
Bake filled crust at 425 degrees for 15 minutes, or just until golden.
Remove from oven; reduce temperature to 350 degrees. In a large
bowl with an electric mixer on high speed, beat cream cheese, sugar,
eggs and vanilla until smooth. Pour over hot pie filling in crust; bake
at 350 degrees for 25 minutes. Filling will be slightly soft in center.
Cool completely on a wire rack. Spread with remaining filling; top
with whipped topping. Serves 8.

A ceramic pie bird keeps juicy fillings from bubbling over in
a double-crust pie. Set it in the center of the unbaked bottom
crust and pour the filling around it. Cut a slit in the center
of the top crust and fit it carefully over the pie bird. Bake as
usual and let cool. You can lift out the pie bird when
the first slice is cut.

Oven & Icebox *Sweets*

Dutch Apple Pie

Christina Hubbell
Jackson, MI

A family picnic favorite that's simple to make.

2/3 c. plus 2 T. all-purpose
   flour, divided
1/2 c. brown sugar, packed
1/3 c. butter
6 c. tart cooking apples, cored,
   peeled and thinly sliced

1 T. lemon juice
3/4 c. sugar
1 t. cinnamon
9-inch pie crust

For crumb topping, combine 2/3 cup flour and brown sugar in a
medium bowl. Cut in butter with a pastry blender or 2 knives until
mixture is the consistency of coarse cornmeal; chill. Place apple slices
in a large bowl; sprinkle with lemon juice and set aside. Combine
remaining flour, sugar and cinnamon; mix well and toss lightly with
apples. Turn apple mixture into unbaked crust, spreading evenly.
Cover with chilled topping. Bake at 400 degrees for 40 to 45 minutes,
until apples are tender. Makes 6 to 8 servings.

Save time when baking. Tuck a measuring cup into
your countertop canisters. It'll be ready to
scoop out flour and sugar in a jiffy.

Million-Dollar Fudge

Dana Nemecek
Skiatook, OK

This fudge recipe is my Mamaw's recipe. She passed away 20 years ago and my children never knew her, so making a pan of her fudge together is a sweet way for me to share her with them.

13-oz. pkg. milk chocolate
   candy bars, broken up
12-oz. pkg. semi-sweet
   chocolate chips
2 c. chopped pecans, toasted
   if desired

12-oz. can evaporated milk
4-1/2 c. sugar
13-oz. jar marshmallow creme
1/2 c. butter
1 t. vanilla extract

Combine chocolate bars, chocolate chips and nuts; set aside. Place evaporated milk and sugar in a large heavy saucepan; bring to a full boil over medium-high heat. Cook for 6 minutes, stirring constantly. Add marshmallow creme, butter and vanilla; stir in chocolate mixture. Beat until creamy and chocolates are melted. Pour into a buttered 13"x9" baking pan. Cool; cut into small squares. Makes about 8 dozen pieces.

A primitive pie safe makes a useful mini pantry for canned goods and boxed mixes. Accent it with embroidered tea towels draped over the pierced-tin doors.

Buttermilk Fudge

Sally Swift
Jacksonville, FL

During the Second World War, my family moved from Iowa to Welch Cove, North Carolina, where my father was an engineer building the Fontana Dam. We were one of many families brought from around the country to help with the war effort, so Mother had many new regional recipes to share and gather. Our next-door neighbor who was from Mississippi gave us a favorite that we still call "Ida Mattie Burns' Buttermilk Fudge." This delicious fudge became a Christmas tradition...it has been in our family now for 62 years. My children, and now grandchildren, look forward each year to this fudge.

1 t. baking soda	2 T. light corn syrup
1 c. buttermilk	1 T. butter
2 c. sugar	1 c. chopped pecans

In a large heavy saucepan, dissolve baking soda in buttermilk. Add sugar, corn syrup and butter. Cook over medium-high heat, scraping sides of pan often, until mixture reaches the soft-ball stage, or 234 to 243 degrees on a candy thermometer. Remove from heat. When pan is cool to touch on the outside, add nuts and beat well. Pour out onto a wax-paper lined paper-lined baking sheet; let stand until set. Fudge should be firm on the outside and creamy on the inside. Cut into squares. Makes 2 to 3 dozen pieces.

Cookie cutters make a whimsical valance for a kitchen window. Secure a tension rod across the top of the window and suspend cookie cutters with ribbons...so clever!

Special Hot Cocoa

Alysson Marshall
Newark, NY

I can still remember my grandma fixing homemade hot cocoa
for me as a child...instant cocoa can't hold a candle to it!

4 c. milk
1/4 c. baking cocoa
1/2 c. sugar
1 t. vanilla extract

1/8 t. salt
Garnish: marshmallows or
    whipped cream

Warm milk in a saucepan over medium-low heat. Add cocoa, sugar, vanilla and salt. Stir constantly until sugar dissolves and milk is just frothing on the top. Serve topped with marshmallows or whipped cream. Makes 4 servings.

Marshmallow Stars

Jill Ball
Highland, UT

My children love making these fun marshmallows for their hot cocoa...
it gives them something to do while the water is heating!

regular-size marshmallows

Roll each marshmallow flat with a rolling pin. Cut a star shape out with a mini cookie cutter. Drop into hot cocoa. Make as many as you like!

Old-fashioned salt shakers make the prettiest little containers
for dusting desserts or hot beverages with a bit of spice.

Oven & Icebox *Sweets*

Family Favorite Frosting

Nichole Martelli
Santa Fe, TX

At our house, we slather this frosting on everything from cakes to cookies...it also makes a yummy filling for homemade cookie sandwiches. My husband calls it "birthday cake frosting" because he says it tastes just like the frosting on the cakes you get at the bakery.

16-oz. pkg. powdered sugar
1 c. butter-flavored shortening

2 T. water
2 t. vanilla extract

Place all ingredients in a large bowl. Beat with an electric mixer on low speed to combine. Increase speed to medium; beat for 5 full minutes. At first it won't look much like frosting, but keep the mixer going for the full 5 minutes. Makes enough to frost a 2-layer cake or a 13"x9" sheet cake.

Angel Mallow Frosting

Becky Jackson
Parkersburg, WV

My mom has made this icing for cakes since I was a little girl and I loved it! Now that I'm grown up, it's still a favorite of mine.

1/2 c. sugar
2 egg whites, beaten
2 T. water

7-oz. jar marshmallow creme
1/2 t. vanilla extract
few drops desired food coloring

Combine sugar, egg whites and water in a double boiler over boiling water. Beat with an electric mixer on high speed until soft peaks form. Add marshmallow creme; beat to stiff peaks. Remove from heat; beat in vanilla. Tint with food coloring. Makes enough to frost a 13"x9" sheet cake.

Fresh from the Farmhouse

Recipe: ....
Servings: ....
....
....
....
....
....

Copy, cut and color to share your own homemade goodies!

Make copies of this recipe card to share your favorites with a friend!

from the kitchen of:

Copy these bookmarks and use to mark your favorite recipes in this or any of your other favorite Gooseberry Patch cookbooks!

RECIPE

★ BOOK ★

PAGE

NOTES ABOUT
THIS RECIPE

★

A delicious secret the next time you make mashed potatoes...substitute equal parts chicken broth and cream for the milk in any favorite recipe.

RECIPE

★ BOOK ★

PAGE

NOTES ABOUT
THIS RECIPE

★

For tomatoes to keep their fresh-from-the-garden taste, they should always be stored at room temperature.

INDEX

Appetizers

Beverages

Breads

Breakfast

Canning & Condiments

INDEX

INDEX

Lemon-Pepper Parmesan Chicken

Karen Hood
Somerset, KY

This is an easy-to-prepare dish I used to serve as one of the plate lunches in my deli, Karen's Konfections & Deli. My customers all loved it and I always ran out by the time lunch was over. I served it with mashed potatoes and brown gravy, green beans with bacon and a yeast roll...wonderful!

1/2 c. butter, melted
1 T. lemon-pepper seasoning
1 c. all-purpose flour
salt to taste

6 boneless, skinless chicken
  breasts
1/2 c. grated Parmesan cheese

In a shallow dish, combine melted butter and lemon-pepper seasoning. In a separate shallow dish, combine flour and salt. Dip chicken into butter mixture, then into flour mixture. Arrange chicken in a lightly greased 13"x9" baking pan. Sprinkle evenly with Parmesan cheese; drizzle with any remaining butter mixture. Cover and bake at 350 degrees for 15 minutes. Uncover; bake an additional 15 to 20 minutes, or until chicken juices run clear. Makes 6 servings.

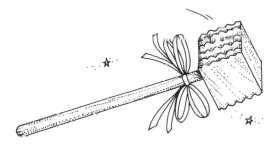

Boneless chicken breasts are a terrific choice for speedy meals. They'll cook up even quicker if placed in a large plastic zipping bag and flattened with a meat mallet.

Easy Chicken & Tomato Rice

Shirley Howie
Foxboro, MA

I like to use rotisserie chicken in this recipe, which makes it delicious and ready to serve in a jiffy.

10-1/2 oz. can chicken broth
14-1/2 oz. can stewed tomatoes
1 t. garlic powder
1 t. dried basil

2 c. cooked chicken, cubed
1-1/2 c. instant rice, uncooked
1 c. peas

In a saucepan over high heat, combine broth, tomatoes with juice and seasonings. Bring to a boil. Add chicken, uncooked rice and peas; return to a boil. Remove from heat. Cover and let stand for 5 minutes, or until most of the liquid is absorbed. Fluff rice with a fork before serving. Serves 4.

Create mini recipe cards listing the ingredients of favorite one-dish dinners. Glue a button magnet on the back and place on the fridge...so handy whenever it's time to make out a shopping list!

30-Minute
☉ Meals ☉

Peppy Pizza Mac & Cheese

Sharon Haddock
Klamath Falls, OR

This recipe was shared by a lady whom I consider an excellent cook and boy, was she right...it's definitely a winner, yet so simple to make. Be prepared for lots of oohs and ahhs!

7-1/4 oz. pkg. macaroni &
   cheese mix
8-oz. can pizza sauce
30 to 40 pepperoni slices

1/2 c. shredded Monterey Jack
   cheese
1/2 c. shredded Cheddar cheese

Prepare macaroni & cheese mix according to package directions. Spread in a 13"x9" baking pan coated with non-stick vegetable spray. Spread with pizza sauce; arrange pepperoni slices on top and sprinkle with cheeses. Bake, uncovered, at 350 degrees for 30 to 35 minutes, until lightly golden and cheese is melted. Let stand 5 minutes before serving. Makes 4 servings.

American Chop Suey

Mary Ludemann
Bronx, NY

My grandmother used to make this simple dish for my mom, and Mom made it for my brother and me. I always asked her to make this for my birthday instead of something fancier! Now my two kids love it...my 8-year-old always gets excited when I make it.

16-oz. pkg. elbow macaroni,
   uncooked
1 lb. ground beef

15-oz. can tomato sauce
2 10-3/4 oz. cans tomato soup

Cook macaroni according to package directions; drain and return to cooking pot. Meanwhile, brown beef in a skillet over medium heat; drain. Add beef and remaining ingredients to macaroni. Cook over medium heat, stirring occasionally, until heated through. Serves 6.

Sophie's Parmesan-Lover's Macaroni

Jenny Bishoff
Mountain Lake Park, MD

This dish was my daughter's first effort at homemade macaroni & cheese. We changed it up to suit her dad's favorite flavors for a special Fathers' Day meal. He loved it, and if you love fresh Parmesan and garlic, you will too! Use rotini pasta if you like.

16-oz. pkg. elbow macaroni, uncooked
1/4 c. butter, sliced
1/4 c. all-purpose flour

2 c. milk
2 to 4 cloves garlic, minced
1 c. shredded Parmesan cheese
salt and pepper to taste

Cook macaroni according to package directions; drain. Meanwhile, melt butter in a medium saucepan over medium heat. Whisk in flour until a smooth paste is formed; cook and stir constantly for one minute. Slowly stir in milk and garlic. Increase heat slightly. Cook, stirring constantly, until mixture boils and thickens to desired consistency. Add cheese, salt and pepper. Stir until cheese is melted; pour over macaroni and stir well. Makes 6 to 8 servings.

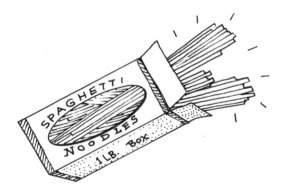

A range of cooking times is often given on packages of pasta. The first cooking time is for al dente (firm to the bite) and the second cooking time is for a softer pasta. You choose!

30-Minute
⊘ Meals ⊘

My Favorite Rice Pilaf

Shirley Howie
Foxboro, MA

This pilaf is delicious served alongside any kind of meat or fish, or even on its own. Very versatile and flavorful! I have been making this for years now and it is my go-to recipe for rice.

2 t. butter
1/2 c. onion, chopped
1/2 c. celery, chopped
1-1/2 c. long-cooking rice,
   uncooked

4 c. hot water
2-1/2 oz. pkg. chicken noodle
   soup mix
1/2 t. dried thyme
1/2 t. dried sage

Melt butter in a large skillet over medium heat. Add onion and celery; sauté until tender. Add rice; cook and stir until lightly golden. Add hot water and soup mix; stir well. Bring to a boil. Reduce heat to low; stir in herbs. Cover and cook for 20 minutes, or until liquid is absorbed, stirring often. Makes 6 servings.

It's not hard to get more veggies into your family's meals. Keep frozen vegetables on hand to toss into favorite pasta or rice dishes...they'll blend right in!

Spicy-Sweet Broccoli

Lisa Ann Panzino DiNunzio
Vineland, NJ

One of my family's favorite side dishes. It's sweet and spicy all in one...we love it!

2 bunches broccoli, cut
   into flowerets
2 T. cider vinegar
2 T. light brown sugar, packed
1/2 t. red pepper flakes

2 T. extra-virgin olive oil
2 cloves garlic, pressed
4 long strips lemon zest
2 T. butter
1/2 t. sea salt

In a large saucepan, bring one inch of water to a boil over high heat. Add broccoli. Reduce heat to medium; cover and cook for 5 minutes, or until fork-tender. Drain and set aside in a large serving bowl; cover to keep warm. In a small bowl, whisk together vinegar, brown sugar and red pepper flakes; set aside. In a large skillet, heat olive oil over medium-high heat. Add garlic and lemon zest to skillet; cook for 30 seconds, or until garlic turns lightly golden. Discard zest. Stir in butter until melted; add vinegar mixture and salt. Stir and remove from heat. Pour hot vinegar mixture over steamed broccoli; toss to coat. Adjust seasoning and drizzle with a little more oil, if desired. Serves 6 to 8.

An oh-so-simple harvest decoration...roll out a wheelbarrow and heap it full of large, colorful squash and pumpkins.

30-Minute Meals

Zucchini Nuggets

Christina Davis
Smithfield, VA

This recipe is special because Mom made these with the zucchini from our family garden while we were growing up. It was one sure way to get us to eat our veggies...there were never any leftovers. We still make them today and now our kids love them!

1 c. zucchini, grated
1 onion, grated
3/4 c. all-purpose flour
1 t. dried parsley

2 eggs, beaten
1/2 c. grated Parmesan cheese
oil for frying

In a bowl, mix together all ingredients except oil. Heat oil in a skillet over medium heat. Add batter by tablespoonfuls. Cook until golden on both sides. Serves 4 to 5.

Zesty Mustard Sauce

Irene Robinson
Cincinnati, OH

Delicious on hot steamed broccoli, asparagus spears or green beans.

3/4 c. mayonnaise
3 T. lemon juice

1-1/2 T. Dijon mustard
1/2 c. heavy cream

In a bowl, mix together mayonnaise, lemon juice and mustard, set aside. In a separate bowl, with an electric mixer on high speed, beat cream until soft peaks form. Fold whipped cream into mayonnaise mixture. Keep refrigerated. Makes about 2 cups.

Create a trail of glowing pumpkins in no time...after carving, tuck a string of outdoor-safe battery-operated lights inside each pumpkin.

Stir-Fried Squash Medley

Ramona Wysong
Barlow, KY

I came up with this tasty recipe years ago, when I wanted to make use of some extra yellow squash and zucchini. It was a hit!

2 T. olive oil
2 c. zucchini, sliced
2 c. yellow squash, sliced
1/2 c. onion, chopped

1 c. tomatoes, diced
1 t. salt
pepper to taste
Optional: 1/4 c. chicken broth

Add olive oil to a wok or large skillet. Heat over medium-high heat for 2 minutes. Add zucchini, squash and onion; cook and stir for 2 minutes. Add tomatoes, salt and pepper. Reduce heat to medium-low. Simmer for 8 to 10 minutes, until vegetables are crisp-tender, stirring occasionally. Add broth if mixture becomes too dry. Makes 4 to 6 servings.

Fall has always been my favorite time of year. I grew up in the suburbs in the 1950s, when burning leaves in the street was still allowed. It was my job to help Dad rake leaves. It took a few hours to rake everything to the front yard and into the street. When we piled our leaves high, Dad would toss that match and they would begin to burn and it smelled so good. It wasn't quite fall until I went into the house and grabbed two potatoes that Dad would place in those burning leaves to roast. When the leaves were burned, our potatoes were done. They were the best potatoes I ever tasted and it was a special time that my Dad and I shared.

– Arden Regnier, East Moriches, NY

30-Minute
☉ Meals ☉

Braised Beans & Tomatoes

Gail Blain
Grand Island, NE

I love this recipe! In the summer I use fresh-from-the-garden ingredients. Once my garden is tucked away for the year, then what I have frozen or canned is perfect for this recipe.

2 T. butter
1 onion, thinly sliced
3 cloves garlic, minced
16-oz. pkg. frozen cut green beans

14-1/2 oz. can diced tomatoes, drained
1 to 1-1/2 c. chicken broth
salt and pepper to taste

Melt butter in a large skillet over medium heat; sauté onion. Add garlic, beans, tomatoes and enough broth to cover everything. Increase heat to high; bring to a boil. Reduce heat to low; cover and simmer for 5 to 10 minutes, until beans are tender. Uncover; simmer for 5 minutes. Season with salt and pepper. Serves 6.

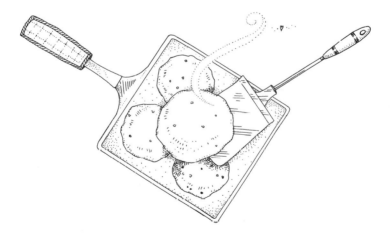

Make crispy potato pancakes with leftover mashed potatoes. Stir an egg yolk and a little minced onion into 2 cups cold mashed potatoes. Form into patties; dust with a little flour and pan-fry in a little oil until golden. Serve with sour cream for a delicious treat.

Honey-Glazed Carrots & Pecans

Paulette Alexander
Newfoundland, Canada

Even finicky eaters like my husband enjoy this side dish. It goes so nicely with practically any meat or fish.

1/3 c. pecans, coarsely chopped
2 T. canola oil, divided
3/8 t. salt, divided
1 T. butter
2 lbs. carrots, peeled, halved
   lengthwise and sliced

1/2 t. chili powder
2 T. honey
salt and pepper to taste

On a rimmed baking sheet, toss pecans with one tablespoon oil and 1/8 teaspoon salt. Toast at 375 degrees for about 5 minutes; set aside. In a large non-stick skillet over medium-high heat, melt butter with remaining oil. Add carrots; reduce heat to medium. Cover; cook for 12 minutes, stirring occasionally. Stir in chili powder and remaining salt. Cover; cook until tender, about one minute. Remove from heat. Stir in honey; season with salt and pepper. Serve carrots with pecans sprinkled on top. Serves 4 to 6.

Sweet Bacon & Brussels

Amy Hunt
Traphill, NC

My niece's mother-in-law Paulette shared this delicious and simple recipe with me. It's a great side dish with any meal.

6 slices bacon
1/2 to 3/4 lb. Brussels sprouts,
   trimmed

6 T. brown sugar, packed

In a skillet over medium heat, cook bacon until crisp. Remove bacon to a paper towel, reserving drippings. Cut any larger Brussels sprouts in half. Add sprouts to drippings; sprinkle with brown sugar. Sauté until tender, 6 to 10 minutes; drain. Transfer sprouts to a serving dish; toss with crumbled bacon. Serves 4.

30-Minute
○ Meals ○

Fried Peppered Cabbage

Irene Robinson
Cincinnati, OH

This simple dish is delicious with pork chops.

1/4 c. butter, sliced
1 head cabbage, coarsely
   chopped

salt and pepper to taste
3 T. sour cream

Melt butter in a large skillet over high heat; add cabbage. Sauté, stirring constantly, for about 2 minutes, until tender-crisp but not wilted. Season with salt and a very generous amount of pepper. Stir in sour cream. Serve immediately. Makes 6 servings.

When I was growing up in Saint Anthony, Idaho, during the 1960s and 1970s, school was let out for a week in October so the farmers could harvest potatoes. If you were old enough, you could get a job riding on the picker and sorting out the leaves and plants from the potatoes. What a dirty job, but so much fun! And the potato dishes were abundant.

–Lisa Seckora, Bloomer, WI

Pan-Roasted Fingerling Potatoes

Krista Marshall
Fort Wayne, IN

We are tater lovin' people. I'm always looking for new ways to prepare them, and these buttery-tasting little potatoes are the perfect side dish to any meal.

1 lb. yellow fingerling potatoes
2 T. olive oil
2 cloves garlic, minced
2 t. dried parsley

1 t. dried rosemary
1 t. dried thyme
salt and pepper to taste
Garnish: additional parsley

Cut any larger potatoes in half. In a Dutch oven or deep skillet, cover potatoes with cold water. Bring to a boil over medium-high heat. Cook until just fork-tender, about 5 to 7 minutes; drain well and set aside. Wipe out pan with a paper towel. Add oil; heat over medium-high heat. Add potatoes and seasonings; stir to combine. Sauté until golden on all sides, stirring often, about 10 to 15 minutes. Garnish with a sprinkle of parsley. Makes 4 servings.

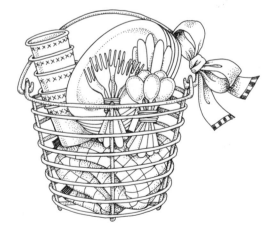

Pick up some paper plates and cups in seasonal designs...
they'll make dinner fun when you're in a hurry and
clean-up will be a breeze.

SPEEDY
Suppers & Sides

Millie's Pepper Steak

Rosemary Hart
Carol Stream, IL

I have so many fond memories of my mother in the kitchen. I remember coming home from school and Mom making this for dinner. She and I would talk about our day while she cooked. This recipe takes me back... it is even tastier the next day!

1 lb. beef sirloin, flank or
    round steak, thinly sliced
1/2 c. all-purpose flour
1 to 2 T. oil
2 cloves garlic, chopped
garlic powder, salt and pepper
    to taste

1 t. dried oregano
1 t. browning and seasoning
    sauce
1 green pepper, sliced
3/4 c. canned diced tomatoes
1 onion, chopped
cooked rice

Dredge beef in flour; set aside. Heat oil in a skillet over medium-high heat. Add beef and cook until browned. Drain; add enough water to cover beef. Stir in garlic, seasonings and sauce; bring to a boil. Reduce heat to low; cover and cook for 30 minutes. Add tomatoes and green pepper; cook an additional 15 minutes, or until beef is tender. Serve over cooked rice. Makes 4 servings.

Let the kids help with meals! Younger children can
scrub vegetables and tear salad greens. Older kids can measure,
chop, stir and take part in meal planning and shopping.
Give 'em a chance...they may just surprise you!

❧ SPEEDY ❧
Suppers & Sides

Comfort Chicken Casserole

Vicki Meredith
Grandview, IN

My mother made this recipe often with leftover chicken or turkey.
It's so easy...you don't even need to cook the noodles first.

10-3/4 oz. can cream of
   mushroom soup
1/2 c. milk
1 c. cooked chicken or turkey,
   cubed
1 c. shredded Cheddar cheese

1/2 c. onion, diced
8-oz. pkg. egg noodles,
   uncooked
1 c. water
1/4 c. soft bread crumbs

In an ungreased 2-quart casserole dish, stir together soup and milk.
Add chicken, cheese and onion; mix well. Stir in uncooked noodles;
pour water over all. Sprinkle with bread crumbs. Bake, uncovered, at
350 degrees for about 50 minutes, or until golden. Serves 4.

At Halloween, my parents made sure that there was plenty of
scary fun to be had for us kids! We'd all go out to a local
pumpkin patch and pick out four of the best-looking pumpkins
to bring home for my dad to carve. The excitement would build
in my mind...Halloween! Mom helped us plan our costumes,
while my sister Michele and I "helped" her in the kitchen as she
created delicious goodies...crispy treat pumpkins, monster toes,
popcorn and caramel apples. Oh, the smells just made me so
excited! On the big night, as Michele and I dressed up, Dad
would greet the trick-or-treaters with his sinister laugh and
recordings of scary sounds. By the time we returned home, our
pillowcases (and tummies) were filled to the brim with candy
and our hearts were happy for another magical Halloween!

—Melissa Fialer, Palo Alto, CA

Simple Ginger Chicken

Kathy Courington
Canton, GA

My daughter's girlfriend says this is the best chicken she has ever had.
A friend shared the recipe with me years ago...every time I serve it,
it disappears! It really is that simple and that good.

6 to 8 chicken thighs
1/2 to 1 onion, chopped
1 c. low-sodium soy sauce

1 c. water
3 T. ground ginger, or to taste
cooked rice

Combine all ingredients except rice in a Dutch oven. Bring to a boil
over medium high heat; reduce heat to low. Cover and simmer for
one hour, or until chicken juices run clear. Check occasionally, adding
more water as needed. May also be cooked in a slow cooker on low
setting for 6 to 8 hours. Serve over cooked rice. Serves 6 to 8.

Sunday Chicken

JoAlice Patterson-Welton
Lawrenceville, GA

This is an easy chicken dish for a busy week. So delicious
and moist...a family favorite!

5 to 6 boneless, skinless
   chicken breasts
1/2 c. sour cream

1/4 c. soy sauce
10-1/2 oz. can French onion
   soup

Arrange chicken in a 13"x9" baking pan coated with non-stick
vegetable spray; set aside. Combine remaining ingredients in a
saucepan. Cook and stir over low heat just until well blended; spoon
over chicken. Cover and bake at 350 degrees for 55 minutes, or until
chicken juices run clear. Serves 5 to 6.

Fresh vegetables will stay bright-colored and tasty if you
add a tablespoon or two of vinegar to the water
when boiling or steaming.

❦ SPEEDY ❦
Suppers & Sides

Hot Cherry Pepper Chicken

Mariann Raftery
Scarsdale, NY

Long and slow is the way to go with this flavorful dish! For adults
I use the whole jar of peppers, because they love the hot spicy
taste. I use fewer peppers when cooking for children.

1 T. olive oil
1 onion, sliced
4 to 6 cloves garlic, chopped
salt and pepper to taste

12 chicken drumsticks, thighs
and wings
32-oz. jar hot cherry peppers,
divided

In an ungreased deep 13"x9" baking pan, combine oil, onion, garlic,
salt and pepper; stir to mix. Add chicken; toss together well. Pour
1/2 jar of cherry peppers with juice over chicken. Bake, uncovered,
at 325 degrees for 45 minutes; turn chicken over. If desired, for a very
spicy dish, pour remaining peppers and juice over chicken. Cook,
uncovered, another 60 minutes, or until chicken juices run clear,
turning chicken over several times. Serves 6 to 8.

Polynesian Chicken

Leslie Kirzner
Ramsey, NJ

This is quick and delicious. I concocted it one night with pantry
ingredients when we were creating a "Tiki Night" for my husband's
birthday, complete with decorations and coconut drinks.

4 chicken breasts
1 c. teriyaki marinade
8-oz. can crushed pineapple

8-oz. can whole-berry cranberry
sauce

Combine chicken and marinade in a large plastic zipping bag; seal
bag. Refrigerate for several hours, turning bag once or twice. Drain,
discarding marinade. Place chicken in a greased 13"x9" baking pan.
Pour pineapple with juice and cranberry sauce over chicken. Bake,
uncovered, at 350 degrees for one hour, or until chicken is golden and
juices run clear. Makes 4 servings.

Pork & Pepper Stir-Fry

Dale Duncan
Waterloo, IA

This delicious one-dish dinner cooks up in a jiffy.
Boneless pork chops may be used instead of pork tenderloin.

1 T. olive oil
1-lb. pork tenderloin, thinly
   sliced
2 green or yellow peppers,
   thinly sliced
1/2 c. orange juice

2 T. soy sauce
1 T. honey
1 T. cornstarch
1/2 t. ground ginger
cooked rice
Optional: chow mein noodles

Heat oil in a large skillet over medium-high heat. Add pork; cook and stir for 4 minutes, until pork is no longer pink. Add peppers; cook and stir another 4 minutes, or until peppers are crisp-tender. In a small bowl, combine remaining ingredients except rice and noodles; mix well and add to skillet. Bring to a boil. Cook and stir until sauce thickens, one to 2 minutes. Serve over cooked rice, garnished with chow mein noodles, if desired. Makes 4 servings.

Start a Thanksgiving tradition. Before dinner, take time to hold hands and ask everyone at the table to share what they're thankful for...some of the sweetest memories will be made.

Suppers & Sides

Bacon & Apple Pork Chops

Becky Drees
Pittsfield, MA

Tart-sweet apples, caramelized onion, salty bacon...
all the savory flavors of autumn at its best!

6 boneless pork chops
garlic powder, salt and pepper
   to taste
2 T. olive oil
3 thick-cut slices bacon, diced

1/2 c. onion, diced
1 to 2 cloves garlic, minced
2 apples, peeled, cored and
   diced
Garnish: honey

Sprinkle pork chops on both sides with seasonings; set aside. Heat oil in a cast-iron skillet over medium-high heat. Add chops; cook just until browned on both sides. Reduce heat to medium-low. Cover and cook until chops are no longer pink in the center; do not overcook. Meanwhile, in a separate skillet over medium heat, cook bacon until crisp. Push bacon to one side of the skillet. Add onion and garlic to the other side; cook until onion starts to soften. Add apples; stir contents of skillet together. Simmer for about 10 minutes, until apples are soft, reducing heat if necessary. To serve, spoon apple mixture over chops; drizzle with a small amount of honey. Serves 6.

A cast-iron skillet is wonderful for cooking up homestyle dinners. If it hasn't been used in awhile, season it first. Rub it lightly with oil, bake at 300 degrees for an hour and let it cool completely in the oven. Now it's ready for many more years of good cooking!

Baked BBQ Ranch Turkey Tacos

Marie Matter
Dallas, TX

Barbecue meets Tex-Mex for these delicious tacos! Baking the tacos allows the cheese to melt and the shells to crisp up perfectly. Your family will go wild over these!

1 T. olive oil
1 lb. ground turkey
2 T. ranch salad dressing mix
1-1/2 c. barbecue sauce

6 crisp corn taco shells
2 c. shredded sharp Cheddar
  cheese
Garnish: diced avocado

In a large skillet, heat oil over medium-high heat. Add turkey and cook just until golden, breaking it up with a spatula. Stir in dressing mix and barbecue sauce. Reduce heat to medium-low; cook and stir for 3 to 4 minutes. Stand up taco shells in an ungreased 8"x8" baking pan. Divide turkey mixture among taco shells; sprinkle with cheese. Bake, uncovered, at 400 degrees for 10 minutes, or until cheese melts. At serving time, garnish with avocado. Makes 6 servings.

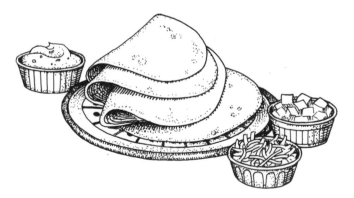

Do you have lots of kids coming over for an after-game party? Make it easy with do-it-yourself tacos or mini pizzas...guests can add their own favorite toppings. Round out the menu with pitchers of soft drinks and a delicious dessert. Simple and fun!

Quick Tamale Pie

Julie De Fusco
Henderson, NV

When a friend of mine shared this with me, I fell in love with it. It's perfect when guests pop in, as most of the ingredients are already in the pantry. It also freezes well if there are leftovers. Save time by using a box of cornbread mix...just follow the package instructions.

1 lb. ground beef or turkey
Optional: 1 onion, chopped
14-1/2 oz. can Mexican or
    Italian-seasoned stewed
    tomatoes
1-1/4 oz. pkg. taco seasoning
    mix

11-oz. can corn, drained
4-oz. can chopped black olives,
    drained
3/4 c. water

In a large oven-safe skillet over medium heat, brown beef with onion, if using; drain. Stir in tomatoes with juice and remaining ingredients. Reduce heat to low and simmer, uncovered, for several minutes, until liquid is reduced. If not using an oven-proof skillet, transfer mixture to a greased 11"x9" baking pan. Pour Cornbread Topping batter over top. Bake, uncovered, at 400 degrees for about 25 minutes, until topping is golden and tests clean with a knife tip. Serves 8.

Cornbread Topping:

1 c. milk
1/4 c. oil
1 egg, beaten
1 c. cornmeal

1 c. all-purpose flour
1 T. baking powder
Optional: 2 T. sugar

Stir together all ingredients until smooth.

Dust off Mom's vintage casserole dishes...they're just right for baking family-pleasing hearty casseroles, with a side dish of sweet memories.

Easy Chicken Manicotti

Becky Holsinger
Belpre, OH

Although I love to cook, I don't claim to be all that great at it. I was given this recipe when I got married and not only is it easy, it tastes great! I know when I make this dish it will be good, no matter what.

26-oz. jar pasta sauce
1/2 c. water
10 boneless, skinless chicken
   tenders
1 t. garlic salt
1/2 t. Italian seasoning

10 manicotti pasta shells,
   uncooked
2 c. shredded mozzarella cheese
Optional: chopped fresh basil
   and oregano

In a bowl, mix pasta sauce and water. Spread 1/3 of sauce mixture in an ungreased 13"x9" inch glass baking pan; set aside. Sprinkle chicken with seasonings. Insert one chicken tender into each uncooked manicotti shell, stuffing from each end, if necessary. Arrange shells over sauce mixture in baking pan. Pour remaining sauce mixture evenly over shells, covering completely. Cover with aluminum foil. Bake at 350 degrees for about an hour, until shells are tender and chicken is no longer pink in the center. Top with cheese. Bake, uncovered, for 5 minutes, or until cheese is melted. Garnish with herbs, if desired. Serves 5 to 7.

Whip up some herb butter to go with hot rolls. Blend 1/2 cup
softened butter, one tablespoon chopped fresh parsley,
1-1/2 teaspoons minced garlic, one teaspoon Italian seasoning
and a squirt of lemon juice. Wrap well and refrigerate or freeze.

🌸 SPEEDY 🌸
Suppers & Sides

Roasted Veggies & Penne Pasta

Ramona Wysong
Barlow, KY

This recipe is great for getting everyone to eat more vegetables! You can vary the veggies with your favorites...I like to use different kinds of peppers from the farmers' market. Sometimes I add more cheese too, since my family likes cheesy dishes. Enjoy!

16-oz. pkg. penne pasta,
   uncooked
2 zucchini, quartered lengthwise
   and sliced 1-inch thick
2 yellow squash, quartered
   lengthwise and sliced
   1-inch thick
2 red peppers, cut into
   1-inch squares

1 onion, cut into
   1-inch squares
1 to 2 T. olive oil
kosher salt to taste
3 c. shredded mozzarella cheese,
   divided
1/4 c. plus 2 T. grated Parmesan
   cheese, divided

Cook pasta according to package directions, just until tender; drain. Meanwhile, combine vegetables in a greased 13"x9" baking pan. Drizzle with oil and season with salt. Bake, uncovered, at 425 degrees for 15 to 20 minutes, stirring once or twice, until golden and caramelized. Add cooked pasta to vegetable mixture along with 2 cups mozzarella cheese and 1/4 cup Parmesan cheese. Toss to mix well. Sprinkle with remaining cheeses. Return to oven for 5 minutes, or until cheese melts. Makes 6 to 8 servings.

Cut the corner from a paper envelope,
then snip off the tip to create a
tiny funnel perfect for filling
salt & pepper shakers.

Deviled Turkey Drumsticks

Teri Lindquist
Gurnee, IL

We love these big flavorful drumsticks! Not only are they fun to eat,
they are budget-friendly and a wonderful surprise anytime.

6 turkey drumsticks
1/4 c. oil
1 T. Worcestershire sauce
2 shakes hot pepper sauce,
   or to taste

1/2 t. garlic powder
1/2 t. onion powder
1/4 t. paprika
1 t. salt
1/2 t. pepper

Place drumsticks in an aluminum foil-lined roasting pan. In a small
bowl, whisk together remaining ingredients; brush evenly over
drumsticks. Bake, uncovered, at 400 degrees for 1-1/4 to 1-1/2 hours,
until drumsticks are golden and no longer pink inside. Baste
occasionally with pan drippings. Remove from oven; let stand
5 minutes. For easier handling, wrap a strip of foil around the end
of each drumstick. Makes 6 servings.

For my daughters Lynda and Elaine and me, fall always signaled
back-to-school time. I was secretary at our local high school for
27 years, so we shared this special time. Buying new fall clothes
and school supplies was the highlight of our year. My daughters
helped get the school ready, putting up fresh fall and sports-
themed bulletin boards. Everywhere there was that special smell
of new clothes, brand spankin' new notebooks and school buses
being prepped for the first day of school. Even now, after being
retired for 15 years, I still feel nostalgic when I see the buses
starting to roll and the students waving, as I remember my own
sweet daughters and the first day of school.

–Bunny Palmertree, Carrollton, MS

Tasty Dijon Pork Chops

Sue Klapper
Muskego, WI

*My mother-in-law was a good but unadventurous cook, so my husband
was a little afraid when I tried new recipes as a newlywed. After tasting
these delicious pork chops, he learned to enjoy my experiments. Thirty
years later, we still love them!*

2 T. Dijon mustard	4 boneless pork chops
2 T. Italian salad dressing	1 onion, sliced
1/4 t. pepper	

Combine mustard, salad dressing and pepper in a small bowl. Brush
over both sides of pork chops; reserve any extra mustard mixture.
Add chops in a skillet sprayed with non-stick vegetable spray. Cook,
covered, over medium heat for about 30 minutes. Turn chops and
baste occasionally with mustard mixture; add a little water if needed.
Add onion during last 5 minutes. Makes 4 servings.

Perfect Pork Chops

Cris Goode
Mooresville, IN

*This is simply the easiest and best way I have found to make
a good pork chop. My family adores our Pork Chop Night
and guests always rave about it!*

4 to 6 center-cut pork chops   seasoned salt to taste

Preheat broiler and broiler pan. Season pork chops on one side with
seasoned salt. Place on hot broiler pan; season other side. Broil for 5
minutes, or until browned. Turn; insert a meat thermometer into a
chop. Broil until internal temperature reaches 145 degrees. Remove
chops to a platter; let stand for 3 minutes. Makes 4 to 6 servings.

Ready, set, cook! When pasta is on the menu, put a big pot
of water on the stove as soon as you get home.
Dinner will be ready in a jiffy!

Sue's Hamburger Pie Deluxe

Susan Whitson
Telford, TN

As a newlywed, I made this for my parents, who said it was a keeper!
It tastes like the great hamburgers you remember as a kid. Add
some French fries and a crisp salad for an easy hearty meal that
everyone loves.

9-inch pie crust
1-1/2 to 2 lbs. ground beef
1 onion, finely chopped
1 green pepper, finely chopped
1 c. all-purpose flour
1/2 c. milk
1 c. shredded Cheddar cheese
1/2 to 1 c. sweet pickle relish

1/4 c. catsup
1/4 c. mustard
dried oregano, salt and pepper
  to taste
Optional: additional cheese
Garnish: catsup, mustard, sliced
  dill pickles and tomatoes

Place pie crust in a 9" deep-dish pie plate sprayed with non-stick
vegetable spray. Bake at 350 degrees for 15 minutes, or until golden;
cool. Meanwhile, brown beef in a skillet over medium heat. Add
onion and pepper when beef is half-done; cook until tender and drain.
Sprinkle with flour and toss to coat; stir in milk. Mixture will be
sticky. Remove from heat. Add remaining ingredients except optional
cheese and garnish. Mix well; spoon into crust. Bake, uncovered,
at 350 degrees for 30 minutes. Top with additional cheese during the
last 5 minutes, if desired. Let stand for 10 minutes. Cut into wedges;
garnish as desired. Makes 6 servings.

Pitch a tent in the backyard on a fall night so the kids
can camp out, tell ghost stories and play flashlight tag.
What a great way to make memories!

152

Veggie Spaghetti Pie

Mary Donaldson
Enterprise, AL

To please my vegetarian guests, I made my favorite spaghetti pie minus the pepperoni slices I usually include. My guests loved it and asked for the recipe.

7-oz. pkg. spaghetti, uncooked
3 T. butter, softened and divided
1 egg, beaten
1 c. grated Parmesan cheese, divided
1/2 c. small-curd cottage cheese

1 onion, chopped
1 yellow pepper, chopped
6-oz. jar artichoke hearts, drained and chopped
4-oz. can sliced portabella mushrooms, drained

Cook spaghetti according to package directions, just until tender; drain. Stir in 2 tablespoons butter, egg and 1/2 cup Parmesan cheese. Press mixture into a 10" pie plate coated with non-stick vegetable spray. Spread cottage cheese over spaghetti mixture; set aside. In a skillet over medium heat, cook onion and yellow pepper in remaining butter until soft. Add artichokes and mushrooms; mix well. Spoon vegetable mixture over cottage cheese; top with remaining Parmesan cheese. Bake, uncovered, at 350 degrees for 25 to 30 minutes, until golden and heated through. Let stand 5 minutes before cutting. Makes 6 to 8 servings.

Create a meal plan for the week, including all of your favorite quick & easy meals...spaghetti on Monday, chicken pot pie on Tuesday and so forth. Post it on the fridge along with a shopping list...making dinner will be a snap!

Cream Cheese-Stuffed Chicken

Paulette Alexander
Newfoundland, Canada

One of our favorite meals! It's so easy to make and leaves everybody quite satisfied. I sometimes make it when cooking as a volunteer with elementary children at our local school.

4 boneless, skinless chicken breasts
1/2 c. cream cheese with chives, softened
4 T. butter, softened and divided
1/2 c. brown sugar, packed
1/4 c. mustard
4 wooden toothpicks, soaked in water
Optional: cooked rice

Place each chicken breast between 2 pieces of plastic wrap. Pound to 1/4-inch thick and set aside. In a small bowl, beat cream cheese and 2 tablespoons butter to a creamy consistency. Blend in brown sugar and mustard. Divide mixture among chicken breasts; spread evenly. Fold chicken over; fasten with toothpicks. Place chicken in a single layer in a lightly greased 9"x9" baking pan. Melt remaining butter and drizzle over chicken. Bake, uncovered, at 350 degrees for 25 to 30 minutes, until chicken juices run clear. Discard toothpicks. Serve with cooked rice, if desired. Makes 4 servings.

A quick fall craft for kids...hot glue large acorn caps onto round magnets for whimsical fridge magnets.

❀ SPEEDY ❀
Suppers & Sides

Bacon-Top Meatloaf

Lori Simmons
Princeville, IL

*Bacon with chili and Worcestershire sauces gives this meatloaf
lots of flavor. Feel free to add more chili sauce and cheese!
Some crumbled crisp bacon may also be added to the beef mixture.*

2 lbs. ground beef
1/2 c. chili sauce
1 T. Worcestershire sauce
2 eggs, beaten

1 onion, chopped
1 c. shredded Cheddar cheese
2/3 c. soft bread crumbs
1/2 lb. bacon

Crumble beef into a bowl; add remaining ingredients except bacon.
Form into a loaf; place on a rack in an ungreased 9"x5" loaf pan.
Arrange bacon slices on top. Bake, uncovered, at 350 degrees for
70 to 80 minutes, until bacon is crisp and meatloaf is no longer pink
inside. Makes 8 to 10 servings.

To mix up a no-mess meatloaf, place all the ingredients in
a large plastic zipping bag. Seal the bag and squish it until
everything is well combined...then just toss the empty bag!

Slow-Cooker Creamed Chicken

Sandra Monroe
Preston, MD

*This is the best creamed chicken our family has ever eaten...
and it takes almost no effort to make!*

4 boneless, skinless chicken
  breasts
1/2 c. water
1-oz. pkg. Italian salad dressing
  mix
8-oz. pkg. cream cheese,
  softened

10-3/4 oz. can cream of
  chicken soup
4-oz. can sliced mushrooms,
  drained
cooked rice or egg noodles

Place chicken in a slow cooker sprayed with non-stick vegetable spray. Combine water and dressing mix in a cup; spoon over chicken. Cover and cook on low setting for 3 hours. In a bowl, blend cream cheese, soup and mushrooms. Spoon over chicken; stir gently. Cover and cook on low setting for one additional hour, or until chicken juices run clear. Serve chicken and sauce over cooked rice or noodles. Makes 4 servings.

A crisp green salad goes well with creamy main dishes.
For a zippy lemon dressing, shake up 1/2 cup olive oil,
1/3 cup fresh lemon juice and one tablespoon of Dijon
mustard in a jar. Chill to blend.

Cheesy Chicken & Tots Casserole   *Dana Rowan*
Spokane, WA

This recipe can be put together in a jiffy, as I always have the ingredients on hand. Feel free to use your own favorite cheese.

32-oz. pkg. frozen potato puffs, divided
1 to 1-1/2 3-oz. pkgs. ready-to-use bacon pieces, divided
2 c. shredded sharp Cheddar cheese
1 lb. boneless, skinless chicken breast, diced
garlic salt and Montreal steak seasoning or salt and pepper to taste
3/4 c. milk

To a slow cooker sprayed with non-stick vegetable spray, add half of the frozen potato puffs. Sprinkle with 1/3 each of bacon pieces and cheese. Add chicken; season as desired. Top with another 1/3 each of bacon and cheese. Arrange remaining potato puffs, bacon and cheese on top. Pour milk evenly over the top. Cover and cook on low setting for 4 to 6 hours. Makes 6 to 8 servings.

Create a fall centerpiece in a snap! Hot glue ears of mini Indian corn around a terra cotta pot and set a vase of orange or yellow mums in the center.

Easy Turkey Dinner

Marlene Burns
Swisher, IA

*A slow-cooker harvest recipe that's easy and good for
the harried cook! Add some cranberry sauce and dinner is served.*

4 to 6 potatoes, peeled and cut
    into large cubes
2 c. carrots, peeled and sliced
1 onion, chopped
2 lbs. boneless, skinless turkey
    thighs

10-3/4 oz. can cream of
    mushroom soup
2/3 c. chicken broth or water
1/4 c. all-purpose flour
2 T. onion soup mix

Place vegetables in a slow cooker; top with turkey. Combine
remaining ingredients in a bowl; spoon over turkey. Cover and cook
on high setting for 30 minutes. Turn setting to low. Cook for an
additional 7 hours, or until turkey juices run clear. Serves 4 to 6.

Bountiful Harvest Relish

Arlene Smulski
Lyons, IL

*I have made this tasty relish often for fall celebrations. It gives warm
rolls a real boost...great as a side dish for poultry too. My family &
friends always scrape out their jars!*

12-oz. pkg. fresh cranberries
2 firm pears, peeled and cored
1/2 lemon, seeds removed

1 T. honey
1/2 c. sugar
1/8 t. salt

Finely chop cranberries, pears and lemon in a food processor or with
a sharp knife. Combine with honey, sugar and salt; mix well. Spoon
into small jars; cover tightly. Keep refrigerated up to 2 weeks. Makes
2 half-pint jars.

For an easy harvest centerpiece, pile Jack-be-Little and
Baby Boo pumpkins on your favorite cake stand.

✿ SPEEDY ✿
Suppers & Sides

Crazy-Day Turkey Breast

*Ali Seay
Baltimore, MD*

This is a great recipe tossed together out of desperation that turned into a family favorite. Slow-cooker juices may be thickened for an easy turkey gravy, if you like.

4-lb. boneless turkey breast
2 to 4 T. butter, sliced

Cajun seasoning or seasoned
   salt to taste

Place turkey breast in a slow cooker, skin-side up. Dot with butter; rub in or spread as evenly as possible over top of breast. Sprinkle generously with desired seasoning. Cover and cook on low setting for 6 to 8 hours, until no longer pink in the center. Remove to a serving platter; let stand for 10 minutes before slicing. Serves 6 to 8.

Skillet Candied Sweet Potatoes

*Krista Marshall
Fort Wayne, IN*

We love sweet potatoes, and I'm always looking for new ways to prepare them. This recipe came about when I was short on time and craving something sweet. It's a winner!

5 T. butter, divided
3 to 4 sweet potatoes, peeled
   and cut into 1-inch cubes

salt and pepper to taste
1/4 c. brown sugar, packed
1-1/2 t. cinnamon

In a Dutch oven, melt 3 tablespoons butter over medium-high heat. Add sweet potatoes. Sauté for 10 to 15 minutes, until golden on all sides, stirring often. Season with salt and pepper. Push potatoes to outer edges of skillet. Melt remaining butter; sprinkle with brown sugar and stir to coat potatoes. Reduce heat to low. Cook for 15 to 20 minutes, until potatoes are fork-tender and glazed. Serves 4.

Shredded Beef over Rice

Joan Mikiten
Shavano Park, TX

My son and his friends love this delicious slow-cooked beef as a second dinner after Friday night football games.

4-lb. boneless beef top
  chuck roast
1-oz. pkg. fajita seasoning
  mix, divided
2 T. canola oil
14-1/2 oz. can diced tomatoes

14-1/2 oz. can Mexican-
  seasoned stewed tomatoes
salt and pepper to taste
3/4 c. water
4 c. cooked rice
2 T. fresh parsley, chopped

Rub both sides of roast with 2 to 3 teaspoons of seasoning mix. Heat oil in a large Dutch oven over medium-high heat. Add roast and brown on all sides, about 5 minutes. Transfer roast to a slow cooker. Add tomatoes with juice, water and remaining seasoning mix. Cover and cook on high setting for 3 to 4 hours. Reduce to low setting; cook for 2 to 3 hours, until roast is very tender. Remove roast and shred, using 2 forks. Pour tomato gravy from slow cooker into a large glass bowl; skim off any fat. Add salt and pepper as needed. Stir shredded beef into tomato gravy. Combine cooked rice and parsley. Serve beef mixture over rice. Makes 8 to 12 servings.

All-day slow cooking works wonders on inexpensive,
less-tender cuts of beef. Chuck roast, round steak and
stew beef cook up juicy and delicious.

❈ SPEEDY ❈
Suppers & Sides

Country-Style Steak

Jewel Sharpe
Raleigh, NC

Easy-peasy in your slow cooker and so delicious. Just a few
ingredients and a side of biscuits to sop up all the gravy!

8 to 10 beef cube steaks
pepper to taste
1.35-oz. pkg onion soup mix
3/4 c. water

2 10-3/4 oz. cans cream of
    mushroom soup
warm biscuits or mashed
    potatoes

Season steaks with pepper; layer in a slow cooker. Stir together soup
mix and water in a cup; spread evenly over steaks. Spoon soup over
steaks; do not stir. Cover and cook on high setting for 5 to 6 hours, or
on low setting for 8 hours, until steaks are tender. Serve steaks and
gravy from slow cooker with biscuits or potatoes. Makes 8 to
10 servings.

My grandparents lived on a small farm in northern Indiana.
I remember that as a small girl I would follow my grandpa all
around. Mom said whenever he picked up his foot, my foot was
right behind his...occasionally he stopped and I would run into
him. He loved it! Of 21 grandkids, I was the only one who did
this. We never talked, I was too shy and he was happy just to
have me there. I remember all the pigs and cows we fed, the
vegetables that we planted and then picked. Another favorite
memory is of making applesauce with Mom's entire family of six
brothers and sisters. All my aunts and uncles along with the
grandkids would come over and we would pick apples. My
grandma, mom and aunts would cut up the apples and put them
in a huge copper kettle over a wood fire. The applesauce cooked
for hours, even all day. I always had so much fun with my family.

–Pam Kollar, South Bend, IN

Autumn Pork Chops

Bianca Erickson
Hidden Valley Lake, CA

This slow-cooker recipe has the perfect flavors for fall!
So tender and juicy, it's sure to be a hit at the dinner table.

4 pork chops, divided
1 acorn squash, cut into 4 to
   6 slices and seeds removed
5 carrots, peeled and chopped
3/4 c. brown sugar, packed
2 T. butter, melted

3/4 t. browning and seasoning
   sauce
3/4 t. salt
1/2 t. orange zest
1 t. orange juice

Arrange 2 pork chops in a slow cooker. Place squash and carrots on top of chops; add remaining chops. In a small bowl, stir together remaining ingredients; spoon over chops. Cover and cook on low setting for 4 to 6 hours, until chops are no longer pink in the center. Makes 4 servings.

Autumn is a good time to check your spice rack for freshness.
Crush a pinch of each spice...if it has a fresh, zingy scent,
it's still good. Toss out any old-smelling spices and
stock up on ones you've used up during the year.

Slow-Cooked Pork Chop Dinner

Helen Adams
Enchanted Oaks, TX

This is a wonderful dish and makes a very thick rich gravy. I used to make it for my children when they were in school. Years later, it has been handed on and they are making for their own families. Be prepared for the heavenly smell while it is cooking!

4 to 6 thick-cut pork chops
2 t. dried thyme, divided
4 Yukon gold potatoes, sliced
1 yellow onion, sliced
12 mushrooms, halved

salt and pepper to taste
6 slices American cheese
10-3/4 oz. can cream of
    mushroom soup
12-oz. can evaporated milk

Season pork chops with one teaspoon thyme. Season vegetables with remaining thyme, salt and pepper; set aside. In a dry skillet over medium-high heat, brown chops on both sides. In a slow cooker, layer chops, potatoes, onion and mushrooms. Arrange cheese slices on top. Mix together soup and milk in a bowl; spoon over cheese. Cover and cook on high setting for 4 hours, or on low setting for 6 hours. Makes 4 to 6 servings.

To get rid of an onion smell after slicing, simply hold
your hands under cold running water along with
a stainless steel spoon or other utensil.

Coal Miners' Stew

Christine Jaworski
Riverside, RI

*This simple dish was one of my father's favorites. After he retired,
he would make it himself and have it waiting in the slow cooker
for my mother when she got home.*

4 potatoes, peeled and sliced
16-oz. pkg. Kielbasa sausage,
  sliced
2 14-1/2 oz. cans green beans,
  drained
1 onion, chopped

2 cloves garlic, minced
2 10-3/4 oz. cans cream of
  mushroom soup
1 to 2 c. shredded Cheddar
  cheese

Layer all ingredients in a slow cooker in the order given. Cover and
cook on low setting for 6 to 8 hours. Makes 6 servings.

Baking Powder Biscuits

Jenna Hord
Mount Vernon, OH

*My grandma and her mother used to make these tender biscuits...
perfect for a hearty breakfast or supper!*

2 c. all-purpose flour
1 T. baking powder
1 t. salt

1/4 c. shortening
3/4 c. milk

In a bowl, sift together flour, baking powder and salt. Cut in
shortening with 2 knives or a fork until mixture is as coarse as
cornmeal. Add milk; stir just enough to make a soft dough. Turn out
dough onto a lightly floured surface; knead for about 30 seconds. Roll
out dough 1/2-inch thick. Cut out biscuits with a floured 2-inch round
cutter. Place biscuits one inch apart on ungreased baking sheets. Bake
at 450 degrees for 12 to 15 minutes, until golden. Makes 15 to 18.

All seasons sweet, but autumn best of all.
–Elinor Wylie

164

❀ SPEEDY ❀
Suppers & Sides

All-in-One Bean Dinner

Kendra Randol
Pella, IA

Old-fashioned flavor made easy by a slow cooker! Serve with a side of cornbread for the ultimate comfort food.

1 smoked ham shank
2 c. cabbage, chopped
1 c. onion, chopped
2 to 3 potatoes, peeled and
    cut into 1-inch cubes

2 carrots, peeled and sliced
    1/2-inch thick
24-oz. jar Great Northern beans
1 c. water
pepper to taste

Place ham shank in a slow cooker. Layer chopped vegetables around ham shank; pour in beans with their liquid. Add water; season with pepper. Cover and cook on low setting for 8 to 10 hours. Remove ham shank; slice meat from the bone and stir into mixture in slow cooker. Serves 4 to 6.

Easy Corn Fritters

Eleanor Dionne
Beverly, MA

These fritters are crisp on the outside and soufflé-like on the inside.

2 eggs, separated
6 ears corn, kernels cut off,
    or 3 c. frozen corn
3 T. milk

2 T. all-purpose flour
1/2 t. salt
Garnish: maple syrup, butter

In a bowl, beat egg yolks until light yellow. Add corn, milk, flour and salt; blend well. In a separate bowl, beat egg whites with an electric mixer on medium speed until soft peaks form. Fold into corn mixture. Drop batter by rounded tablespoonfuls onto a hot greased griddle. Cook until golden on both sides. Serve hot with maple syrup and butter. Serves 4.

Harvest Chicken & Apples

Kathleen Bell
Clovis, CA

*An easy and delicious slow-cooker recipe to make after
a visit to your favorite apple orchard.*

2 c. onions, thickly sliced
2 to 3 apples, peeled, cored and
    thickly sliced
2 lbs. bone-in chicken pieces
2 T. fresh rosemary, chopped
1/2 t. salt

1/4 t. pepper
10-3/4 oz. can cream of celery
    soup
1 c. chicken broth
cooked rice

Arrange onions and apple slices in a slow cooker. Season chicken
pieces with rosemary, salt and pepper; arrange over apples. Whisk
together soup and broth in a bowl; spoon over chicken. Cover and
cook on low setting for 6 to 8 hours, or on high setting for 3 to
4 hours. Serve over cooked rice. Serves 4 to 6.

Come, ye thankful people, come,
Raise the song of harvest home!

–Henry Alford

SPEEDY
Suppers & Sides

Slow-Cooker Scalloped Potatoes

*Jessica Shrout
Flintstone, MD*

*A rich and cheesy adaptation of a favorite baked recipe.
It's wonderful for potlucks and get-togethers. Sometimes I'll add
a few unpeeled, sliced redskin potatoes for a bit of color.*

4 lbs. potatoes, peeled, sliced
   and divided
2 T. butter, sliced
1 onion, diced and divided
16-oz. pkg. thick-cut bacon,
   diced and divided
3 c. shredded Cheddar cheese,
   divided

8-oz. pkg. cream cheese, cubed
   and divided
2 10-3/4 oz. cans cream of
   chicken soup
dried parsley, salt and pepper
   to taste

Arrange half of the potato slices in a large slow cooker; dot with
butter. Top with half each of the onion, uncooked bacon and cheeses;
repeat layers. Top with soup and seasonings. Cover and cook on low
setting for 8 to 10 hours, until bubbly and potatoes are tender. Makes
8 to 10 servings.

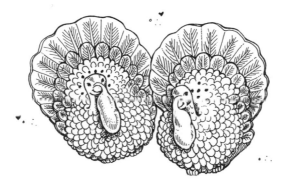

A frozen turkey needs to begin thawing about 4 days before it's
roasted. Just tuck it in the back of the refrigerator where it's
coolest. Oops...you forgot? Place the turkey in a large picnic
cooler and cover with cold water, changing the water once
an hour. A 12 to 14-pound bird will thaw in about 8 hours.

167

Baked Butternut Squash

Mary King
Ashville, AL

I can still smell the cinnamon baking when my mother and grandmother used to make this recipe. I have served this yummy squash to my husband and he loves it too. One medium butternut squash serves two, so it's simple to double this recipe.

1 butternut squash, halved and
    seeds removed
2 T. butter

2 to 4 T. brown sugar, packed
2 t. cinnamon

Place squash halves cut-side down on an ungreased baking sheet. Bake at 350 degrees for 15 to 20 minutes. Turn squash halves over; top each half with one tablespoon butter, one to 2 tablespoons brown sugar and one teaspoon cinnamon. Bake at 350 degrees for an additional 30 to 40 minutes, until fork-tender. Makes 2 servings.

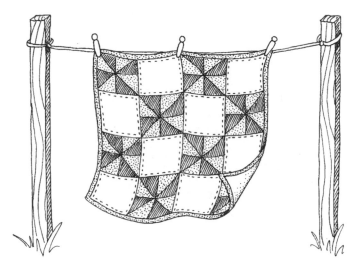

On clear, crisp autumn days, freshen household quilts and blankets for winter. Simply shake them out and spread over a porch rail or fence. Sunshine and fresh air will quickly chase away any mustiness that they've picked up in storage.

Fried Autumn Apples

Hollie Moots
Marysville, OH

We have been taking family trips to the apple orchard for many years. This quick dish is a favorite year 'round, but is extra special made with apples we picked together!

6 apples, peeled, cored
   and sliced
1 t. lemon juice
1/4 c. butter, sliced

1/4 c. brown sugar, packed
1 t. cinnamon
1/4 t. nutmeg
1/4 t. salt

In a bowl, toss apples with lemon juice; set aside. Melt butter in a skillet over medium-low heat. Add apples; top with brown sugar, spices and salt. Sauté, uncovered, for about 15 minutes, until apples are tender, stirring occasionally. Makes 6 servings.

Sprinkle the inside of your Jack-o'-Lantern with some pumpkin pie spice. It will smell delicious when the candle is lit!

Farm-Style Green Beans

Cindy Neel
Gooseberry Patch

Good old-fashioned simmered green beans are delicious! Long cooking over low heat is the secret to the farm-style taste. The beans simmer on the stove while you're doing other things...it's not a recipe to rush! In the summertime, follow these directions using about four pounds of fresh green beans.

4 slices center-cut bacon   1/4 c. butter, sliced
4 14-1/2 oz. cans whole green   1/8 t. salt
    beans, partially drained

In a large saucepan over medium heat, cook bacon until crisp. Reserve bacon and drippings in skillet. Add green beans along with enough of their liquid to cover the beans. Add butter and salt. Reduce heat to low. Cover and simmer over low heat for 2 to 3 hours. Stir occasionally, checking to make sure beans are still covered with liquid. Makes 8 to 10 servings.

Let the kids help out with the Thanksgiving feast.
Something as simple as setting the table and folding napkins
means time spent together, making memories.

🍂 SPEEDY 🍂
Suppers & Sides

Spinach & Cheese Puff

Regina Wickline
Pebble Beach, CA

Spinach is dressed up for the holiday table in this creamy,
cheesy dish. It takes just a few minutes to put together.

3 10-oz. pkgs. frozen chopped
   spinach, thawed and
   squeezed dry
1-1/2 c. half-and-half
3 eggs, beaten

1-1/2 c. shredded Swiss cheese,
   divided
2 t. salt
1/8 t. pepper
1/4 t. nutmeg

In a large bowl, combine spinach, half-and-half, eggs, one cup cheese
and seasonings; stir to combine. Spread mixture evenly in a lightly
greased shallow 2-quart casserole dish. Top with remaining cheese.
Bake, uncovered, at 350 degrees for 30 to 35 minutes, until set and
golden on top. Makes 8 servings.

Younger guests will feel so grown-up when served bubbly
sparkling cider or ginger ale in long-stemmed plastic glasses.
Decorate with curling ribbon just for fun.

Vickie's Country Sage Dressing

Vickie
Gooseberry Patch

My own tried & true recipe! Toss the bread mixture well
to make sure all the bread is coated in buttery goodness.

1-lb. loaf country white
  sandwich bread, torn
1 c. butter, sliced
1 c. onion, chopped
1 c. celery, chopped

8 to 10 fresh sage leaves,
  chopped
5 T. fresh parsley, chopped
salt and pepper to taste
1-1/2 to 2 c. chicken broth

The day before, place bread pieces on a baking sheet; allow to dry overnight. Melt butter in a skillet over medium heat. Sauté onion and celery until softened, about 5 minutes. In a large bowl, combine bread, onion mixture, herbs, salt and pepper. Toss gently to coat bread well. Spoon into a greased deep 13"x9" baking pan or a roaster pan. Pour 1-1/2 cups broth over the top; add remaining broth if a moister consistency is preferred. Cover; bake at 350 degrees for 30 minutes. Uncover during the last 10 minutes to allow the bread to crisp. Makes 8 to 10 servings.

Do you have lots of leftover turkey? It freezes well for up to three months. Cut turkey into bite-size pieces, place in plastic freezer bags and pop in the freezer...ready to stir into hearty casseroles and soups whenever you are.

❧ SPEEDY ❧
Suppers & Sides

Patty's Mushroom Supreme

Jennifer Salberg
Helendale, CA

One Thanksgiving, my husband's sister Patty introduced me to this recipe. I was not a big fan of mushrooms, but this is such a wonderful combination of flavors that it's a special treat. Sadly, Patty passed away before the following Thanksgiving. It is now on the menu for every holiday dinner we prepare in our home.

2 cubes beef bouillon
1/2 c. boiling water
1 lb. whole mushrooms,
   trimmed
1/2 c. butter, divided
2 T. all-purpose flour
1/2 c. whipping cream

1/8 t. salt
1/8 t. pepper
1/2 c. dry bread crumbs or
   cracker crumbs
1/2 to 1 c. grated Parmesan
   cheese

In a cup, combine bouillon cubes and boiling water; set aside. In a large skillet over medium-high heat, sauté mushrooms in 1/4 cup butter. Transfer mixture to a greased 2-quart casserole dish; set aside. Melt remaining butter; blend with flour in a large bowl. Stir in cream, bouillon mixture, salt and pepper. Pour cream mixture over mushrooms. In a small bowl, mix crumbs and cheese; sprinkle on top. Bake, uncovered, at 350 degrees for 30 minutes, until bubbly and golden. May bake the day before, cover and refrigerate for reheating. Serves 6 to 8.

Make your own bread crumbs. Save leftover bread slices (the "heels" are fine) and freeze in a plastic bag. When you have enough, bake the slices in a 250-degree oven until dry and crumbly, then tear into sections and pulse in a food processor or blender.

Yellow Squash Casserole

Lisanne Miller
Canton, MS

*A light casserole for Thanksgiving dinner that tastes wonderful!
You can use fresh or frozen yellow squash. This may be made
ahead and it's easy to double.*

2 to 3 c. yellow squash,
   thinly sliced
1/2 c. mayonnaise
1/2 c. shredded Cheddar cheese
1/4 c. green pepper, minced
2 T. green onions, minced

1 egg, beaten
pepper to taste
1 sleeve round buttery crackers,
   crushed
1/4 c. butter, melted

In a large saucepan, bring one inch of water to a boil over high heat.
Add squash. Reduce heat to medium; cover and cook for 3 to
5 minutes, or until fork-tender. Drain well and let cool; transfer
squash to a large bowl. Add remaining ingredients except crackers
and butter; mix well. Spoon squash mixture into a lightly greased
2-quart casserole dish. Mix crackers with melted butter in a separate
bowl; spread on top. Bake, uncovered, at 350 degrees for 20 to
25 minutes, until golden. Serves 4 to 6.

If it's Thanksgiving now, Christmas can't be far away.
Why not double any must-have casseroles or side dishes and
freeze half for Christmas dinner...you'll be so glad you did!

❀ SPEEDY ❀
Suppers & Sides

Savory Baked Potatoes

Martha Stephens
Covington, LA

*I'm always looking for different new ways to fix potatoes instead of
the same ol' baked potatoes. So I created this...my kids love it!*

5 to 6 russet potatoes, very
   thinly sliced and divided
1/4 c. extra-virgin olive oil,
   divided
2 t. garlic powder

2 t. seasoned salt
1/2 t. celery salt
2 t. salt
2 t. pepper
Garnish: dried parsley

Arrange half of the potato slices in a greased 13"x9" glass baking pan.
Drizzle with half of the oil. Combine all seasonings except garnish;
sprinkle half of mixture over potatoes. Repeat layers; sprinkle parsley
on top. Cover with aluminum foil. Bake at 375 degrees for 35 to
45 minutes, until potatoes are tender. Serves 6.

A day or two before Turkey Day, set out all the serving platters,
baskets and dishes and label them..."Judy's Cranberry Sauce,"
"Grandma's Muffins" and so on. When the time arrives,
you'll be able to get dinner on the table in a jiffy.

Festive Broccoli Salad

Crystal Shook
Catawba, NC

This crunchy salad goes well with just about any meal. It's perfect for school potlucks, tailgating parties and even Thanksgiving.

3 bunches broccoli, cut into
    bite-size flowerets
1/2 c. sweetened dried
    cranberries
1/3 c. toasted almonds
    or pecans

1 onion, chopped
1 c. mayonnaise
1/3 c. sugar
2 T. cider vinegar
6 slices bacon, crisply cooked
    and crumbled

In a large bowl, toss together broccoli, cranberries, nuts and onion; set aside. In a separate bowl, mix mayonnaise, sugar and vinegar; spoon over broccoli mixture and toss to mix. Top with bacon. Cover and refrigerate for 2 to 4 hours. Serves 8 to 10.

Lynn's Nutty Slaw

Lynn Foley
Branson, MO

This slaw may sound a little unusual, but it's delicious, oh-so easy to make and keeps really well in the fridge.

16-oz. pkg. coleslaw mix
1/3 c. salted cocktail peanuts
1/3 c. raisins

1/2 c. mayonnaise
1 T. red wine vinegar
1 t. sugar

Combine slaw mix, peanuts and raisins in a large bowl; set aside. In a separate small bowl, combine mayonnaise, vinegar and sugar; stir until well blended. Fold mayonnaise mixture into slaw and combine well. Cover and refrigerate at least one hour before serving. Makes 6 to 8 servings.

Apple Orchard Salad

Lynn Williams
Muncie, IN

I used to love my mom's Waldorf salad, but with a sweet dressing and tiny marshmallows, it needed a bit of updating. This version is fruity and refreshing.

2 apples, peeled, cored
  and diced
1/2 c. golden raisins or
  sweetened dried cranberries

2 stalks celery, sliced
1/2 c. chopped walnuts
1/4 c. mayonnaise
2 T. orange juice

Combine all ingredients in a serving bowl; toss to mix well. Cover and chill until serving time. Makes 6 to 8 servings.

When I was in first grade, at Thanksgiving we sang, "Over the river and through the woods, to Grandmother's house we go." I thought the song was written about my grandmother because we really did have to cross a river and go through the woods to get to her home! We traveled in a car rather than a sleigh, but no matter...it seemed to me that most details were correct! When we got to her old farmhouse, we would see a table that was groaning from all the food placed on it. There was always a big roast goose, many vegetable casseroles, fluffy mashed potatoes, gravy and other delights. Cakes, pies and puddings were brought in after we had eaten the main course. Everyone talked, laughed and just enjoyed being together. What fond memories I have of those times

–Dee Lakes, Mansfield, OH

Creamy Cranberry Salad

Lynda Robson
Boston, MA

An easy make-ahead for your Thanksgiving buffet.

14-oz. can whole-berry
  cranberry sauce
1 c. boiling water
3-oz. pkg. strawberry gelatin
  mix

1 T. lemon juice
1/2 c. mayonnaise
1 apple, peeled, cored and diced
1/4 c. chopped pecans

Spoon cranberry sauce into a small saucepan over low heat; cook until melted. Strain, reserving cranberry juice; set cranberries aside. In a bowl, combine reserved cranberry juice, boiling water and dry gelatin mix; stir until dissolved. Stir in lemon juice. Cover and refrigerate until gelatin begins to set. Add mayonnaise; beat with an electric mixer on low speed until fluffy. Fold in reserved cranberries, apple and pecans; pour into a 4-cup mold. Cover and refrigerate until set. Turn out of mold onto a serving plate. Makes 6 servings.

Picture-perfect portions of a favorite gelatin salad are
handy for buffets or potlucks. Spoon the gelatin mixture
into paper muffin liners and set in a baking pan. Chill until
firm, then peel off liners.

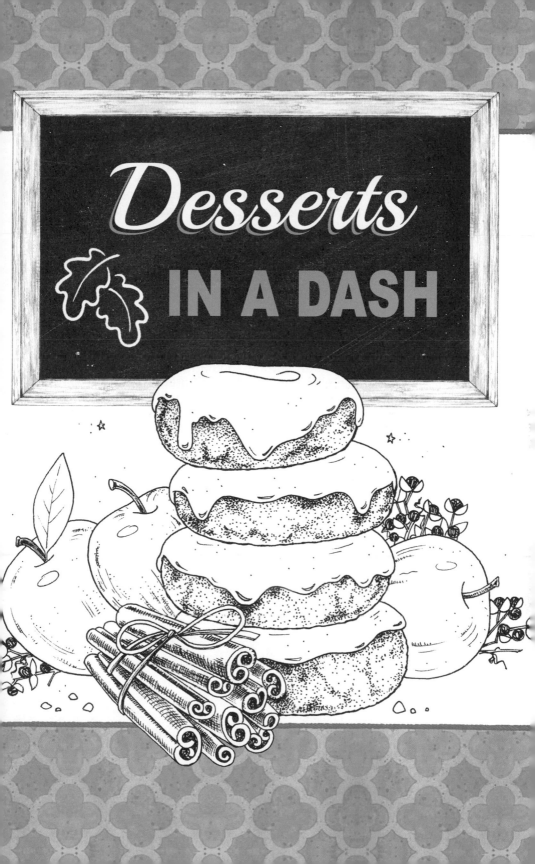

Desserts
IN A DASH

Nanny's Peanut Butter Goblins

Beverly Mahorney
Cynthiana, KY

Every year on Halloween my family hosts an open house. My mom always made these simple but scrumptious cookies for it. We lost her in 2005, but when I make her cookies, I feel like she's still with us.

1-1/2 c. all-purpose flour
1/2 t. baking soda
1/2 t. salt
1/2 c. butter, softened
1 c. crunchy peanut butter

1/2 c. brown sugar, packed
1 c. sugar, divided
1 egg, beaten
1 t. vanilla extract

In a bowl, mix together flour, baking soda and salt; set aside. In a separate large bowl, combine butter, peanut butter, brown sugar and 1/2 cup sugar. Beat with an electric mixer on medium speed until blended; stir in egg and vanilla. Add flour mixture; stir until a stiff dough forms. Roll dough into balls by tablespoonfuls. Roll balls in remaining sugar; place 2 inches apart on greased baking sheets. With a fork dipped in sugar, flatten balls in a criss-cross pattern. Bake at 375 degrees for 10 to 12 minutes, until golden. Makes 3 dozen.

Parchment paper is a baker's best friend! Place it on a baking sheet to keep cookies from spreading and sticking. Clean-up is a breeze too. Generally, the paper can be reused at least once... when it starts to darken, toss it.

Speedy Little Devils

Sherry Cecil
South Point, OH

When I was a child. this was my "special treat" that Mom made for me. Little did I know back then how just a few simple ingredients could make such a delicious rich dessert. Now that I have my own family, this has become one of my kids' favorite desserts and always takes me back to fond memories from my childhood!

18-1/4 oz. pkg. devil's food
   cake mix
1/2 c. butter, melted

1/2 c. creamy peanut butter
7-oz. jar marshmallow creme

In a large bowl, combine dry cake mix with melted butter; mix well. Reserve 1-1/2 cups of cake mixture for topping. Press remaining cake mixture into the bottom of an ungreased 13"x9" baking pan. In a separate bowl, blend peanut butter and marshmallow creme; gently spread over cake mixture. Sprinkle remaining cake mixture over top. Bake at 350 degrees for 20 minutes. Cool; cut into squares. Makes one dozen.

When I think of harvest time, it brings such wonderful memories of my mother. She was a great cook and our house was filled with the best smells. Coming in the back door after a crisp fall walk home from school, I was always greeted by my mother in her ruffled apron and the smell of homemade breads, cakes and cookies, yum! But my best 'smell' memory was her bread pudding. The egg custard mixed with bread, plump raisins and the cinnamon with just a dash of nutmeg added to it. Oh my goodness, my mouth just waters when I think of it.

–Ann Viviano, St. John, IN

Fruity Sugar Cookies

Rita Jefferis
Anthony, KS

A co-worker gave me this great recipe more than 20 years ago. These bright-colored cookies are beautiful for any special occasion. I've used it for many school parties. It's an easy dough for beginning bakers to handle. Finish it simply by sprinkling the tops with a little sugar before baking, if you wish to skip the decorator icing.

3 c. all-purpose flour
1 t. baking powder
1 t. salt
1 c. sugar
3-oz. pkg. favorite-flavor
    gelatin mix

3/4 c. shortening
2 eggs, beaten
Optional: additional sugar
    for sprinkling, decorator
    frosting

In a bowl, mix together flour, baking powder and salt; set aside. In a separate bowl, combine sugar and dry gelatin mix; stir well. Add shortening and eggs; mix until smooth. Add flour mixture; stir well until a soft dough forms. Roll out dough on a lightly floured surface. Cut out desired shapes with cookie cutters. Arrange cookies on baking sheets lightly sprayed with non-stick vegetable spray. Sprinkle with sugar, if desired. Bake at 375 degrees for 6 to 8 minutes. Cool cookies on wire racks; decorate with frosting, if desired. Makes 4 dozen.

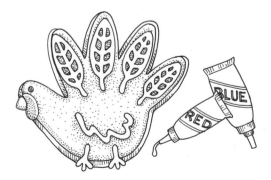

When rolling out cookie dough, sprinkle powdered sugar
on the work surface. So much tastier than using flour
and it works just as well!

Desserts ❀
IN A DASH

Judy's Brownie Cookies

Judy Borecky
Escondido, CA

My husband loves these cookies...and who wouldn't,
with chocolate chips, cranberries and crunchy oats?

20-oz. pkg. brownie mix
1-1/2 c. quick-cooking oats,
   uncooked
1/2 c. oil
2 eggs, beaten

1/2 c. semi-sweet chocolate
   chips
1/2 c. sweetened dried
   cranberries
Optional: pecan halves

In a large bowl, combine dry brownie mix, oats, oil and eggs; mix
well. Stir in chocolate chips and cranberries. Drop dough by rounded
teaspoons onto ungreased baking sheets. If desired, press 3 to
4 pecan halves onto the top of each cookie. Bake, one sheet at a time,
at 350 degrees for 15 to 17 minutes. Let cookies cool for 2 minutes;
remove to wire racks and cool completely. Makes 2 dozen.

Nut Macaroons

Rebecca Etling
Blairsville, PA

One of my favorite quick & easy cookie recipes.

2/3 c. sweetened
   condensed milk
1 c. sweetened flaked coconut

1 c. chopped nuts
1 t. vanilla extract
3/4 t. almond extract

In a bowl, mix all ingredients in the order given. Drop by teaspoonfuls
onto well greased baking sheets. Bake at 350 degrees for 10 to
12 minutes, until dry around the edges. Makes 2 dozen.

When baking two sheets of cookies
at once, remember to reverse the
top and bottom sheets halfway
through the baking time to
ensure they bake evenly.

Butterscotch Cherry Cookies

Renae Scheiderer
Beallsville, OH

A friend shared the recipe for these cookies...they are delicious!

2 c. all-purpose flour
1 t. baking soda
1 t. salt
1 c. butter, softened
1 c. sugar

1 t. vanilla extract
6-oz. pkg. butterscotch chips
1/2 c. chopped pecans
1/2 c. maraschino cherries,
    well drained and chopped

Combine flour, baking soda and salt in a bowl; mix well and set aside. In a separate large bowl, combine butter and sugar; beat until creamy. Blend in vanilla. Add flour mixture and stir well. Fold in butterscotch chips, pecans and cherries. Drop dough by rounded teaspoonfuls onto ungreased baking sheets. Bake at 375 degrees for 10 to 12 minutes, until golden. Makes 7 dozen.

Little ones love to help out in the kitchen, so tuck
a set of measuring spoons, oven mitt and mini rolling pin
in the pocket of a child-size apron...everything
a little helper needs.

✿ *Desserts* ✿
IN A DASH

Lemon Pecan Dainties

Cassie Hooker
La Porte, TX

You'll love these tender, lemony cookies...perfect with a cup of tea.

2 c. all-purpose flour
1 t. baking powder
1/2 t. salt
3/4 c. shortening
1 c. sugar

1 egg, beaten
1 T. lemon zest
1 T. lemon juice
1 c. pecans, finely chopped

In a bowl, mix together flour, baking powder and salt; set aside. In a separate large bowl, combine shortening and sugar; blend very well. Add egg, lemon zest and lemon juice; beat well. Add flour mixture and mix well; stir in pecans. Shape dough into rolls, 2 inches thick. Wrap in plastic wrap; chill thoroughly. Slice very thinly, about 1/4-inch thick. Place on greased baking sheets. Bake at 350 degrees for 12 to 15 minutes. Cool slightly before removing from baking sheets. Makes 4 dozen.

Slice 'n Bake
Sugar Cookie Dough

Such a thoughtful gift for a busy mom! Wrap up a roll of your best cookie dough along with fun decorations...colorful sprinkles, candy-coated chocolates and of course a cookie cutter or two. She'll love it!

Delicious Cranberry Bars

Susan Wilson
Johnson City, TN

My husband loves these bar cookies any time of the year. They are especially good with a cup of hot coffee.

2 c. all-purpose flour
2 c. long-cooking oats,
    uncooked
1 c. sugar

1 t. baking powder
1 c. butter, melted
2 14-oz. cans whole-berry
    cranberry sauce

In a large bowl, combine all ingredients except cranberry sauce; mix until large crumbs form. Reserve 1-1/2 cups of crumb mixture for topping. Press remaining crumb mixture into the bottom of a greased and floured 13"x9" baking pan. Spread cranberry sauce over top. Sprinkle with reserved crumb mixture; pat gently. Bake at 350 degrees for 25 minutes. Cool and cut into bars. Store in refrigerator. Makes 1-1/2 dozen.

Serve up a Bucket o' Bones at your next Halloween party! Press a mini marshmallow into each end of a pretzel stick and dip in melted white chocolate.

☺ *Desserts* ☺
IN A DASH

Beth's Toffee Bars

Beth Richter
Canby, MN

This recipe gets taken everywhere! From the first time I made these bars, they have always been in high demand. At family gatherings, they often disappear as fast as they hit the table...they're that good!

18-1/2 oz. pkg. yellow cake mix
1 egg, beaten
1/3 c. butter, melted and slightly
  cooled

6-oz. pkg. toffee bits
14-oz. can sweetened
  condensed milk

In a large bowl, stir together dry cake mix, egg and butter. Gently pat into a 13"x9" baking pan. Sprinkle with toffee bits; spread condensed milk over the top. Bake at 350 degrees for about 25 minutes. Cool; cut into squares. Makes about 16 bars.

A vintage black lunchbox makes a clever Halloween candy holder...just fill with tasty treats for little goblins to choose from.

Delectable Peanut Butter Squares

Lyn Peters
Olive Hill, KY

*When I was in grade school, our cafeteria had these melty peanut butter
& chocolate squares. After searching for years for the recipe, I decided
that it was time to tackle the task myself. After much trial & error,
I have come close to the ones I remember as a child.*

1/2 c. butter
1/2 c. brown sugar, packed
2 c. creamy or crunchy peanut
  butter

1 t. vanilla extract
2-1/2 c. powdered sugar
6-oz. pkg. semi-sweet chocolate
  chips

Melt butter in a large saucepan over low heat, stirring to prevent
burning. Add brown sugar; stir until completely dissolved. Add peanut
butter and vanilla; mix thoroughly. Add powdered sugar; stir well.
Press mixture into a 13"x9" baking pan sprayed with non-stick
vegetable spray; let cool. Melt chocolate chips in a double boiler over
low heat; spread evenly over peanut butter layer. Let cool completely;
cut into squares. Makes one to 2 dozen.

Slice bar cookies into one-inch squares and set them in
frilly paper candy cups. Guests will love sampling "just a bite"
of several different treats.

Marbled Chocolate Bars

Darlene Hartzler
Marshallville, OH

This super-easy recipe is a lunchbox favorite for my kids.

18-1/4 oz. pkg. German
   chocolate cake mix
8-oz. pkg. cream cheese,
   softened

1/2 c. sugar
3/4 c. milk chocolate chips,
   divided

Prepare cake batter according to package directions. Spread in a greased 15"x10" jelly-roll pan; set aside. In a separate bowl, beat together cream cheese and sugar; stir in 1/4 cup chocolate chips. Drop mixture by tablespoonfuls over batter; cut through batter with a knife to swirl. Sprinkle with remaining chocolate chips. Bake at 350 degrees for 25 to 30 minutes, until a toothpick inserted in the center comes out clean. Cool in pan on a wire rack. Cut into bars. Makes 3 dozen.

Warm up dinner with friends by hosting a casual fireside supper. Toast sandwiches in pie irons and make s'mores for dessert...so cozy!

Mom's Pumpkin Brownies

Linda Renderer
Ocala, FL

*Mom always made these terrific brownies on Halloween
before we went out trick-or-treating.*

4 eggs, room temperature
2 c. sugar
1 c. butter, melted and slightly
  cooled
1 c. canned pumpkin
1 t. vanilla extract

1-1/2 c. all-purpose flour
1-1/2 t. pumpkin pie spice
1/2 t. cinnamon
Garnish: vanilla or cream cheese
  frosting

In a large bowl, beat eggs well with an electric mixer on medium speed. Beat in sugar, butter, pumpkin and vanilla on medium speed. Add flour and spices; beat on low speed. Spread batter in a lightly greased 9"x9" baking pan. Bake at 350 degrees for 40 minutes. Cool; frost as desired and cut into squares. Makes 8 to 10.

Save the sprinkles! Before adding candy sprinkles to cookies,
cover the table with a length of wax paper. Return any excess
sprinkles to their jars by simply folding the paper in half, gently
shaking sprinkles to one side and sliding them into the jar.

☙ *Desserts* ☙
IN A DASH

7-Layer Brownie Bars

Becky Holsinger
Belpre, OH

*My husband came home from work one day, talking about some
delicious brownies that his co-worker had brought to work. I told him
to get me the recipe and he was right...these are wonderful!*

1/2 c. butter, melted
18-oz. pkg. double chocolate
   brownie mix
1 c. sweetened flaked coconut
1 c. butterscotch chips

1 c. semi-sweet chocolate chips
1 c. chopped pecans
14-oz. can sweetened
   condensed milk

Spread melted butter in the bottom of a 13"x9" baking pan; sprinkle
dry brownie mix over butter. Top with coconut, butterscotch chips,
chocolate chips and pecans. Drizzle with condensed milk. Bake at
350 degrees for 30 to 35 minutes, until edges are bubbly. Cool
completely before cutting into bars. Makes one dozen.

Just for fun, slip a little note of encouragement
into your child's lunchbox each week.

Halloween Candy Pie

Elizabeth Cassinos
Paradise Valley, NV

I used to make this simple treat all the time for my girls when they were little. Their little faces really lit up when I served to them in a real pizza box!

12-oz. pkg. semi-sweet
   chocolate chips

1 c. dry-roasted peanuts
1 c. candy corn

Line an 8" or 9" round cake pan with parchment paper or wax paper; set aside. In a saucepan, melt chocolate chips over low heat; stir in peanuts. Pour into cake pan. Decorate with candy corn as desired. Cover and chill until firm. Turn "pizza" out of pan; peel off paper. Slice into wedges. Makes 8 servings.

Ask your neighborhood pizza parlor for a new pizza box
to put your Halloween Candy Pie in. Decorate the lid
with colorful craft paper cut-outs and stickers...don't forget
to tie on a pizza cutter!

192

Taffy Apple Pizza

Lori Simmons
Princeville, IL

A fun fall dessert that everyone is sure to like.

16-1/2 oz. pkg. refrigerated
   sugar cookie dough
8-oz. pkg. cream cheese,
   softened
3/4 c. brown sugar, packed

2 t. vanilla extract
4 to 6 apples, cored and sliced
Garnish: caramel ice cream
   topping
Optional: chopped peanuts

Press cookie dough into an ungreased pizza pan. Bake at 350 degrees for 10 to 12 minutes, until golden; let cool. In a bowl, blend cream cheese, brown sugar and vanilla; spread over cooled crust. Arrange apple slices on top; drizzle caramel topping over the apples. If desired, sprinkle with peanuts. Cover and chill; cut into wedges. Makes 8 to 10 servings.

Every year when fall came with apple season, we loaded the bushel baskets into our 1946 Oldsmobile, packed bologna sandwiches and Mason jars of water and headed to a neighboring orchard to pick apples. My daddy always insisted only on Jonathan apples that were almost too ripe. He cooked his apple butter in a cast-iron Dutch oven instead of a slow cooker as I do now. Daddy said his Indian grandmother would cook it over an open fire, starting before daylight and finishing up around midnight. He also taught me how to make "cathead" biscuits which we would cover with homemade Guernsey butter and the apple butter. It was delicious on just about anything. I just loved eating it out of the jar...unless I got caught!

–Cheryl Bone, Millington, TN

Sopapilla Cheesecake

Dorothy Keichler
Friendswood, TX

This recipe is the answer when you need a big tasty dessert, fast!
Mix & match your choice of fruit fillings...apple, strawberry, cherry,
blackberry, raspberry and blueberry are all wonderful.

2 8-oz. tubes crescent rolls,
  divided
3 8-oz. pkgs. cream cheese,
  softened
1-1/2 c. plus 1 T. sugar, divided

1-1/2 t. vanilla extract
2 21-oz. cans fruit pie filling,
  divided
1/2 c. butter, melted
2 T. cinnamon

Spray a 13"x9" glass baking pan with non-stick vegetable spray.
Unroll one can of crescent rolls in the bottom of pan; set aside.
Combine cream cheese, 1-1/2 cups sugar and vanilla in a large bowl.
Beat with an electric mixer on medium speed until soft and fluffy.
Spread half of cream cheese mixture over rolls. Spread one can of pie
filling on half of the cream cheese mixture, to one side, and the
remaining can on the other half. Spread remaining cream cheese
mixture over pie filling; lay remaining crescent rolls on top. Drizzle
with melted butter. Mix remaining sugar with cinnamon; sprinkle over
butter. Bake at 350 degrees for 45 minutes, or until golden. Cool
slightly; cut into squares. Makes 20 servings.

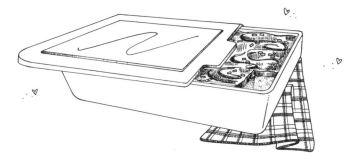

If you see a vintage cake pan with its own slide-on lid
at a tag sale, snap it up! It's indispensable for toting cakes
and bar cookies to picnics and potlucks.

Fruit Cocktail Cake

Nan Calcagno
Grosse Tete, LA

This old favorite is delicious and so easy...good for
family gatherings and church dinners.

2 c. all-purpose flour
1 t. baking soda
2-1/2 c. sugar, divided
2 eggs, beaten
15-oz. can fruit cocktail in syrup

1/2 c. brown sugar, packed
1/2 c. chopped pecans
1 c. evaporated milk
1/2 c. butter, sliced

In a large bowl, stir together flour, baking soda and 1-1/2 cups sugar. Add eggs and fruit cocktail with syrup; beat well. Pour batter into a greased 13"x9" baking pan. Sprinkle with brown sugar and pecans. Bake at 325 degrees for 30 to 40 minutes; remove from oven. In a saucepan, combine remaining sugar, evaporated milk and butter over medium heat. Bring to a boil; cook and stir for several minutes, until thickened. Drizzle over warm cake; cut into squares. Makes 15 servings.

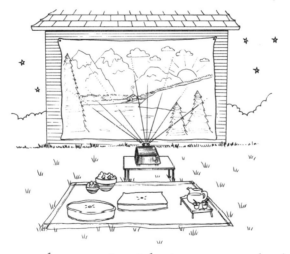

Host an outdoor movie night in your own backyard!
Great fun for watching the big game on TV too. Call a local
camera or rental store for a video projector...simply hook it
to a DVD player and project your favorite movie on
a painter's canvas dropcloth. Sure to be a hit!

Pumpkin Pudding

Joyce Stackhouse
Cadiz, OH

This recipe is really quick to make and scrumptious...perfect for a light dessert after a big meal. If you are watching your calories, you can use sugar-free pudding mix and skim milk.

2 c. milk
3.4-oz. pkg. instant vanilla
  pudding mix
1 c. canned pumpkin

1 t. vanilla extract
1 t. pumpkin pie spice
1/2 t. cinnamon
Optional: whipped cream

Combine milk and dry pudding mix in a large bowl. Beat with an electric mixer on low speed for one to 2 minutes, until smooth. Add pumpkin, vanilla and spices; mix well. Spoon into individual dessert bowls; cover and chill. If desired, garnish with dollops of whipped cream at serving time. Makes 6 to 8 servings.

Pumpkin pie is scrumptious topped with homemade whipped cream. For the fluffiest whipped cream possible, always make sure the bowl and beaters are chilled.

☻ *Desserts* ☻
IN A DASH

Pumpkin Gingersnap
Ice Cream

Paula Purcell
Plymouth Meeting, PA

*An old-fashioned shop near us used to sell this ice cream in the fall.
When the shop went out of business, I had to come up with a substitute.
We think my version is even better! A great harvest dessert, especially
for Thanksgiving.*

14-oz. container vanilla
   ice cream, softened
15-oz. can pumpkin
1 sleeve gingersnap cookies,
   crushed

Optional: whipped cream,
   additional gingersnaps,
   candy corn

In a large bowl, combine ice cream and pumpkin; blend well by hand.
Stir in crushed cookies. Cover and freeze. If desired, garnish scoops of
ice cream with a dollop of whipped cream, a gingersnap cookie and
several pieces of candy corn. Makes 6 to 8 servings.

Looking for a new no-mess way to decorate Jack-o'-Lanterns?
Try duct tape! It comes in lots of fun colors and is super-easy
to cut into shapes...great for kids to craft with. Later, the uncut
pumpkin can even be re-purposed for pies.

Apple-Cranberry Crostada

Wendy Ball
Battle Creek, MI

A wonderful dessert using pantry ingredients! So simple, it can be baked while you're eating dinner. Some canned apple pie fillings have more filling than apples...in those cases, I add an extra apple.

21-oz. can apple pie filling
1/2 c. whole-berry cranberry
   sauce
Optional: 1 Golden Delicious
   apple, peeled, cored and
   sliced

9-inch pie crust, room
   temperature
1 egg white
1 t. water
2 to 4 T. raw or regular sugar
Garnish: ice cream

Combine pie filling and cranberry sauce in a bowl. Add sliced apple if pie filling is thin; set aside. Unroll pie crust on a sheet of wax paper. Cover with another piece of wax paper; roll out crust slightly larger. Place rolled-out pie crust onto a baking sheet that has been sprayed with non-stick spray. Spoon fruit mixture into center of pie crust, leaving a 2-inch rim. Fold edge of crust over fruit mixture, pleating crust as necessary. In a separate bowl, whisk together egg white and water. Brush crust with egg white mixture; sprinkle with sugar. Bake at 425 degrees for 15 to 18 minutes, until golden and bubbly. Leave crust uncovered to prevent softening. Serve warm, garnished as desired. Makes 6 servings.

Stir up some Grizzly Gorp for snacking and tucking into lunchboxes. Just toss together 2 cups bear-shaped graham crackers, one cup mini marshmallows, one cup peanuts and 1/2 cup seedless raisins. Yum!

Desserts
IN A DASH

Apple Crisp with a Twist

Natasha Crevier
London, Ontario

An old family recipe that's so simple, anyone can do it.

4 c. tart apples, cored and sliced
1/3 c. butter, softened
1 c. brown sugar, packed
3/4 c. all-purpose flour

cinnamon to taste
Optional: ice cream or whipped
  cream

Arrange apple slices in a lightly greased 8"x8" baking pan; set aside. In a bowl, mix butter, brown sugar and flour until crumbly; sprinkle over apples. Add cinnamon to taste. Bake at 350 degrees for about one hour. Serve warm, garnished as desired. Makes 6 servings.

Roly Polys

Pam Halter
Pennsville, NJ

Whenever my mom made pie, she would make these treats from the leftover crust. We kids liked them better than the pie! A few years ago, I discovered refrigerated pie crust, which is perfect for making Roly Polys. Now we can enjoy them anytime!

9-inch pie crust, room
  temperature
2 t. butter, melted

1/2 c. sugar
1 t. cinnamon

Unroll pie crust; brush with melted butter. Combine sugar and cinnamon in a cup; sprinkle over crust. Roll up crust; slice 1/2-inch thick. Place rolls cut-side up on an ungreased baking stone or a greased baking sheet. Bake at 400 degrees for 15 minutes, or until golden. Makes about 1-1/2 dozen.

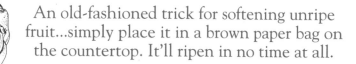

An old-fashioned trick for softening unripe fruit...simply place it in a brown paper bag on the countertop. It'll ripen in no time at all.

Lemon Crunch Pound Cake

Sharon Jones
Fountain, FL

This is the best lemon pound cake I've ever made...everyone loves it!
I enjoy serving it to special morning coffee guests...my mom,
a neighbor or a group of ladies from church. I hope you love it too!

18-1/4 oz. pkg. yellow cake mix
3-oz. pkg. lemon gelatin mix
2/3 c. oil
4 eggs, beaten

3/4 c. water
1 t. lemon extract
1/2 t. salt
1/2 c. chopped pecans

In a large bowl, combine dry cake and gelatin mixes. Add remaining ingredients except pecans; beat well until smooth. Spray a Bundt® pan with non-stick vegetable spray; sprinkle with flour and shake out loose flour. Sprinkle pecans in bottom of pan; pour in batter. Bake at 325 degrees for 45 to 55 minutes, until a toothpick tests clean. Cool cake completely; turn out of pan onto a serving plate. Drizzle with Powdered Sugar Glaze shortly before serving. Makes about 12 servings.

Powdered Sugar Glaze:

2 c. powdered sugar
3 T. milk

1/2 t. vanilla extract

Mix together powdered sugar and milk to desired thickness for drizzling; stir in vanilla.

A party without cake is really just a meeting.

–Julia Child

Poppy Seed Cake

Pamela Bennett
Whittier, CA

*I have been making this cake for parties, showers, cake walks,
fundraisers...you name it, for years! For a flavorful change,
sprinkle the greased pan with cinnamon-sugar instead of flour.*

18-1/2 oz. pkg. white or
   yellow cake mix
3.4-oz. pkg. instant lemon
   pudding mix
1 c. water

1/2 c. oil
4 eggs, beaten
1/4 c. poppy seed
1 t. almond extract

In a large bowl, mix together dry cake and pudding mixes. Add water
and oil; beat well with an electric mixer on medium speed. Beat in
eggs, one at a time. Add poppy seed and extract; beat until smooth.
Pour batter into a well greased and floured Bundt® pan. Bake at
350 degrees for about 45 minutes, until a toothpick comes out clean.
Allow cake to cool in pan for 15 minutes before removing. Drizzle
with Lemon Glaze, if desired; cake is also delicious served plain.
Makes 10 to 12 servings.

Lemon Glaze:

2 c. powdered sugar
3 T. milk

1/2 t. lemon extract

Mix together powdered sugar and milk to desired thickness for
drizzling; stir in extract.

Cover the tube in a Bundt® pan
with a small paper cup. When you
pour in the batter, it won't spill
down the center hole.

Festive Cranberry Pie

Gladys Kielar
Whitehouse, OH

For something so delicious, this takes no time at all.

2 c. fresh or frozen cranberries
1-1/2 c. sugar, divided
1/2 c. chopped walnuts
    or pecans
2 eggs

1 c. all-purpose flour
1/4 c. shortening, melted and
    slightly cooled
1/2 c. butter, melted and
    slightly cooled

Spread cranberries in a 10" deep-dish pie plate sprayed with non-stick vegetable spray. Sprinkle with 1/2 cup sugar and nuts; set aside. In a bowl, beat eggs well; gradually add remaining sugar and beat thoroughly. Add flour, shortening and butter; mix well and pour over cranberries. Bake at 325 degrees for one hour, or until bubbly and crust is golden. Makes 8 servings.

Fresh cranberries can be kept frozen up to 12 months, so if you enjoy them, stock up every autumn when they're available and pop unopened bags in the freezer. You'll be able to add their fruity tang to recipes year 'round.

Sweet Potato Pie

Lisa Barber
Tyler, TX

*My mom makes this pie every year at Thanksgiving and Christmas.
It is a favorite of several family members. My son says he doesn't like
sweet potato pie, but every year he eats it and loves it because he
thinks it is pumpkin!*

3 sweet potatoes, peeled
   and sliced
1/4 c. butter, softened
1/8 t. salt
1 c. sugar, or more to taste

2 eggs, well beaten
1 c. evaporated milk
1 t. cinnamon
1 t. vanilla extract
9-inch pie crust

In a saucepan, cover sweet potatoes with water. Bring to a boil over
medium-high heat; boil potatoes until tender. Drain; mash potatoes
with butter, salt and sugar. Add eggs, evaporated milk, cinnamon and
vanilla; mix well. Pour into unbaked pie crust. Bake at 350 degrees
for 45 minutes. Reduce heat to 300 degrees; bake another 15 minutes,
or until pie is set. Cool before serving. Makes 8 servings.

Take time to share family stories and traditions with
your children. A cherished family recipe can be
a great conversation starter.

Pumpkin Crunch Cream Pie

Eleanor Dionne
Beverly, MA

This is a special favorite of mine every fall...it's perfect for Thanksgiving and so simple to make.

3/4 c. whole milk
3.4-oz. pkg. instant vanilla
   pudding mix
1/2 c. canned pumpkin
3/4 t. pumpkin pie spice
2/3 c. semi-sweet chocolate
   chips

2/3 c. slivered almonds
12-oz. container frozen whipped
   topping, thawed and divided
9-inch graham cracker crust
Optional: chocolate curls

Pour milk into a bowl; add dry pudding mix. Beat with a whisk until well blended; let stand for about 5 minutes. Blend in pumpkin, spice, chocolate chips, almonds and 2 cups whipped topping. Spoon into pie crust. Cover and chill for about 4 hours. Just before serving, garnish with remaining whipped topping and chocolate curls, if desired.

Chocolate shavings look so delicate but are really simple to make. Just pull a vegetable peeler across a bar of chocolate and watch it curl!

Desserts
IN A DASH

Harvest Apple Parfait Crunch

Shirl Parsons
Cape Carteret, NC

*Enjoy the flavor of fresh caramel apples in a layered dessert.
It only looks like it took a lot of effort!*

8-oz. pkg. Neufchâtel cheese,
  softened
3/4 c. dark brown sugar,
  packed and divided
1 T. milk
1/2 c. granola cereal nuggets

3/4 c. dry-roasted peanuts,
  finely chopped
3 T. margarine, melted
4 red apples, cored and chopped
Garnish: whipped topping

Mix Neufchâtel cheese, 1/2 cup brown sugar and milk in a bowl until
well blended; set aside. In a separate small bowl, combine cereal,
peanuts and remaining brown sugar; stir in melted margarine until
well blended. Spoon half of the apples into 6 parfait glasses; cover
with half each of cheese mixture and cereal mixture. Add a dollop of
whipped topping. Repeat layering, ending with topping. Serve
immediately, or cover and chill. Makes 6 servings.

It's easy to make your own crumb crust. Mix 1-1/2 cups fine
crumbs, 1/4 cup sugar and 1/2 cup melted butter; press into
a pie plate. Chill for 20 minutes, or bake at 350 degrees for
10 minutes. For the crumbs, use vanilla wafers or graham
crackers, of course...try gingersnaps or pretzels too!

Ruth's Oatmeal Pie

Gloria Land
Southlake, TX

My mother used to make this recipe. It is like a pecan pie, but made with oatmeal instead of nuts...so simple. I have shared this with friends who have allergies to nuts and don't want to miss out on a Thanksgiving day favorite.

2/3 c. long-cooking oats, uncooked
2/3 c. sugar
2 eggs, beaten
1/3 c. light corn syrup
1/3 c. dark corn syrup

2/3 c. margarine, melted and slightly cooled
1 t. vanilla extract
1/4 t. salt
8-inch pie crust

In a bowl, combine all ingredients except pie crust; mix well. Pour into unbaked crust. Bake at 350 degrees for one hour. Let cool completely before slicing. Makes 8 servings.

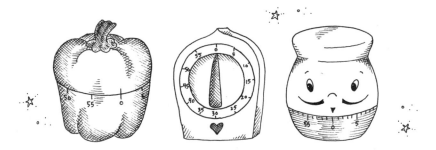

Ovens can vary, so set a kitchen timer when the pan goes into the oven. Check for doneness after the shortest baking time given...if a little more time is needed, be sure to watch closely.

✿ *Desserts* ✿
IN A DASH

Autumn Spice Streusel Cake

Ellie Levesque
Upland, CA

This is a family favorite. I make it in October because it has the flavors of fall. It's a hit with my Bible study group too!

18-1/4 oz. pkg. spice cake mix
1 sleeve graham crackers, crushed
3/4 c. brown sugar, packed

1/2 c. butter, melted
2 t. cinnamon
Garnish: powdered sugar

Prepare cake mix according to package directions; set aside batter. In a separate small bowl, mix graham cracker crumbs, brown sugar, butter and cinnamon; set aside. Lightly coat a 12-cup Bundt® pan with non-stick vegetable spray. Pour half of batter into pan. Add all of crumb mixture; pour remaining batter on top. Bake at 350 degrees for 35 to 40 minutes, until cake tests done with a toothpick. Let cool. Turn out cake onto a cake plate; dust with powdered sugar. Serves 8 to 10.

One cool crisp fall day, my dad asked me to bring the grandchildren to the farm to pick apples. The apples were very small, but just right to can for pies and cobblers. Well, I talked a friend into helping me and we peeled our hearts out. The apples were so small by the time you peeled them, they were the size of a small egg! But they were free and we had a good time together. We made the best-tasting apple pies, small ones that were more like pocket pies for our children's small hands. My children still remember how much fun they had that day at Grandpa Curly's farm.

–Sandy Perry, Bakersfield, CA

Caramel Apple Pie Dump Cake

MaryAlice Dobbert
King George, VA

This recipe takes about five minutes to put together!
Great fall flavors and aromas will warm your kitchen.

2 21-oz. cans apple pie filling
1/4 c. caramel ice cream topping
18-1/2 oz. pkg. yellow cake mix

1/2 c. butter, melted
Garnish: whipped cream or
   vanilla ice cream

Spray a 13"x9" baking pan with non-stick vegetable spray. Add pie
filling and caramel topping; swirl mixture with a quick stir. Sprinkle
dry cake mix evenly over the top; drizzle with melted butter. Bake at
350 degrees for 30 to 35 minutes. Let cool. Garnish portions with
whipped cream or ice cream. Makes 8 to 10 servings.

Cherry Fluff Pie

Kim Jasper
Lancaster, OH

I love this tasty recipe because it's so easy! It's great for when
company pops in, or the kids tell you at the last minute
that they need something to take to school.

21-oz. can cherry pie filling
8-oz. container frozen whipped
   topping, thawed

9-inch graham cracker crust

Gently mix together pie filling and whipped topping; spoon into crust.
Cover and chill for about one hour. Serves 8.

Serve hot spiced coffee with sweet
autumn treats. Simply add
3/4 teaspoon pumpkin pie spice
to 1/2 cup ground coffee
and brew as usual.

208

☺ *Desserts* ☺
IN A DASH

Apple Pie Cobbler

Mary Casasanta
Tracy, CA

*I have an apple tree in my backyard, and one year I ended up
with about 50 pounds of apples! When I found a cobbler recipe,
I decided to make my own version using my apples.*

1 c. self-rising flour
1-1/4 c. sugar, divided
1 c. milk
3/4 c. butter, melted and divided

6 Granny Smith apples, cored
   and chopped
1 t. cinnamon

In a bowl, mix together flour, one cup sugar, milk and 1/2 cup butter.
Pour batter into a greased 11"x7" baking pan; set aside. Toss apples
with cinnamon and remaining sugar. In a skillet over medium heat,
sauté apples in remaining butter until tender; spoon over batter in
pan. Sprinkle with Streusel Topping. Bake at 375 degrees for
40 minutes. Serves 8.

Streusel Topping:

1 c. long-cooking oats,
   uncooked
3/4 c. brown sugar, packed

1/2 c. self-rising flour
1/2 c. chopped pecans
1/2 c. butter, softened

Mix together all ingredients with a fork until crumbly.

For delicious apple pies and cakes, some of the best apple
varieties are Granny Smith, Gala and Jonathan as well as
old-timers like Rome Beauty, Northern Spy & Winesap.
Ask at the orchard...the grower is sure to have tips for you!

S'mores Cobbler

Audra Vanhorn-Sorey
Columbia, NC

A unique twist on a family favorite...it's sure to be a hit!

5-oz. pkg. cook & serve
   chocolate pudding mix
1 c. whole milk
6 whole graham crackers,
   broken in half
1/2 c. mini semi-sweet chocolate
   chips

18-1/2 oz. pkg. chocolate cake
   mix
1/2 c. butter, sliced
10-oz. pkg. marshmallows

Prepare pudding mix with milk according to package directions; cool slightly. Spoon pudding into an ungreased 13"x9" baking pan. Arrange graham crackers over pudding, with some space between crackers. Sprinkle with chocolate chips; spread dry cake mix over top and dot with butter. Bake at 350 degrees for 25 minutes. Remove from oven; stir slightly to ensure all ingredients are moistened. Top with marshmallows. Bake for an additional 8 to 10 minutes, until marshmallows are melted. Makes 10 servings.

One of the best ways to give thanks is to help someone else. Volunteer, lend a neighbor a hand, leave a surprise on someone's doorstep...there are lots of thoughtful ways to show you care.

✿ *Desserts* ✿
IN A DASH

Tina's Marshmallow Pie

Tina Goodpasture
Meadowview, VA

I love mallow cups and think of them whenever I serve this creamy pie!

10-oz. pkg. mini marshmallows
1/2 c. milk
1/4 c. butter, sliced
1 c. frozen whipped topping,
   thawed

9-inch graham cracker crust
Garnish: chopped chocolate
   pieces or chocolate syrup

In a saucepan over low heat, combine marshmallows, milk and butter. Cook and stir until marshmallows are melted. Let cool; stir in whipped topping. Spoon into pie crust. Cover and chill. Garnish with chocolate pieces or drizzle with chocolate syrup, as desired. Makes 8 servings.

A quick & easy harvest decoration for cupcakes!
Flatten red, yellow and orange fruit roll-ups and cut with
a leaf-shaped cookie cutter, then press the "leaves"
onto frosted cupcakes.

Creamy Maple Rice Pudding

Andrea Heyart
Savannah, TX

Creamy rice pudding flavored with real maple syrup and
brown sugar...pure comfort!

3/4 c. water
3/4 c. instant rice, uncooked
2-3/4 c. whole milk
1 egg, beaten
1/3 c. maple syrup

1/3 c. brown sugar, packed
1 T. butter
1/2 t. cinnamon
Optional: 1/8 t. salt

Bring water to a boil in a large saucepan over medium-high heat. Stir
in rice. Remove from heat; cover and let stand for 10 minutes, or until
most of water is absorbed and rice is tender. Add milk to rice in
saucepan and return to a low boil, stirring occasionally. In a small
bowl, beat together egg, maple syrup and brown sugar. Slowly add
2 tablespoons of warm rice mixture to egg mixture; stir and add all
of mixture to saucepan. Stir in butter, cinnamon and salt, if desired.
Simmer over low heat, stirring constantly, for another 10 minutes, or
until thickened. Serve warm, or cover and refrigerate until chilled.
Makes 4 to 6 servings.

Press whole cloves into the surface of a pillar candle to form
a pattern...just right for a dessert buffet.

212

Desserts
IN A DASH

Butterscotch Chocolate Pudding
Shala Kerrigan
Anchorage, AK

My family loves pudding! They like the packaged kind, but they love it when I make pudding from scratch. My kids are 16 and 20 now, and they still run to the kitchen looking for the bowls and whisk to "clean" for me.

1/2 c. semi-sweet chocolate
   chips
1/4 c. butterscotch chips
1 egg, lightly beaten
2 c. milk
1/4 c. brown sugar, packed

1/4 c. baking cocoa
2 T. cornstarch
1 t. vanilla extract
1/8 t. salt
Garnish: whipped cream

Place chocolate and butterscotch chips in a large heatproof bowl; add egg and set aside. In a large saucepan, combine remaining ingredients except garnish; whisk well. Cook over medium heat, whisking constantly, until thickened. Pour hot milk mixture over chocolate chip mixture. Stir constantly until well combined and chips are melted. Spoon pudding into individual dessert bowls; cover and chill. Serve topped with whipped cream. Serves 6.

Before displaying gourds and pumpkins as a centerpiece, a quick wash will help them last longer. Stir together a tablespoon of bleach in a gallon of water, then gently wash and pat dry.

Pumpkin-Chocolate Chip Muffins

Carrie Kelderman
Pella, IA

Most of us cook with pumpkin only in autumn, but these muffins are a welcome treat any time of year. Our family loves them!

1 c. canned pumpkin
1/2 c. brown sugar, packed
1/4 c. butter, melted and slightly
    cooled
2 eggs, beaten

2 c. all-purpose flour
2 t. baking powder
1/2 t. salt
1 c. semi-sweet chocolate chips

In a large bowl, mix all ingredients in the order given. Spoon batter into paper-lined muffin cups, filling about 3/4 full. Bake at 375 degrees for 20 minutes, or until muffins test done with a toothpick. Makes one dozen.

Honey Cups

Jill Nikunen
Kalispell, MT

Several years ago I received this recipe from a patient where I worked. It is so easy and tasty! Perfect for school snacks, hiking trips or anytime. I almost always have to share the recipe!

3 c. long-cooking oats,
    uncooked
2 c. sweetened flaked coconut
1 c. whole-wheat flour, or
    1-1/3 c. all-purpose flour

2 c. chopped almonds
1 c. butter, sliced
1/2 c. honey
1 c. brown sugar, packed
1 t. vanilla extract

In a large bowl, combine oats, coconut, flour and almonds; set aside. In a saucepan over medium-low heat, combine butter, honey, brown sugar and vanilla. Bring to a boil; boil for one minute. Pour over oat mixture; mix well. Spoon batter into greased mini muffin cups, filling about 3/4 full. Bake at 350 degrees for 8 to 10 minutes, until golden. Cool muffins in tin for 5 minutes; remove to a wire rack. Makes about 4 dozen.

☺ *Desserts* ☺
IN A DASH

Cotton Candy Muffins

Brenda Huey
Geneva, IN

I came up with this recipe after we went to a county fair.
I love cotton candy and thought this combination would make
a wonderful muffin...it sure did!

2 c. sugar	1 t. salt
1 c. margarine, softened	1 t. baking soda
1-1/2 c. sour cream	4 c. all-purpose flour
4 eggs, beaten	3 T. nonpareil sprinkles
1/2 c. maraschino cherry juice	Garnish: additional sprinkles

In a large bowl, combine sugar, margarine, sour cream and eggs. Add cherry juice, salt, baking soda and flour. Beat until well combined; stir in sprinkles. Pour into paper-lined muffin cups, filling 3/4 full. Bake at 325 degrees for 10 to 12 minutes, until muffins test done with a toothpick. Cool; frost with Buttercream Icing and top with a few extra sprinkles. Makes 1-1/2 dozen.

Buttercream Icing:

1/2 c. butter, softened	2 t. vanilla extract
4 c. powdered sugar	Optional: red or blue food
1/2 c. milk	coloring

In a large bowl, combine butter, powdered sugar and milk. Beat with an electric mixer on medium speed until smooth; beat in vanilla. If too thin, add more sugar. If desired, tint pink or blue with a few drops of food coloring to look like cotton candy.

When taking along snacks for the ride, slice cupcakes in half, frost and put them back together so that the frosting is in the middle...neat and tidy.

Potato Doughnuts

Nancy Diem
East Earl, PA

My mother-in-law gave me this recipe many years ago.
Very good. The doughnut holes are my favorite!

2 c. sugar
4 c. all-purpose flour
4 t. baking powder
1/2 t. salt
1 c. whole milk
1 c. cold mashed potatoes

1 T. butter, softened
3 eggs, beaten
oil for deep frying
Garnish: powdered sugar or
   cinnamon-sugar

In a large bowl, mix together sugar, flour, baking powder and salt.
Add milk, potatoes, butter and eggs; mix thoroughly. Roll out dough
on a well floured surface, about 3/4-inch thick. Cut out doughnuts
and holes with a doughnut cutter; set aside. Add 4 inches oil to a
large heavy saucepan. Heat to medium-high, about 360 degrees on a
candy thermometer. Carefully add doughnuts to oil, 2 to 3 at a time.
Cook, turning over, until golden on all sides. Cook doughnut holes the
same way. Drain well on paper towels. Sprinkle with powdered sugar
or cinnamon-sugar while still warm. Makes about 3 dozen.

It's the perfect time of year to share some tasty treats with
teachers, librarians and school bus drivers...let them know
how much you appreciate them!

✿ *Desserts* ✿
IN A DASH

Amber's Cinnamon Bread

Denise Webb
Newington, GA

This recipe was always my daughter's favorite quick bread.
Now as a mommy, she loves to make it for her kids.

1 egg, beaten
1/4 c. oil
1-1/2 c. sugar, divided
2 c. all-purpose flour

1/2 t. salt
1 t. baking soda
1 c. buttermilk
1 T. cinnamon

In a large bowl, beat together egg, oil and one cup sugar; set aside. In a separate bowl, mix together flour, salt and baking soda. Add flour mixture to egg mixture alternately with buttermilk, stirring well. Combine cinnamon and remaining sugar in a cup. Spoon half of batter into a greased 9"x5" loaf pan; sprinkle with half of cinnamon-sugar. Repeat layers; swirl with a knife. Bake at 350 degrees for one hour. Cool for 10 minutes; turn out of pan. Makes one loaf.

For the tenderest quick breads and muffins,
don't overmix...just stir the batter until moistened.
A few lumps won't matter.

Index

Index

Find Gooseberry Patch
wherever you are!

www.gooseberrypatch.com

Email   Blog   You Tube

Call us toll-free at 1·800·854·6673

homecoming parades · colorful leaves

drives in the country

casual get-togethers

craft fairs

moonlit hayrides

crackling bonfires · community suppers

U.S. to Metric Recipe Equivalents

Volume Measurements

1/4 teaspoon	1 mL
1/2 teaspoon	2 mL
1 teaspoon	5 mL
1 tablespoon = 3 teaspoons	15 mL
2 tablespoons = 1 fluid ounce	30 mL
1/4 cup	60 mL
1/3 cup	75 mL
1/2 cup = 4 fluid ounces	125 mL
1 cup = 8 fluid ounces	250 mL
2 cups = 1 pint =16 fluid ounces	500 mL
4 cups = 1 quart	1 L

Weights

1 ounce	30 g
4 ounces	120 g
8 ounces	225 g
16 ounces = 1 pound	450 g

Oven Temperatures

300° F	150° C
325° F	160° C
350° F	180° C
375° F	190° C
400° F	200° C
450° F	230° C

Baking Pan Sizes

Square

8x8x2 inches	2 L = 20x20x5 cm
9x9x2 inches	2.5 L = 23x23x5 cm

Rectangular

13x9x2 inches	3.5 L = 33x23x5 cm

Loaf

9x5x3 inches	2 L = 23x13x7 cm

Round

8x1-1/2 inches	1.2 L = 20x4 cm
9x1-1/2 inches	1.5 L = 23x4 cm